Cooperative Learning Activities Manual with Manipulatives and Technology

COOPERATIVE LEARNING ACTIVITIES MANUAL WITH MANIPULATIVES AND TECHNOLOGY

Heidi A. Howard

Florida Community College—Jacksonville

Mathematics for Elementary School Teachers

Phares O'Daffer
Illinois State University

Randall Charles
San Jose State University

Thomas Cooney
University of Georgia

John A. Dossey
Illinois State University

Jane Schielack
Texas A&M University

Reproduced by Addison-Wesley from files supplied by the author.

Copyright © 2003 Pearson Education, Inc.

All rights reserved. No part of this publication may be reproduced, stored in a retrieval system, or transmitted form or by any means, electronic, mechanical, photocopying, recording, or otherwise, without the prior writte mission of the publisher.

Printed in the United States of America.

ISBN   0-201-73689-6

1 2 3 4 5 6 7 8 9 10 VHG 05 04 03 02

CONTENTS

Chapter 1: Viewing Mathematics
INVESTIGATIONS
1.1	Analyzing What We Think Mathematics Is	page	1
1.2	Analyzing Problem Solving	page	2
1.3	Mix It Up	page	3
1.4	Analyzing Statements	page	4
1.5	Patterns in Ancestry	page	5
1.6	Ratios in U.S. Flags	page	6
1.7	Addition of Unit Fractions	page	7
1.8	Using Mathematical Reasoning	page	8

MANIPULATIVE ACTIVITIES
1.1	Connecting Squares and Cubes	page	9
1.2	Cutting Verses Folding Paper	page	10
1.3	Turning Squares into Boxes	page	11
1.4	Piling Up Cubes	page	12

TECHNOLOGY ACTIVITIES
1.1	Communicating Mathematical Data	page	13
1.2	Exploring Figures with a Fixed Perimeter	pages	14-15
1.3	Exploring the Fibonacci Sequence	page	16
1.4	Using Sequencer to Draw Conclusions	page	17
1.5	Graphing Calculator Representations	page	18
1.6	Using Graphit to Draw Conclusions	page	19

Chapter 2: Sets and Whole-Number Operations and Properties
INVESTIGATIONS
2.1	Set Ideas	page	21
2.2	Names and Symbols	pages	22-23
2.3	Different Bases in Everyday Units	page	24
2.4	Counting in Different Bases	page	25
2.5	Braille Numerals	pages	26-27
2.6	Operations in Base-Six	page	28
2.7	Comparing Numeration Systems *WEB*	page	29
2.8	Expansion of the Babylonian Numeration System	page	30
2.9	Mayan System	page	31
2.10	Representing Numbers on an Abacus (or Two)	pages	32-33

v

MANIPULATIVE ACTIVITIES
- 2.1   Determining Features of Sets — page 34
- 2.2   Meaning of Subtraction — page 35
- 2.3   Meaning of Division — page 36
- 2.4   Representing the Same Value in Different Bases — page 37
- 2.5   Race to a Red — pages 38-39

TECHNOLOGY ACTIVITIES
- 2.1   Venn Diagrams — page 40
- 2.2   Pizza and Pascal — pages 41-42
- 2.3   Repeated Subtraction — page 43
- 2.4   Sums of Odds and Evens — page 44
- 2.5   Playing with Numbers — page 45
- 2.6   What Day Was That? — pages 46-47

Chapter 3: Estimation and Computation

INVESTIGATIONS
- 3.1   Planning a Trip *WEB* — page 49
- 3.2   Compatible Numbers, Compensation, and Lattice Multiplication in Other Bases — pages 50-51
- 3.3   A Weighty Problem (or Two) — page 52
- 3.4   Looking a Gift Horse in the Mouth — page 53
- 3.5   Walk-a-Thon — page 54
- 3.6   A Cross to Bear — page 55
- 3.7   Egyptian and Russian Peasant Multiplication — page 56
- 3.8   A Couple Mental Multiplications — page 57

MANIPULATIVE ACTIVITIES
- 3.1   Chip Trading Addition *WEB* — page 58
- 3.2   Chip Trading Subtraction *WEB* — page 59
- 3.3   Finger Multiplication — pages 60-62
- 3.4   Race to 500 Game *WEB* — page 63
- 3.5   Race to 0 Game *WEB* — page 64
- 3.6   Five Digit Challenge *WEB* — page 65
- 3.7   Other Base Blocks *WEB* — page 66

TECHNOLOGY ACTIVITIES
- 3.1   Patterns Through Calculations — page 67
- 3.2   Sums and Differences of Whole Numbers — page 68
- 3.3   Expense Report Errors — page 69
- 3.4   Using Caesar Cipher to Encrypt a Message — pages 70-71
- 3.5   Using Caesar Cipher II to Determine Encryption Rules — pages 72-73

Chapter 4: Number Theory

INVESTIGATIONS
4.1	Divisibility	page	75
4.2	GCF and LCM	page	76
4.3	Sums of Odd Numbers	page	77
4.4	Divisibility Tests	page	78
4.5	Three Short Problems	page	79
4.6	Factor Rainbows	pages	80-81
4.7	Same Numbers, Same Operations, Different Results	page	82

MANIPULATIVE ACTIVITIES
4.1	Factors of 2 through 50 *WEB*	page	83
4.2	Colored Rods *WEB*	page	84
4.3	Prime Factor Game *WEB*	page	85
4.4	Pick's Theorem	page	86

TECHNOLOGY ACTIVITIES
4.1	Five Factors	page	87
4.2	A Bigger Cross to Bear	pages	88-89
4.3	Square Patterns	page	90
4.4	Ulam's Algorithm	pages	91-92
4.5	Using Coloring Multiples in Pascal's Triangle *WEB*	pages	93-94
4.6	Using Coloring Remainders in Pascal's Triangle	pages	95-96
4.7	Playing with Numbers II	page	97

Chapter 5: Understanding Integer Operations and Properties

INVESTIGATIONS
5.1	Whole Numbers and Integers	page	99
5.2	Integer Operations	page	100
5.3	Pascal and Company	pages	101-102
5.4	Sums and Differences of Consecutive Integer	page	103
5.5	Integer Towers *WEB*	page	104
5.6	Three Short Problems II	page	105

MANIPULATIVE ACTIVITIES
5.1	Integer Addition and Subtraction Encounters *WEB*	page	106
5.2	Number Lines and Cars *WEB*	pages	107-108
5.3	Integer "Football" *WEB*	page	109
5.4	Adding and Subtracting Integers with PopCubes®	pages	110-111

TECHNOLOGY ACTIVITIES
- 5.1 Sums and Differences of Integers — page 112
- 5.2 A Twist on Ulam's Algorithm — pages 113-114
- 5.3 Sequencer and Integers — pages 115-116
- 5.4 Powers of Negative Integers — page 117
- 5.5 Playing with Numbers III — page 118

Chapter 6: Rational Number Operations and Properties

INVESTIGATIONS
- 6.1 Rational Numbers as Quotients — page 119
- 6.2 Adding and Subtracting Fractions — page 120
- 6.3 Multiplying and Dividing Fractions — page 121
- 6.4 Comparing Fractions — page 122
- 6.5 Comparing Fractions II — page 123

MANIPULATIVE ACTIVITIES
- 6.1 Which Fraction is Greater? *WEB* — page 124
- 6.2 Cover a Unit *WEB* — pages 125-126
- 6.3 Modeling Fractions *WEB* — page 127
- 6.4 Mixed Up by Mixed *WEB* — pages 128-129

TECHNOLOGY ACTIVITIES
- 6.1 The In-Between Game — page 130
- 6.2 Sums and Differences of Rational Numbers — page 131
- 6.3 Simplifying Continued Fractions — pages 132-133
- 6.4 The Rebounding Ball: How Far Does It Go? — pages 134-135
- 6.5 Pi, Pi, and More Pi — page 136
- 6.6 Using Converter — pages 137-138
- 6.7 And the Winner is…… — pages 139-140

Chapter 7: Proportional Reasoning

INVESTIGATIONS
- 7.1 A "Griddy" Problem — pages 141-142
- 7.2 Pieces of Eight — page 143
- 7.3 Flying Ratios — pages 144-145
- 7.4 Half-Baked Ratios — page 146
- 7.5 Three Short Problems III — page 147
- 7.6 Summing Terms with a Common Ratio — pages 148-149

MANIPULATIVE ACTIVITIES
7.1	Representing Proportional Relationships *WEB*	pages	150-151
7.2	Popping the Question(s) *WEB*	page	152
7.3	Going in Circles *WEB*	page	153
7.4	A Body of (in) Great Proportions *WEB*	pages	154-155
7.5	Expanding and Shrinking Rectangles *WEB*	page	156

TECHNOLOGY ACTIVITIES
7.1	Summing Terms with a Common Ratio II	pages	157-158
7.2	Representing Proportional and Inverse Relationships	page	159
7.3	Sierpinski's Triangle *WEB*	pages	160-162
7.4	Playing with Pies	page	163
7.5	A Topic of Interest	pages	164-166

Chapter 8: Analyzing Data
INVESTIGATIONS
8.1	Population Data	page	167
8.2	…And the Older gets Older	pages	168-169
8.3	Speed Skating Times	pages	170-171
8.4	Three Short Problems IV	page	172
8.5	How Honorable is Honorable?	page	173

MANIPULATIVE ACTIVITIES
8.1	Take a Survey	page	174
8.2	Trendy Lines *WEB*	page	175
8.3	How Many Reds? *WEB*	page	176
8.4	Three Coin Toss	page	177
8.5	A Dicey Game *WEB*	page	178

TECHNOLOGY ACTIVITIES
8.1	Sled Dog Race Times	page	179
8.2	First Digit Analysis	pages	180-181
8.3	Hot is Hot and Cold is Cold	pages	182-183
8.4	Top Tunes	pages	184-185
8.5	Harrison Ford's Films	pages	186-187
8.6	TV Junkies	page	188

Chapter 9: Probability

INVESTIGATIONS

9.1	A Gate to Somewhere or Nowhere	page	189
9.2	Three Short Problems V	page	190
9.3	How Fortunate We Are	page	191
9.4	Conditional Probability and Venn Diagrams	page	192
9.5	Other Dicey Games *WEB*	page	193
9.6	Benford's Law	pages	194-195

MANIPULATIVE ACTIVITIES

9.1	Taking Your Chances *WEB*	page	196
9.2	It All Depends *WEB*	page	197
9.3	Take a Walk	pages	198-199
9.4	Making the Lineup *WEB*	page	200
9.5	One-Son Policy	page	201

TECHNOLOGY ACTIVITIES

9.1	Funny Funnel	pages	202-203
9.2	It's Perfectly Normal	pages	204-208
9.3	The Birthday Problem	pages	209-210
9.4	Spinning Around	page	211
9.5	Hit the Target	pages	212-216

Chapter 10: Introducing Geometry

INVESTIGATIONS

10.1	What's in a Name?	page	217
10.2	Polygon Angles	page	218
10.3	Network Traversability	page	219
10.4	Quadrilateral Generalizations	page	220
10.5	What's Right is Right	page	221

MANIPULATIVE ACTIVITIES

10.1	Try a Different Angle! *WEB*	page	222
10.2	Disappearing and Appearing Units *WEB*	pages	223-225
10.3	The Pythagorean Connection	page	226
10.4	Right, Obtuse, Acute, or None *WEB*	page	227
10.5	Dominos, Triomonos, Tetrominos, and More	page	228

TECHNOLOGY ACTIVITIES
10.1 Inscribed Quadrilaterals   page   229
10.2 Parallelograms and Squares   pages   230-231
10.3 Right Triangle Relationships   pages   232-233
10.4 Property Lines   page   234
10.5 Triangle Explorer   page   235
10.6 Triangles in Triangles   pages   236-237

Chapter 11: Extending Geometry
INVESTIGATIONS
11.1 Magnification   page   239
11.2 Tessellations from Tessellations   page   240
11.3 Euler's Formula   page   241
11.4 Symmetries in the Alphabet   page   242
11.5 Three Short Problems VI   page   243

MANIPULATIVE ACTIVITIES
11.1 The Box Pattern Report *WEB*   page   244
11.2 Showing Pattern and Cube Symmetry *WEB* page 245
11.3 Try Some Tiling! *WEB*   page   246
11.4 Flipping Out!   page   247
11.5 Footprints in the Sand *WEB*   page   248

TECHNOLOGY ACTIVITIES
11.1 Transformations   page   249
11.2 Create Your Own Tessellations   page   250
11.3 Regular Polygons   page   251
11.4 Perspective Drawings   page   252
11.5 Tessellate!   page   253

Chapter 12: Measurement
INVESTIGATIONS
12.1 Analyzing The Concept of Measure   page   255
12.2 Analyzing the Concept of Area *WEB*   page   256
12.3 Analyzing Measure of Surface Area and Volume page 257
12.4 Sewing a Flag   page   258
12.5 Area and Perimeter Connections   page   259

MANIPULATIVE ACTIVITIES
12.1 Determining Volume   page   260
12.2 Surface Area of Similar Solids *WEB*   page   261
12.3 Volumes of Solids   page   262
12.4 Tangram *WEB*   page   263
12.5 Looking at a Cone from a Different Angle   pages   264-265

TECHNOLOGY ACTIVITIES
12.1 Watering a Garden   page   266
12.2 Pick a Box   page   267
12.3 Heron's Formula   page   268
12.4 Shape Explorer   page   269
12.5 Surface Area and Volume   page   270

Chapter 13: Exploring Ideas of Algebra and Coordinate Geometry
INVESTIGATIONS
13.1 Garden Expressions   page   271
13.2 The Ups and Downs of Life   page   272
13.3 Seeing Double *WEB*   page   273
13.4 The Eyes Have It   page   274
13.5 Changing Population Densities   page   275

MANIPULATIVE ACTIVITIES
13.1 Expression Strips *WEB*   page   276
13.2 Solving Equations with Cubes   page   277
13.3 Bouncing Ball Experiment   page   278
13.4 Towers of Brahma *WEB*   page   279
13.5 Flatten that Circle *WEB*   pages   280-281

TECHNOLOGY ACTIVITIES
13.1 What's One More Degree?   pages   282-283
13.2 Another Fibonacci Sequence   page   284
13.3 Rectangles and Areas   page   285
13.4 Linear and Quadratic Graphs   page   286
13.5 Possible or Not?   page   287

WEB indicates download available at http://wps.aw.com/aw_odaffer_mathematic_2

INTRODUCTION

This manual provides instructional experiences designed to extend understanding of important mathematics concepts and skills introduced in *Mathematics for Elementary Teachers*, Second Edition, by O'Daffer, Charles, Cooney, Dossey, and Schielack. In addition to extending your understanding of important mathematics, the activities in this manual also introduce you, as a prospective elementary school teacher, to three kinds of instructional activities likely to be encountered in a powerful elementary school curriculum: Investigations, Manipulative Activities, and Technology Activities. Thus, your work on the activities in this manual will strengthen your preparation for teaching mathematics by helping you to develop a deep understanding of mathematics through instructional activities similar to those you will be expected to use as a teacher. We have all heard the statement that "teachers teach as they were taught." The investigations and activities in this manual, when used as an important part of the course, can help prospective teachers develop dispositions toward the teaching and learning of mathematics needed to be a successful teacher of elementary school mathematics.

Some Ways to Use These Activities

The following are some ideas for ways the activities in this manual might be used. Of course, many combinations of these suggestions are also possible and make sense for this course.

Use for Supplemental Instruction from the Textbook

The activities in this book can be used as follow-up experiences tied to the presentations of the concepts and skills in the text. After key ideas and skills have been presented, selected activities can be used as part of the regular course or through a laboratory component to reinforce and exemplify the ideas and skills presented.

Use to Introduce Concepts and Skills

Rather than being used as a follow-up instruction, these activities can be used as the vehicle for *introducing* content. First, students can do investigations from this manual. Then, using their reflections on the activity, students can make connections to the key ideas and skills in the text.

Use for Small-group Projects

These investigations can be the seeds of rich extending projects. One focus could be to make connections between these investigations and activities to other mathematical ideas. Another intent might be to connect the mathematics in the investigation to the elementary and middle school mathematics curricula.

While all of the activities in this manual are designed for individual or small-group work, some can be modified for whole-class demonstrations. There are three different types of activities in this manual: Investigations, Manipulative Activities, and Technology Activities.

Investigations

The accompanying textbook for this manual contains numerous Mini-Investigations. Investigations are designed to elicit reasoning about an important mathematical idea or to help discover an important relationship or fact. When you have to reason, think, and make sense of important mathematical ideas, those ideas are more likely to be better understood and not as easily confused or forgotten. The investigations contained in this manual are similar to those in the textbook, but are more extensive with regard to the amount of time needed to complete them and are usually more involved with regard to the complexity of the mathematical thinking needed. Some of the activities have an icon (*WEB*) in the table of contents indicating that a download is available at http://wps.aw.com/aw_odaffer_mathematic_2. The majority of these Investigations downloads are designed to help students better organize their responses.

Manipulative Activities

These experiences model closely the kinds of activities that might be used with elementary school children to develop understanding through the use of manipulatives. Many of the activities involve the use of PopCubes®, which can be purchased separately. Also, many of the activities can be performed with the aid of downloads that are available at http://wps.aw.com/aw_odaffer_mathematic_2. Activities that have a download available are indicated in the table of contents by an icon (*WEB*). Some require the use of a color printer.

Manipulatives Help Us Understand Problems

Representing a problem with manipulatives models the situation, helping us "see it" and thus better understand it. Understanding a problem is essential in moving toward a solution.

Manipulatives Help Us Develop a Deeper Understanding of a Concept

For example, a fourth-grade child comes to understand division through solving real-world division problems using manipulatives. When students use manipulatives to solve the two main types of division problems (sharing and partitioning), the actions with the manipulatives mirror the actions in the real-world situations. Physically moving the manipulatives helps a student "feel" the actions associated with the operation, thus leading to a better understanding of that operation.

Manipulatives Help Us Make Sense of Mathematical Procedures

Students can often use the same manipulatives they used to develop understanding of a concept to extend that understanding to a related mathematical procedure. For example, we can use manipulatives to understand the meaning of division, then use the same manipulatives to model the steps in a division algorithm to help children make sense of the steps in the symbolic algorithm.

Technology Activities

The textbook, *Mathematics for Elementary Teachers*, Second Edition, is integrated with technology examples, activities, investigations, and problems. This integration of technology emphasizes the appropriate uses of technology as tools for teaching and learning mathematics. The activities in this manual reinforce, supplement, and extend the concepts and skills of each chapter. The Technology Activities mainly rely on four tools: the Interactivate disk which accompanies the text, spreadsheet software such as Excel®, a graphing calculator such as a TI-83, and geometry exploration software such as The Geometer's Sketchpad®. Some of the activities have an icon (*WEB*) in the table of contents indicating that a download is available at the website http://wps.aw.com/aw_odaffer_mathematic_2. These downloads are designed to help students better organize their responses.

The textbook contains two technology appendices that provide instruction in the use and application of graphing calculators and geometry exploration software. Also, detailed instruction is given in many of the activities that rely on different forms of technology.

Available to the instructor are solutions and suggested responses to questions posed in the activities of this manual. These solutions are password protected. Contact your local Addison Wesley Longman representative for further details and your access code.

CHAPTER 1:   VIEWING MATHEMATICS

INVESTIGATION 1.1

Analyzing What We Think Mathematics Is

Rate each of the following problems using the scale of 1 to 10 in terms of the extent to which the problem reflects what you think is important about mathematics.

Let 1 represent "This is very *unimportant* in terms of what I think mathematics is all about."

Let 10 represent "This is very *important* in terms of what I think mathematics is all about."

   A. $3\frac{1}{2} + 5\frac{2}{3} = ?$

   B. What are three different ways to find $2 \div 3$?

   C. Mark, Carlos, and Cindy ordered a large pizza. Mark will eat three times as much pizza as Carlos. Carlos will eat twice as much pizza as Cindy. If the pizza is cut into 36 slices, how many slices will each person get?

   D. A newspaper reporter found that 25% of American families own Toyotas, 20% own Hondas, 15% own Nissans, and 10% own other foreign-made cars. The reporter wrote a story and created the following headline:

   Only 30% of American families own American cars.

   Should the reporter's editor allow the headline? Why or why not?

   E. If a circle is inscribed in a square 6 cm on a side, how many square centimeters are outside the circle but inside the square?

Summary Questions:
1. What are comparisons that can be made between your ratings and a classmate's?

2. Why do you think your ratings were different (or the same) as those of your classmates?

Chapter 1: Viewing Mathematics

INVESTIGATION 1.2

Analyzing Problem Solving

Consider the following statements and react to them on the basis of strongly disagree, disagree, undecided, agree, or strongly agree. Then, working in a small group, compare your responses with those of others and discuss how you could communicate the group results.

	strongly disagree	disagree	un-decided	agree	strongly agree
A. Mathematical problem solving means solving word problems.					
B. Most mathematical problems can be solved in more than one way.					
C. Solutions to mathematical problems consist of a single number.					
D. There are some mathematical problems that have no solutions.					
E. There is always a best way to solve a mathematical problem.					

Summary Questions:
1. Was there an agreement to the questions? If not, how did the responses differ?

2. How would you describe your attitude toward problem solving in mathematics?

3. What do you think is the attitude of other group members toward problem solving in mathematics?

4. Can you communicate a summary of the group response for each question? Consider assigning numerical results to individual responses.

INVESTIGATION 1.3

Mix It Up

With a calculator, use the guess-and-check strategy to solve this problem. Making a table may be helpful.

A school club wants to create a mix of cashews and peanuts to sell during the holidays. Peanuts sell for $1.50 per pound and cashews sell for $6.50 per pound. If the club wants to create a 100-pound mix of peanuts and cashews to sell for $4.51 per pound, how many pounds of peanuts and how many pounds of cashews will the club need?

Number of pounds of cashews	Number of pounds of peanuts	Cost per pound of mixture

Part A Summary Questions:
1. How did you use your results from one guess to help make your next guess?

2. If the price per pound of the two different kinds of nuts were close, how would that affect your initial guess?

3. If the price per pound of one kind of nut was very high and the other was very low, how would that affect your initial guess if the mixture had a relatively low price per pound?

4. If the price per pound of one kind of nut was very high and the other was very low, how would that affect your initial guess if the mixture had a relatively high price per pound?

This problem can also be solved by solving a equation by introducing a variable. Solve this problem by letting x be the number of pounds of peanuts and $100 - x$ be the number of pounds of cashews.

Part B Summary Question:
What are some of the advantages and disadvantages about each approach (guess-and-check strategy verses the writing an equation strategy)?

4 Chapter 1: Viewing Mathematics

INVESTIGATION 1.4

Analyzing Statements

Create two statements for each of the following conditions and provide examples that satisfy the conditions.

    a. A mathematical statement that is always true.

    b. A mathematical statement that is sometimes true and sometimes false.

    c. A mathematical statement that is always false.

Part A Summary Questions:
1. What do the examples all have in common?

2. In what way do the examples differ?

3. How would you explain to someone how a statement can be true for some examples and not true for others in terms of the hypotheses and conclusions of the statements?

Consider the following statement about a small town with just one barber.

    The barber only shaves men and only those men that do not shave themselves.

Part B Summary Questions:
1. Can you restate this statement as a conditional? If so, restate it.

2. Does the barber shave himself?

3. This is an example of a paradox. After examining Question 2 in Part B, can you describe what you believe a paradox to be? If so, describe it.

INVESTIGATION 1.5

Patterns in Ancestry

Under the assumption that a child is born to two parents (a male and a female), a child would have 2 ancestors (parents) one generation back. Each of that child's parents would have 2 ancestors (parents) one generation back. So that child has 4 ancestors two generation back. The family tree would look like this:

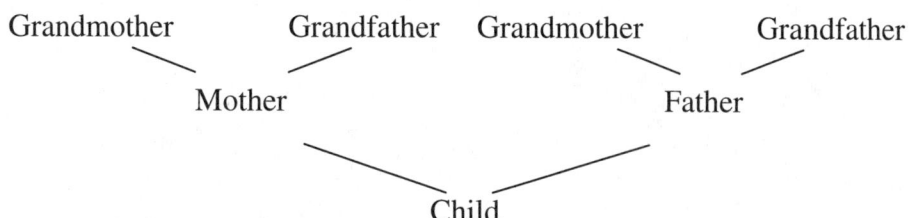

Draw a tree to show how many ancestors that child has three and four generations back.

Part A Summary Questions:
1. How many ancestors does that child has in the 10th generation back?

2. Can you identify what kind of sequence is formed in examining the number of ancestors in the previous generations?

Male bees are produced from unfertilized eggs from the queen bee. So a male bee has only one "parent" (a female). A female bee is produced when a male bee and the queen bee mate. So a female bee has two parents (a male and a female). The "family tree" would look like this:

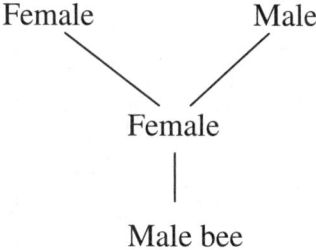

Draw a tree to show how many "ancestors" a male bee would have three and four generations back.

Part B Summary Questions:
1. How many "ancestors" does that bee have 10th generations back?

2. Can you describe the pattern that is formed in this sequence of numbers of the ancestors in the previous generations?

6 Chapter 1: Viewing Mathematics

INVESTIGATION 1.6

Ratios in U.S. Flags

In order to make a U.S. flag in correct proportions, the ratio of the width of a flag to its length should be 10 to 19. The following yields this specification along with others pertaining to the stars and stripes.

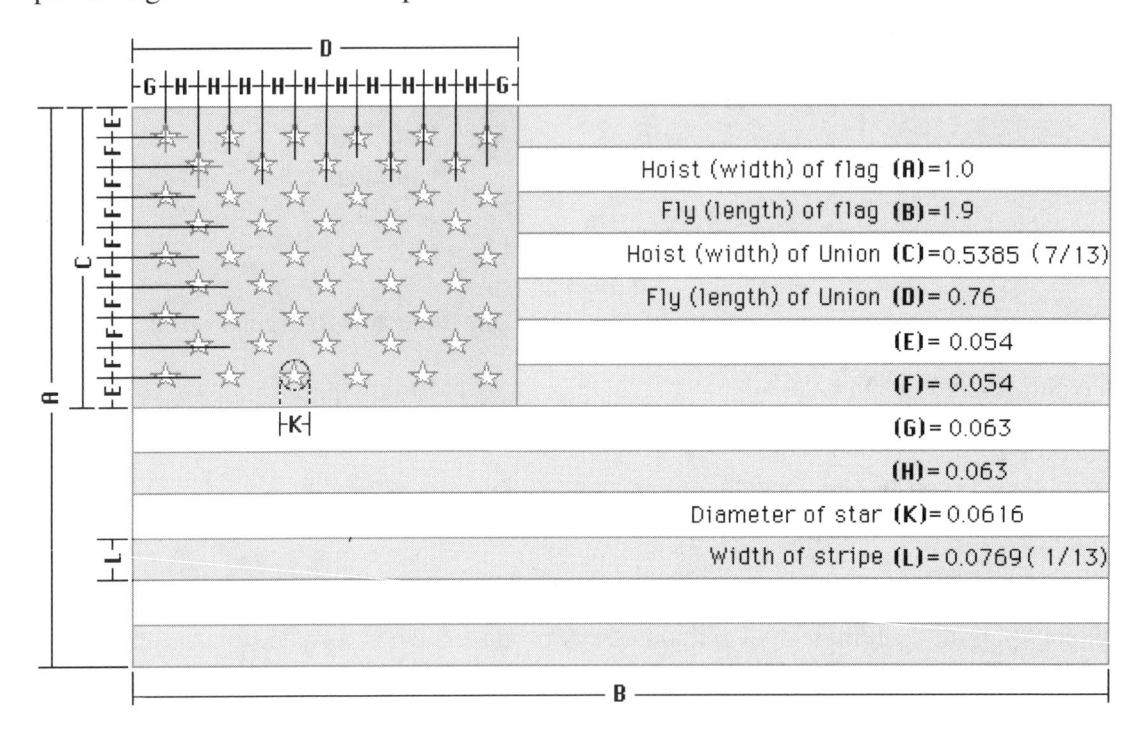

Hoist (width) of flag **(A)** = 1.0
Fly (length) of flag **(B)** = 1.9
Hoist (width) of Union **(C)** = 0.5385 (7/13)
Fly (length) of Union **(D)** = 0.76
(E) = 0.054
(F) = 0.054
(G) = 0.063
(H) = 0.063
Diameter of star **(K)** = 0.0616
Width of stripe **(L)** = 0.0769 (1/13)

A flag company offers U.S. flags in various sizes and prices as shown below.

Size	2x3'	3x5'	4x6'	5x8'	5x9.5'	6x10'
Cost	$22.50	$32.00	$45.00	$70.00	$75.00	$95.00

Size	8x12'	10x15'	12x18'	15x25'	20x30'	30x50'
Cost	$160.00	$250.00	$350.00	$550.00	$800.00	$1600.00

Summary Questions:
1. Which of the sizes are in the correct ratio of width to length?

2. Why do you think the sizes that are not in the correct ratio have the given widths and lengths?

3. Are there any similarities between the flags that are not in the correct ratio? If so, what are they?

INVESTIGATION 1.7

Addition of Unit Fractions

A unit fraction is a fraction where the numerator is 1. Look at the following examples of addition of unit fractions:

$$\frac{1}{2} + \frac{1}{3} = \frac{5}{6} \qquad \frac{1}{3} + \frac{1}{4} = \frac{7}{12}$$

$$\frac{1}{6} + \frac{1}{7} = \frac{13}{42}$$

$$\frac{1}{5} + \frac{1}{7} = \frac{12}{35} \qquad \frac{1}{10} + \frac{1}{13} = \frac{23}{130}$$

Summary Questions:

1. Can you describe a pattern in the addition of fractions? If so, what is the pattern?

2. What kinds of restrictions, if any, do you place on these fractions?

3. Can you make a generalization about the sum $\frac{1}{a} + \frac{1}{b}$, where $a, b \neq 0$? If so, what is it?

4. Do you think the pattern found in the response to Question 1 would also be true if you have three or more unit fraction being summed? Explain.

5. If the denominators were both the same non-zero value, would the pattern you found be valid? Give a formal justification for your response using variables.

Chapter 1: Viewing Mathematics

INVESTIGATION 1.8

Using Mathematical Reasoning

Consider adding together the first 100 natural numbers. The sum would be given by

$$1 + 2 + 3 + \ldots + 98 + 99 + 100.$$

Part A Summary Questions:
1. What happens when you sum the first and the last terms together?

2. What happens when you sum the second and the second to last terms together?

3. How many times can you group the terms in this fashion?

4. What would the sum of all 100 terms be?

This problem is attributed to the famous mathematician Carl Gauss who as a child used this type of addition pattern to arrive at the sum instead of adding term after term.

Part B Summary Questions:
1. What would the general formula be for finding the sum of the first n natural numbers?

2. Consider using the pairing technique attributed to Gauss for the following.

$$5 + 12 + 19 + 26 + 33 + 40 + 47 + 54$$

   What is the sum?

3. Does the same technique work for the following? First try the pairing and then add up the terms with a calculator.

$$5 + 12 + 19 + 26 + 33 + 40 + 47$$

   What is the sum?

4. This technique can be used for finding the sum of the terms of an arithmetic sequence. Recall from Section 1.2 in the text, an arithmetic sequence is a sequence that has a common difference between consecutive terms. Can you find a generalized formula or procedure in finding the sum of the terms of an arithmetic series? If so, what is it?

MANIPULATIVE ACTIVITY 1.1

Connecting Squares and Cubes

Use PopCubes® to make a cube consisting of 8 smaller cubes. If PopCubes® are not available, sugar cubes or blocks could be used. Compare the cube consisting of 8 smaller cubes to a cube consisting of 1 smaller cube. Rearrange all of the smaller cubes from both solids in one layer so that they cover a 3x3 square.

  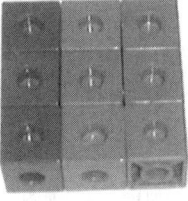

Build three cubes made up of 1, 8, and 27 smaller cubes. Arrange all the smaller cubes from the three solids in one layer so that they cover a square.

Part A Summary Question:
What size square do they cover?

Build four cubes made up of 1, 8, 27, and 64 smaller cubes. Arrange all the smaller cubes from the four solids in one layer so that they cover a square.

Part B Summary Questions:
1. What size square do they cover?

2. Consider the number of smaller cubes that make up each of the cubes. What do you observe about the number of these smaller cubes?

3. Consider the number of smaller cubes that cover each of the squares. What do you observe about the number of these smaller cubes?

4. Based on your observations, what is a generalization about the relationship between sums of cubes and squares?

10   Chapter 1: Viewing Mathematics

MANIPULATIVE ACTIVITY 1.2

Cutting Verses Folding Paper

For this activity you will need two 8 ½ " x 11" pieces of paper and scissors (the paper can be folded and torn if scissors are not available).

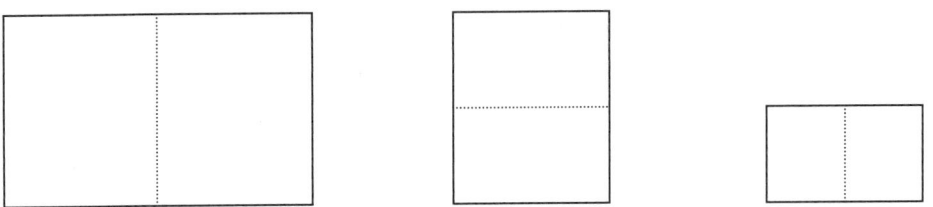

Take a piece of paper and cut it into two halves. Take one half and set it down. Take the other half and cut it into two halves. Place one of these pieces on top of the first piece and continue cutting and piling the pieces up until it is not longer practical (i.e. the pieces are too small to cut). Keep tract of how many times you cut the paper.

With the second piece of paper, fold the paper in half and do not cut. Fold the paper again in half, again without cutting. Continue this process until it is not longer practical (i.e. it is too hard to fold the paper over). Keep tract of how many times you folded the paper.

A package of 20-lb 8 ½ " x 11" office paper contains 500 sheets. The height of this stack is approximately $1\frac{29}{32}$". Use a calculator to determine the approximate thickness of one sheet of paper.

Summary Questions:
1. How high would the stacked cut paper be if you performed the cutting 25 times?

2. How thick would the paper be if you could fold it 25 times?

3. What kinds of sequences of numbers are formed in the two experiments?

Helpful information:
There are 12 inches in 1 foot and 5280 feet in one mile.

MANIPULATIVE ACTIVITY 1.3

Turning Squares into Boxes

Consider the following figures. Use a geometry drawing tool to make these figures larger on a separate piece of paper. If one is not available, a ruler and pencil can be used.

Summary Questions:
1. Which of these figures can be folded up into a cubical box if you are not allowed to disconnect the pieces? Try to use spatial reasoning on each of the figures. Cut the figures out to confirm your results.

2. Can you find some common features of the figures that can be turned into cubical boxes that the others don't have?

12 Chapter 1: Viewing Mathematics

MANIPULATIVE ACTIVITY 1.4

Piling Up Cubes

A grocer wants to pile up cubical boxes in a corner in the pattern as shown below. Recreate the four figures with PopCubes®. If PopCubes® are not available, sugar cubes or blocks could be used.

One block

Four blocks (One is hidden.)

Ten blocks (Four are hidden.)

Twenty blocks (Ten are hidden.)

Summary Questions:
1. If the grocer wants to make such a stacking which is 6 cubes high, how many cubes are visible and how many cubes are hidden behind the visible cubes?

2. If the grocer wants to make such a stacking which is 10 cubes high, how many cubes are visible and how many cubes are hidden behind the visible cubes?

3. If the grocer wants to make such a stacking that is 100 cubes high, *discuss how* to determine the number of cubes visible and the number of cubes hidden behind the visible cubes. What kinds of patterns are formed?

TECHNOLOGY ACTIVITY 1.1

Communicating Mathematical Data

Collect the last four digits from the social security numbers of you and your classmates.

Go to the Histogram feature on the Interactivate disk.

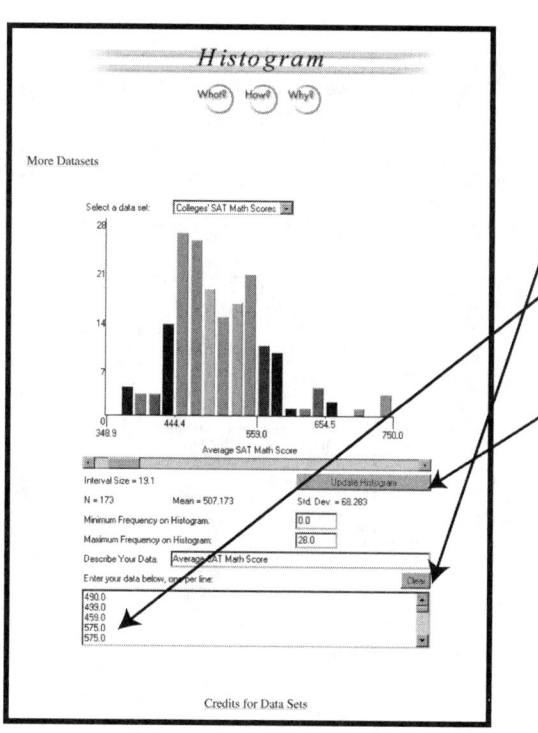

1. Clear the data that is given.
2. Enter each of the four digits separately. For example, if there are five people in your group you will have 20 pieces of data.
3. Click "Update Histogram"
4. Adjust the Interval size until the graph best represents the data.

Summary Question:
Why do you believe that your choice of interval length is best? Compare it to other interval sizes.

Chapter 1: Viewing Mathematics

TECHNOLOGY ACTIVITY 1.2

Exploring Figures with a Fixed Perimeter

This activity can be performed with the software, The Geometer's Sketchpad®, in order to draw a conclusion. If you refer to Appendix B in your text (pages 782-793) an introduction to geometry exploration software is given. This activity can also be done using graph paper if the software is not available.

With The Geometer's Sketchpad®, draw a 3, 4, 6, and 8 sided figure with equal lengths (or as close as possible) with a perimeter of 24 centimeters. For each of these figures, determine the area in the interior.

Summary Questions:
1. What estimate did you find for the area of each figure? Fill in the table below.

Number of sides	Length of each side	Area in interior
3		
4		
6		
8		

2. What conclusion can you make about the area of a figure with congruent sides when the number of sides increases and the perimeter is held constant?

Drawing Figures with The Geometer's Sketchpad®

Below is an example of a six-sided figure with a perimeter of 12 centimeters with equal length sides. This was drawn by plotting six dots in order (either clockwise or counter-clockwise) in approximately the correct positions. Under Edit, choose **Select All** and then under Construct, choose **Polygon Interior** (for a triangle through a hexagon it will give the name of the polygon, so here it would be Hexagon Interior). This will create a six-sided figure with the interior shaded. Choose the Selection Arrow and click somewhere outside the figure. To determine the length of one of the sides, hold down the shift key and click on the two ends (dots) of a side. Under Measure, choose **Distance**. Click somewhere outside the figure and then click on one of the two ends of the segment you measured. Drag this end until you get the desired length. Click somewhere outside the figure and then choose the next length (work either clockwise or counter-clockwise) to measure. To alter this second length, you will want to move the end that is not common to the two measured lengths. Keep altering the sides until you have gone all the way around. The last side is often the hardest. It may be necessary to adjust other sides. After you have succeeded to get a figure with all sides the same measure, click somewhere in the interior of the figure. Under Measure, choose **Area** and record the results. Under File you can choose **New Sketch** to do another if you wish to refer back to your drawing.

Section Arrow

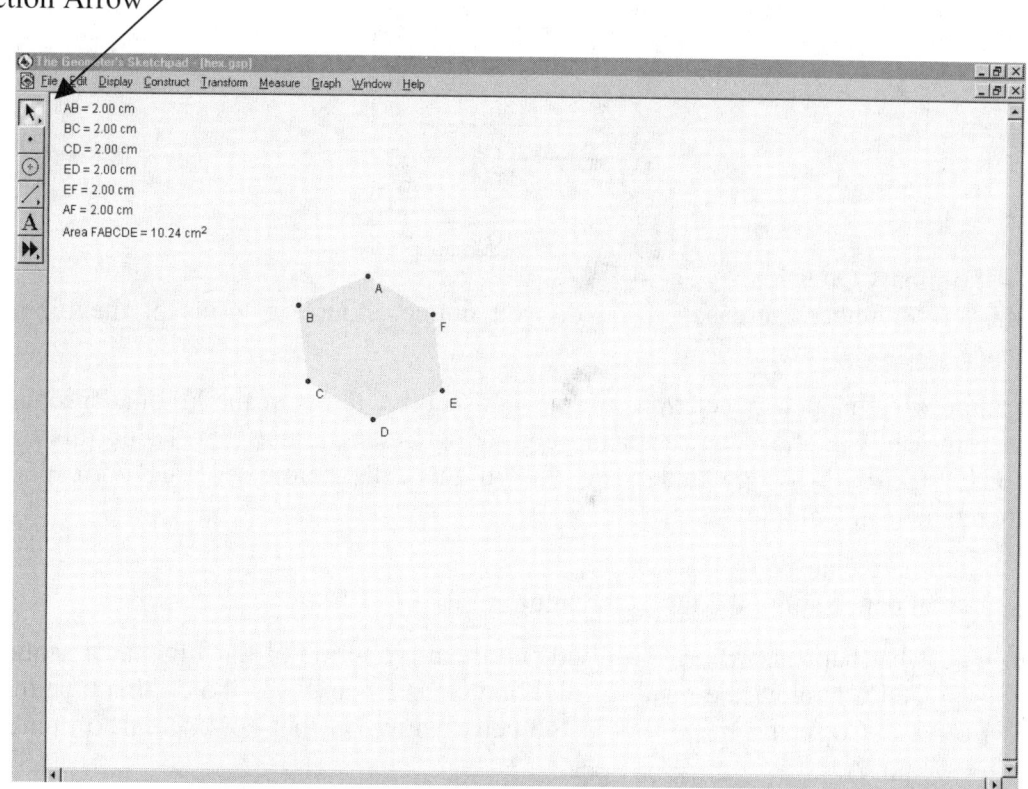

TECHNOLOGY ACTIVITY 1.3

Exploring the Fibonacci Sequence

This activity can be performed with spreadsheet software such as Excel® in order to draw a conclusion. A calculator can also be used if this software is not available.

The terms of the *Fibonacci Sequence* can be generated by adding two consecutive terms to get the next. When the first term is 1 and the second term is 1, the third term is $2 = 1 + 1$, the fourth term is $3 = 1 + 2$, and the fifth term is $5 = 2 + 3$. The next five terms are 8, 13, 21, 34, and 55. Use a computer spreadsheet to create a table similar to the one shown here, where Column A shows the term numbers and Column B shows the Fibonacci sequence. Include at least the first 20 Fibonacci numbers. If you are using Excel®, enter the numbers 1 through 20 in Column A and the first two terms of the Fibonacci sequence in Column B (This would be Cells B2 and B3). In Cell B4 type "=B2+B3" (without the quotation marks) and hit enter. The number 2 should be calculated in this cell. Click on Cell B4 and copy it to the remaining cells in Column B (as many as you labeled in Column A). The Fibonacci sequence should be calculated.

	A	B
1	Term #	Fib. #
2	1	1
3	2	1
4	3	2
5	4	3
6	5	5
7	6	8
8	7	13
9	8	21
10	9	34
11	10	55

Part A Summary Question:
As the term number increases, what do you notice about the terms of the Fibonacci sequence?

Determine what happens when you subtract consecutive terms of the Fibonacci sequence. Starting in Cell C3, show the result of subtracting Cells B3 and B2. To do this type in Cell C3 "=B3-B2". Copy and paste this in the cells below C3 that correspond to numbered cells in Column A.

Part B Summary Question:
What do you notice about the terms in Column C?

Determine what happens when you divide consecutive terms of the Fibonacci sequence. Starting in Cell C3, show the result of dividing Cells B3 and B2. To do this type in Cell C3 "=B3/B2". Copy and paste this in the cells below C3 that correspond to numbered cells in Column A.

Part C Summary Question:
What do you notice about the terms in Column C?

TECHNOLOGY ACTIVITY 1.4

Using Sequencer to Draw Conclusions

Suppose you were contracted to work for 10 days. You are offered a choice in your salary.

Choice 1: You can be paid $1000 for each day worked.

Choice 2: You can be paid $1 on the first day and for each of the remaining days, be paid triple the previous day. So on day 2, you would earn $3 and on day 3 you would earn $9.

Go to the Sequencer feature on the Interactiviate disk. Use Sequencer to find the salary for each of the 10 days with Choice 2.

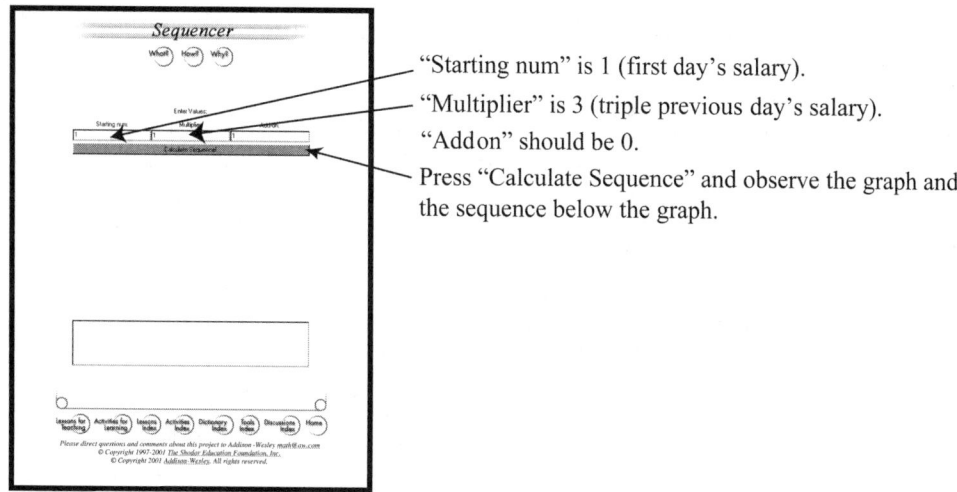

"Starting num" is 1 (first day's salary).
"Multiplier" is 3 (triple previous day's salary).
"Addon" should be 0.
Press "Calculate Sequence" and observe the graph and the sequence below the graph.

Part A Summary Questions:
1. What is the **total** salary you would receive for the 10 days under Choice 1?

2. What is the **total** salary you would receive for the 10 days under Choice 2?

3. Which is the better choice?

Now suppose a firm wanted to hire you for a 10-day contract and you have the same choices as before for payment. One stipulation in the contract is if you take a day off, you will be paid $1 for that day.

Part B Summary Questions:
1. If you have to miss a day of work with Choice 1, what day (if any) is best to miss?

2. If you have to miss a day of work with Choice 2, what day (if any) is best to miss?

3. If you know that you will be missing one day of work, which Choice is best?

4. If you know that you will be missing two days of work, which Choice is best?

18   Chapter 1: Viewing Mathematics

TECHNOLOGY ACTIVITY 1.5

Graphing Calculator Representations

The screens below show three different representations of a relationship as viewed with a graphing calculator.

- The first is a *symbolic* representation, Y1=3X+1.
- The second is a *graph* of that relationship in the viewing window [-10,10] horizontally by [-10,10] vertically. This is called a *visual* representation.
- The third screen shows part of a table of values, or a *numerical* representation.

Use a graphing calculator to replicate these three representations. Screens may vary slightly depending on which model of graphing calculator you are using.

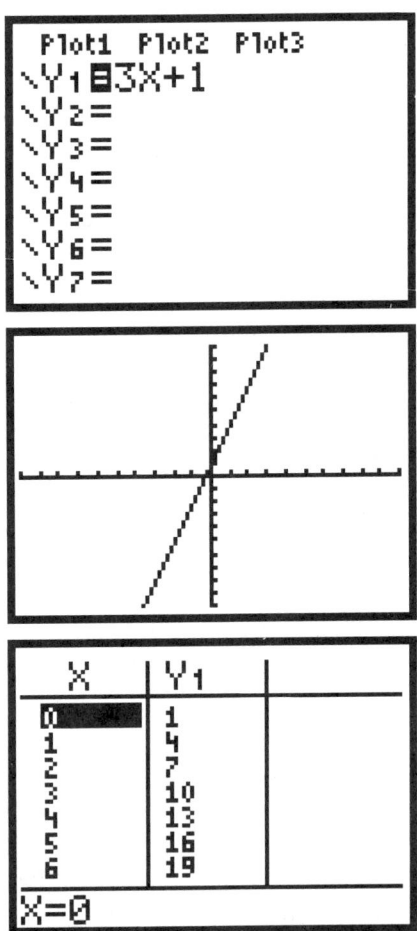

Summary Questions:
1. What are some advantages and disadvantages of each representation?

2. When might each type of representation be most useful?

TECHNOLOGY ACTIVITY 1.6

Using Graphit to Draw Conclusions

Consider the following sets of data.

A: $\{(-3.1, -5.21), (-1.9, -2.91), (-1.1, -1.19), (0.1, 1.23), (0.8, 2.58), (2.2, 5.51), (2.9, 6.83)\}$

B: $\{(-3.1, 10.63), (-1.9, 4.55), (-1.1, 2.23), (0.1, 1.21), (0.8, 1.68), (2.2, 5.88), (2.9, 9.46)\}$

C: $\{(-3.1, -0.21), (-1.9, -4.73), (-1.1, -4.46), (0.1, 0.49), (0.8, 3.59), (2.2, 4.04), (2.9, 1.19)\}$

Go to the Graphit feature on the Interactiviate disk.

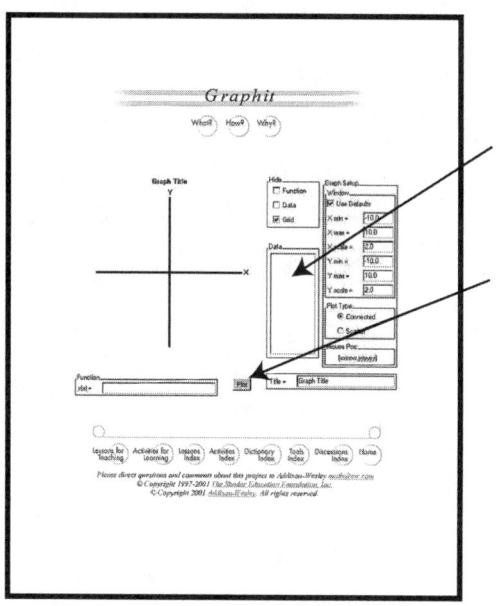

For each set,

1. Enter the data as ordered pairs. A comma must go between the elements of each pair. Hit enter after each pair.

2. Plot the data.

3. Observe the graph. Make sure the old data is deleted before plotting new data.

Summary Questions:

1. What kind of relation, if any, seems to be between the elements of the ordered pairs in Set A?

2. What kind of relation, if any, seems to be between the elements of the ordered pairs in Set B?

3. What kind of relation, if any, seems to be between the elements of the ordered pairs in Set C?

CHAPTER 2: SETS AND WHOLE-NUMBER OPERATIONS AND PROPERTIES

INVESTIGATION 2.1

Set Ideas

Use examples and the definitions of subsets and equal sets to explore and verify the following statement:

For sets A and B, $A = B$ if and only if A is a subset of B and B is a subset of A.

Summary Questions:

1. What examples for sets A and B did you use? Do your examples prove the statement is true?

2. What if you use the empty set as an example for one or both sets? Does the statement still hold? How does that change your reasoning or affect your verification?

3. How does this statement compare to the definition of equal sets? Could it be used as a definition for equal sets? Why or why not?

4. How does this statement relate to the idea of one-to-one correspondence and its role in the definition of whole numbers?

5. Would the statement still be true if it said "proper subset" instead of "subset"? Why or why not?

Chapter 2: Sets and Whole-Number Operations and Properties

INVESTIGATION 2.2

Names and Symbols

In this chapter, many names, properties, and symbols were introduced. A possible explanation for the ten symbols that are used in the Hindu-Arabic numeration system has to do with the number of angles that are represented.

Part A Summary Question:
If you consider an angle to be less than 180^0, where are the angles in each numeral? Is the number of angles consistent with what the numeral represents?

Besides the operations of addition and multiplication of whole numbers, several properties of these operations on the whole numbers were given.

Part B Summary Questions:
1. What is the meaning of the title *Closure Property* in everyday language?

2. What is the meaning of the title *Identity Property* in everyday language?

3. What is the meaning of the title *Commutative Property* in everyday language?

4. What is the meaning of the title *Associative Property* in everyday language?

In the discussion of sets, the term *disjoint* was introduced (page 75).

Part C Summary Questions:
1. What is the meaning of the term *disjoint* in everyday language?

2. A condition placed on Sets *A* and *B* in the *Definition of Addition of Whole Numbers* (page 77) was that the two sets are disjoint. Why is this a necessary condition?

3. The condition that Sets *A* and *B* must be disjoint was not placed on these sets in the *Definition of Multiplication of Whole Numbers* (page 90). Why is this not a necessary condition? If the sets are disjoint, does this affect the definition?

Inequalities can be separated into two groups, strict inequalities and weak inequalities. The strict inequalities are < and >. The weak inequalities are ≤ (less than or equal to) and ≥ (greater than or equal to). The weak inequalities are called such because they have a less restrictive condition.

Part D Summary Question:
How do the two types of inequalities compare to the symbols that are used for *subset* and *proper subset?*

In Chapter 2, the names of the components involved in the four basic operations as well the names of the results are given. The names involving addition are given on page 77, page 83 for subtraction, page 90 for multiplication, and page 97 for division.

Part E Summary Questions:
1. Which operations have names of the components different?

2. Which operations have names of the components the same?

3. What properties (or lack there of) could justify why an operation has components with different or the same names?

Chapter 2: Sets and Whole-Number Operations and Properties

INVESTIGATION 2.3

Different Bases in Everyday Units

Consider the following conversions.

1 gallon = 4 quarts
1 quart = 4 cups
1 hour = 60 minutes
1 minute = 60 seconds
1 meter = 10 decimeters
1 decimeter = 10 centimeter
1 centimeter = 10 millimeters

Part A Summary Questions:
1. What are

$$\begin{array}{r} 3 \text{ quarts } 2 \text{ cups} \\ + 2 \text{ quarts } 3 \text{ cups} \\ \hline \end{array}$$ and $$\begin{array}{r} 1 \text{ gallon } 2 \text{ quarts } 1 \text{ cup} \\ - \phantom{1 \text{ gallon }} 3 \text{ quarts } 2 \text{ cups} \\ \hline \end{array}$$?

2. What are

$$\begin{array}{r} 39 \text{ minutes } 28 \text{ seconds} \\ + 24 \text{ minutes } 49 \text{ seconds} \\ \hline \end{array}$$ and $$\begin{array}{r} 1 \text{ hour } 10 \text{ minutes } 28 \text{ seconds} \\ - \phantom{1 \text{ hour }} 42 \text{ minutes } 29 \text{ seconds} \\ \hline \end{array}$$?

3. What are

$$\begin{array}{r} 1 \text{ m} \phantom{3 \text{ dm}} 7 \text{ cm } 2 \text{ mm} \\ + \phantom{1 \text{ m}} 3 \text{ dm } 5 \text{ cm } 9 \text{ mm} \\ \hline \end{array}$$ and $$\begin{array}{r} 1 \text{ m} \phantom{6 \text{ dm}} 2 \text{ cm } 6 \text{ mm} \\ - \phantom{1 \text{ m}} 6 \text{ dm } 7 \text{ cm } 9 \text{ mm} \\ \hline \end{array}$$?

Part B Summary Questions:
1. What base was used in each of the questions in Part A?

2. Are any of these bases used elsewhere? If so, explain where.

INVESTIGATION 2.4

Counting in Different Bases

In base-ten, counting by 5's is fairly easy. The pattern of 5, 10, 15, 20, 25, 30, etc can be generated rather quickly. To determine if there are similar patterns in other bases, generate the first one hundred counting numbers in base-five, -six, -seven, and -eight. You may choose to assign a different base to members of the group.

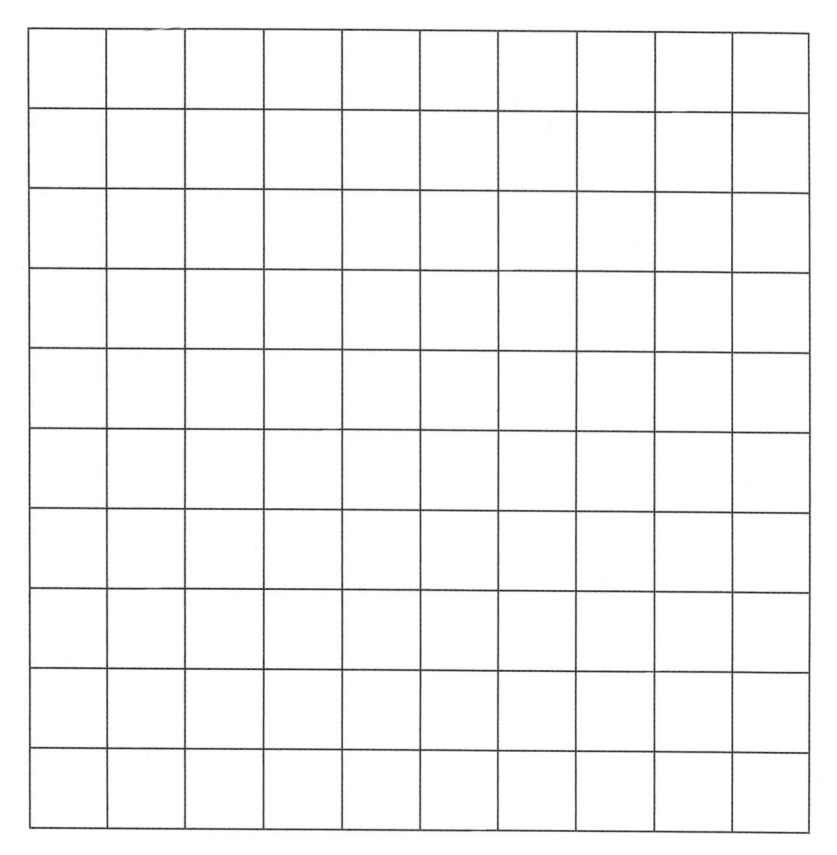

Summary Questions:
1. Which of the bases have the type of pattern found when counting by 5's in base-ten?

2. What is a common feature among these bases? Why is this a common feature?

3. If you wanted to count by 6's in base-twelve, what would the first twenty-four numerals in the pattern be? In base-twelve, twelve symbols are needed to represent the twelve digits. A standard that is used is 0, 1, 2, 3, 4, 5, 6, 7, 8, 9, T, and E where T converts to 10 and E converts to 11 in base-ten.

26 Chapter 2: Sets and Whole-Number Operations and Properties

INVESTIGATION 2.5

Braille Numerals

Another way to express numerals is the Braille System. It was developed by Louis Braille who at the age of 3 became blind due to an accident. The system is used for letters and punctuation as well as representing numbers. It consists of raised dots in various combinations. The numerals 0, 1, 2, 3, 4, 5, 6, 7, 8, and 9 are represented as follows.

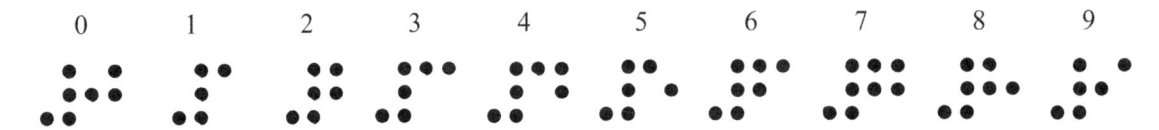

```
  0     1     2     3     4     5     6     7     8     9
```

Each of these numerals is preceded by a "backwards L". So if one wants to represent a number that has more than one digit, the "backwards L" need only be written on the first digit. Also, these numerals (without the "backwards L") correspond to the first 10 letters of the Braille Alphabet with 1 corresponding to "a", 2 corresponding to "b", etc. The 0 corresponds to the 10th letter of the alphabet, "j".

Part A Summary Question:
How would you represent the numeral 1234567890 in Braille?

When the numerals in Hindu-Arabic represent large quantities, commas are included to separate periods. In Braille, these periods are separated by a dot in the middle row.

Part B Summary Question:
How would you represent the numeral 1,234,567,890 in Braille?

In this system the alphabet and numerals (without the "backwards L") uses just 6 raised dots in different combinations. The dots are enumerated

1	4
2	5
3	6

.

Part C Summary Questions:
1. What dots are the raised for each the numerals 0 through 9 in Braille?

2. What is a common feature among the representations of each of these Braille numerals?

Letters in the Braille alphabet include a raised dot in the 3 or 6 positions for letters "k" through "z" whereas letters "a" through "j" do not. If you restrict the dots to the 1, 2, 4, and 5 locations, there are potentially 15 different representations that can be made with 1, 2, 3, or 4 dots.

Part D Summary Questions:
1. How many potential combinations can be made with 1 dot?

2. How many potential combinations can be made with 2 dots?

3. How many potential combinations can be made with 3 dots?

4. How many potential combinations can be made with 4 dots?

Discuss which combinations were not used in the representation of numerals 0 through 9 in Braille and possible explanations why.

28 Chapter 2: Sets and Whole-Number Operations and Properties

INVESTIGATION 2.6

Operations in Base-Six

In base-six, the symbols used are 0, 1, 2, 3, 4, and 5. Make a table showing the addition facts for a Hindu-Arabic base-six numeration system.

+	0	1	2	3	4	5
0						
1						
2						
3						
4						
5						

Part A Summary Questions:
1. What strategies, if any, did you use in making the addition facts table? What mathematical properties of addition do these strategies illustrate?

2. How can you use these addition facts to do subtraction in base-six? Have members of your group make up subtraction problems (in base-six) and detail its solution in terms *Using Addition to Define Subtraction* as described on page 82 of your text.

Make a table showing the multiplication facts for a Hindu-Arabic base-six numeration system.

x	0	1	2	3	4	5
0						
1						
2						
3						
4						
5						

Part B Summary Questions:
1. What strategies, if any, did you use in making the multiplication facts table? What mathematical properties of multiplication do these strategies illustrate?

2. How can you use these multiplication facts to do division in base-six? Have members of your group make up division problems (in base-six) and detail their solutions in terms *Using Multiplication to Define Division* as described on page 96 of your text.

3. Using your multiplication facts table, how can you create division problems that have a remainder?

INVESTIGATION 2.7

Comparing Numeration Systems

While working with two other classmates, write down the first one hundred counting numbers in the Egyptian, Babylonian (use the blank space symbol, ✸), and Roman numeration systems. Each student can start with "one" in the upper left hand corner of a 10x10 grid and work across the rows. If you wish, you may visit http://wps.aw.com/aw_odaffer_mathematic_2 for a larger printable numbered-grid. Compare the charts.

Summary Questions:
1. Why do you think there have been different numeration systems developed over time?

2. What strategies, if any, did you use in filling out the charts? What mathematical characteristics of your numeration system do those strategies illustrate?

3. What patterns do you see in your chart? What do the patterns show about the mathematics of the numeration system?

4. How are the patterns in the charts alike? How are they different from each other?

Chapter 2: Sets and Whole-Number Operations and Properties

INVESTIGATION 2.8

Expansion of the Babylonian Numeration System

The Babylonians had a symbol for "subtraction" in their numeration system. The symbol was a combination of the two symbols and it was ▼̄. For example, the numeral ◀▼̄▼ represents 10 − 1 = 9.

Write the following Babylonian numerals as Hindu-Arabic numerals.

◀◀▼▼   ◀▼̄▼   ◀◀▼̄▼▼   and   ◀▼̄▼▼▼   ◀◀▼̄▼   ▼▼

Write the following Hindu-Arabic numerals as Babylonian numerals two ways, without and with the subtraction symbol.

        7,990   and   49,168

Summary Questions:
1. What other system uses subtraction in their numeral representations?

2. What are some advantages of including such a subtraction symbol in this sexagesimal (base-sixty) system?

3. When would you use the subtraction symbol?

INVESTIGATION 2.9

Mayan System

The Mayans had a numeration system that included the concept of zero. The Mayans, who lived on the Yucatan Peninsula, had three basic symbols which were a shell (clam), line (bar), and a dot. The symbols and each of their value are as follows.

⊘ 0   ——— 5   ● 1

The positional system created numeric representations in a vertical fashion. Starting on the bottom and progressing upwards, the position in which a symbol appeared determined its meaning. A dot in the first position would represent 1, in the second position 20, in the third position 360, in the fourth position 7200, in the fifth position 144000, etc. The following is a Mayan numeral.

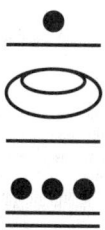

It would be translated to Hindu-Arabic as $43{,}200 + 0 + 100 + 13 = 43{,}313$

$7200 \cdot (5 + 1) = 7200 \cdot 6 = 43{,}200$

$360 \cdot 0 = 0$
$20 \cdot 5 = 100$

$1 \cdot (5 + 5 + 3) = 1 \cdot 13 = 13$

Summary Questions:

1. What would a dot in the sixth, seventh, and eighth positions represent?

2. What would a clam with a dot over it represent?

3. Is there a difference between

    ●● and ●
    ⊘   ●
              ⊘   ? Explain.

4. What are some advantages and disadvantages of this system over the Babylonian, Egyptian, and Roman numeration systems?

5. What other systems studied in Section 2.4 have the feature of being a positional system?

Chapter 2: Sets and Whole-Number Operations and Properties

INVESTIGATION 2.10

Representing Numbers on an Abacus (or Two)

The Hindu-Arabic base-ten numbers can be represented on a variety of devises. The Chinese abacus (suan-pan) which consists of seven beads in columns, separated into groups of 2's and 5's is a common type of abacus. Each of the two upper deck beads (which is said to represent heaven) has a value of 5. Each of the five lower deck beads (which is said to represent earth) has a value of 1. Because of the arrangement of the beads, this is also called a 2/5 abacus. Also manufactured is a 1/5 abacus (one bead on the top deck and 5 on the bottom) as well as a 1/4 abacus as variations of the same type of representation of numbers in base-ten.

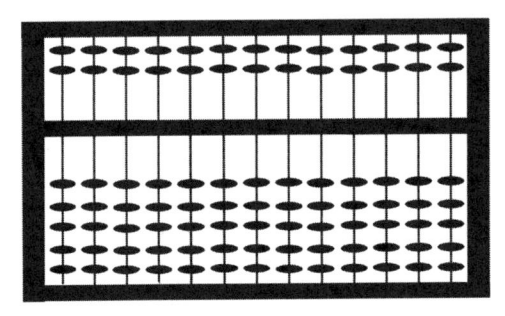

This "decimal" abacus displays a base-ten system number in which the right-most column is the ones column; the next column is the tens column, then the hundreds, etc. You move beads towards the bar that separates the two decks. When 5 beads are moved in the lower deck, the result is "carried" to the upper deck. When the two beads in the upper deck are moved, the result is carried to the next column to the left.

Part A Summary Questions:
1. Can you determine why there are two types are "carrying over" between decks and columns? If so, explain.

2. What base-ten Hindu-Arabic number would be represented by the following?

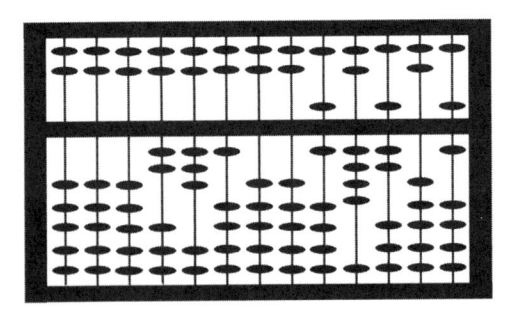

3. How could you represent the numeral 102,359 on a 2/5 abacus?

4. The 1/5 and 1/4 arrangements of an abacus are the same as the 2/5 in terms of the values of the beads on the upper and lower decks. Why do you think such variations were developed and how do they differ from the 2/5 arrangement?

Investigation 2.10   33

A variation on the abacus is the 3/4 abacus. Whereas the 2/5, 1/5, and 1/4 arrangements are all "decimal" arrangements, the 3/4 abacus can be a "vigesimal" arrangement. It does however use the same multiples on the upper and lower decks. When the base is the same (the other arrangements have been base-ten), the abacus represents regular place-value column values.

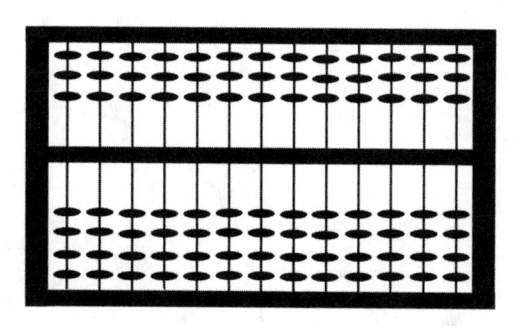

Part B Summary Questions:
1. Assuming regular place-value column values, what would the base be?

2. What would the representation of the numeral 61,996 be on the 3/4 abacus?

3. What similarities does the 3/4 abacus have with the 2/5 abacus?

4. Which abacus (the 2/5, 1/5, or 1/4) is the 3/4 abacus most similar to and why?

This same "vigesimal" 3/4 abacus can represent numbers that use the calendric place-value column values. The first column (on the right) represents the ones, then moving towards the left the columns represents 20, $18 \cdot 20$, $18 \cdot 20^2$, $18 \cdot 20^3$, etc.

Part C Summary Questions:
1. Why is this system not a regular place-value column values system?

2. Why is this system called a calendric place-value column values system? Discuss what you believe calendric refers to.

3. What number is represented by the following 3/4 abacus using the calendric place-value column values system?

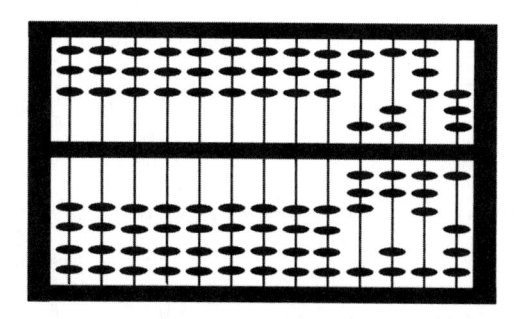

MANIPULATIVE ACTIVITY 2.1

Determining Features of Sets

Place into a bag a set of 50 PopCubes®. Randomly take out ten groups of PopCubes® two at a time and link them together. Then take out the remaining thirty PopCubes® in groups of three and link them together. You should have ten groups of two and ten groups of three PopCubes®.

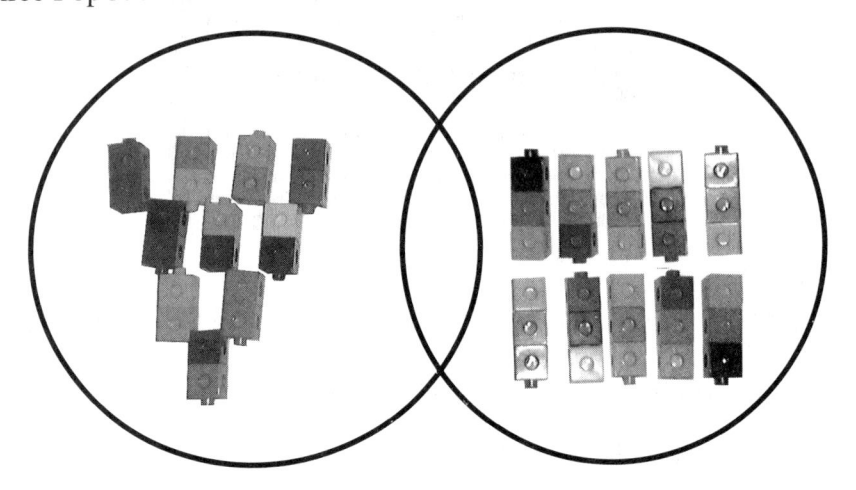

To sort this collection into two disjoint subgroups one could create a set that is made up of elements that have two PopCubes® and a set that is made up of elements that have three PopCubes®.

Create two rules of these same linked PopCubes®. One rule should have the PopCubes® sorted into two disjoint sets. The second rule should have the PopCubes® sorted into two non-disjoint sets. You may want to make use color in your sorting rule (a particular color or repeating of colors, for example). Answer the following Summary Questions for both the disjoint and non-disjoint sets.

Summary Questions:
1. What attributes would you use to describe each of the two sets?

2. How well do your descriptions name or describe the sets? Test your description by removing one object from one set and give it to a classmate in another set. Describe the two tests to him/her and ask them to place the object in the correct set.

3. Which of the sets has more items? How can you determine this without actually counting the objects in the set?

4. Without counting, how could you find a person who has made a set equivalent to one of yours?

Discuss and write a brief paragraph explaining why is it useful to be able to count and assign a whole number to sets.

MANIPULATIVE ACTIVITY 2.2

Meaning of Subtraction

Consider the subtraction expression $20 - 12$.

A. Have one member of your group demonstrate with PopCubes® the action this expression represents as a take-away situation. Have a different member of your group make up a story to go with it.

B. Have one member of your group demonstrate with PopCubes® the action this expression represents as a comparison situation. Have a different member of your group make up a story to go with it.

Part A Summary Questions:
1. How does the physical representations of the take-away situation differ from the comparison situation? How are they alike?

2. How do the two subtraction situations relate to the physical representation of addition (joining)?

3. What is alike about the two situations that allow us to use subtraction to describe them both?

Demonstrate by the take-away situation that the subtraction expression $12 - 20$ will not result in a whole number.

Part B Summary Questions:
1. In the comparison situation, can one "compare" the values of 12 and 20? If so, will this lead to an incorrect answer? Explain.

2. If you were to demonstrate the subtraction expression $12 - 12$ by the comparison situation, what physical attribute of the PopCube® arrangements allows you to come to the conclusion that $12 - 12 = 0$? Explain.

Chapter 2: Sets and Whole-Number Operations and Properties

MANIPULATIVE ACTIVITY 2.3

Meaning of Division

Consider the division expression $35 \div 5$.

A. Have one member of your group demonstrate with PopCubes® the action this expression represents as a repeated-subtraction situation. That is, given the size of the group to subtract determine how many times the group is subtracted. Have a different member of your group make up a story to go with it.

B. Have one member of your group demonstrate with PopCubes® the action this expression represents as a measurement situation. That is, given the size of the groups determine how many groups there are. Have a different member of your group make up a story to go with it.

C. Have one member of your group demonstrate with PopCubes® the action this expression represents as a sharing situation. That is, given how many groups there are determine the size of each group. Have a different member of your group make up a story to go with it.

Part A Summary Questions:
1. How are the physical representations of the repeated-subtraction situation, measurement situation, and sharing situation different? How are they alike?

2. How do the repeated-subtraction, measurement, and sharing situations relate to the physical representations of multiplication? (repeated-addition, arrays, area, or Cartesian product)

3. What is alike about the three situations that allows us to use division to describe them?

Consider the division expression $35 \div 6$.

Go through the demonstration of the three situations as described in A, B, and C with the PopCubes®.

Part B Summary Questions:
1. How does the repeated-subtraction situation demonstrate that $35 \div 6$ is not a whole number?

2. How does the measurement situation demonstrate that $35 \div 6$ is not a whole number?

3. How does the sharing situation demonstrate that $35 \div 6$ is not a whole number?

MANIPULATIVE ACTIVITY 2.4

Representing the Same Value in Different Bases

Take 50 PopCubes® and separate them to represent the same value, but in different bases. If PopCubes® are not available, you could use items like coins. To represent 50 in base-nine, for example, we have five groups of nine cubes and five groups of single cubes. This implies that $50 = 55_{nine}$.

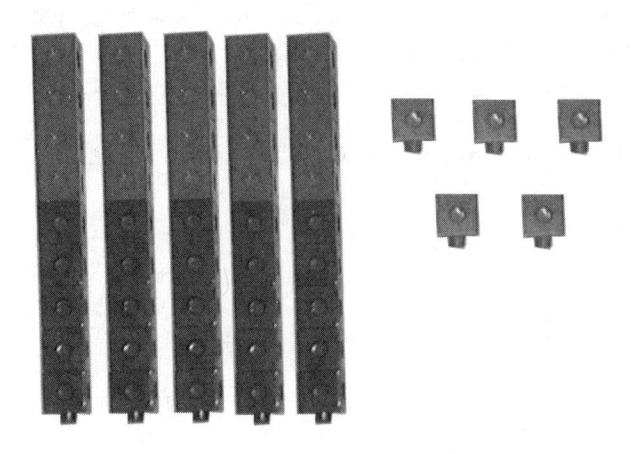

Summary Questions:
1. Using the PopCubes®, what are the representations of 50_{ten} in the following bases?

Base	Representation
Eight	
Seven	
Six	
Five	
Four	
Three	
Two	

2. Which of the following is more difficult and why, to give the representation of the fifty cubes in a higher or lower base?

3. Could you describe the appearance of the representations of fifty in different bases to be "bigger" when the base is smaller? Discuss.

Chapter 2: Sets and Whole-Number Operations and Properties

MANIPULATIVE ACTIVITY 2.5

Race to a Red

For this activity, you will need a die and PopCubes®. If PopCubes® are not available you can use four colors of chips or other counters (for the first player) and grid paper (for the second player). If a die is not available, see the end of this activity on how you can use your graphing calculator to simulate the roll of a die.

A. Find a partner. Separate the PopCubes® so that one player gets the red, white, orange and blue cubes (there should be five of each color in the set). Have the second player choose five of the other six colors of cubes. The second player should have 25 cubes.

B. The first player will be working with the following table.

red	white	orange	blue

C. The second player will be rolling the die while keeping track of the total number rolled by assembling his/her PopCubes® into a 5x5 square. When a square is completed, separate the cubes and start again, but keep track of how many complete squares were constructed. Most likely the second player will have to finish one square and continue the next square in a single roll.

D. In this game, we will use a grouping rule of five. On the first roll of the die, the first player starts on the right-hand column of the table. With a grouping rule of five, if 1 through 4 is rolled then this player will place that number of blue cubes in the blue-cube column. If 5 or 6 is rolled, then 5 blues are grouped to make 1 orange.

During each roll of the die, each player should make note of what position he or she is in relation to the other player. The game is over when the first player places a red cube in the red-cube column.

Part A Summary Questions:
1. What is the relationship between Player 1's table and Player 2's creation of squares?

2. What does one cube in the blue-cube column represent?

3. What does one cube in the orange-cube column represent?

4. What does one cube in the white-cube column represent?

5. What does the cube in the red-cube column represent?

6. How could you use numerals to record the different quantities shown after each roll?

Play this game again using a grouping rule of three. Switch roles of two players. Since the grouping rule is three, the player rolling the die will be making 3x3 squares.

Part B Summary Questions:
1. How does the size of the grouping rule affect the game?

2. How does the size of the grouping rule affect how you would record the quantities with numerals?

If a die is not available, you can use your graphing calculator to simulate the roll of a die. When you press the MATH button you will see the first screen on a TI-83.

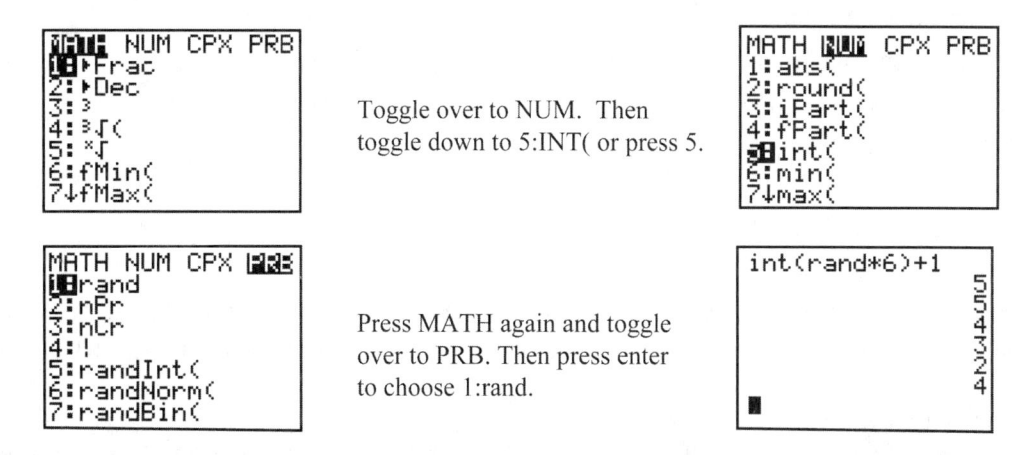

Toggle over to NUM. Then toggle down to 5:INT(or press 5.

Press MATH again and toggle over to PRB. Then press enter to choose 1:rand.

Type in the rest of the expression as shown is the last screen. If you continue to hit enter, the calculator will display the digits 1 through 6 randomly.

Chapter 2: Sets and Whole-Number Operations and Properties

TECHNOLOGY ACTIVITY 2.1

Venn Diagrams

Go to the Venn Diagrams feature on the Interactiviate disk.

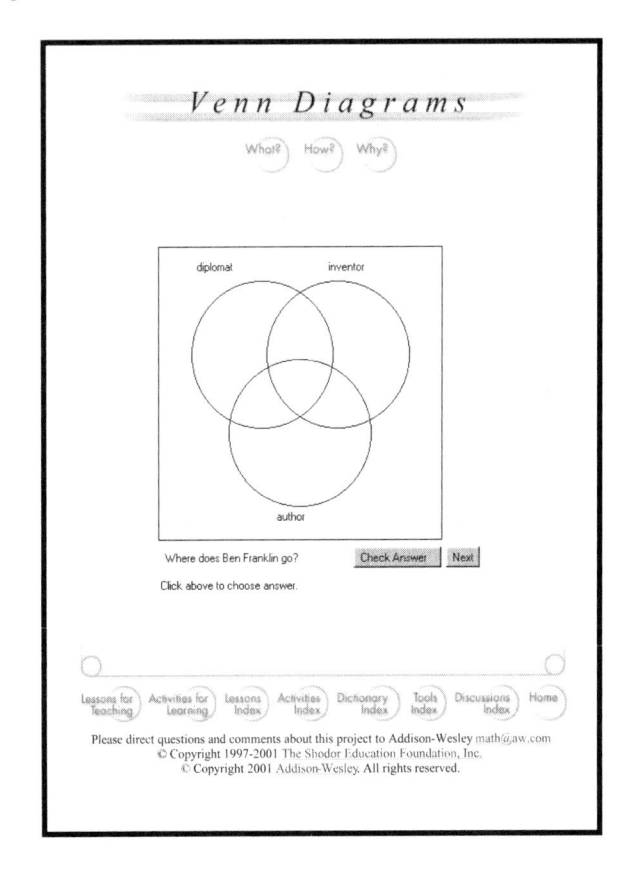

There are twenty exercises. Perform the exercises that ask the following questions.

A) Where does a triangle go?
B) Where does one quarter go?
C) Where does a graph go?
D) Where does 5.25 go?
E) Where does one day go?
F) Where does 13 go?

After you answer each question and determine the correct region, create a different question with different sets that has the same response (the same shaded region).

Summary Question:
Is it more difficult to deal with problems that have 3 circles verses 2 circles? Why or why not?

TECHNOLOGY ACTIVITY 2.2

Pizza and Pascal

Pascal's Triangle can be used to determine how many subsets of a given set will have a specified number of elements. For example, if you have a set with three elements such as $\{a,b,c\}$. The subsets are

$$\{\ \},\ \{a\},\ \{b\},\ \{c\},\ \{a,b\},\ \{a,c\},\ \{b,c\},\text{ and }\{a,b,c\}.$$

There is 1 set with no elements, 3 sets with 1 element, 3 sets with 2 elements, and 1 set with 3 elements. This reflects the line "1 3 3 1" in Pascal's Triangle.

Now a restaurant that serves pizza offers the following toppings:

> Anchovies
> Pepperoni
> Green Olives
> Black Olives
> Canadian Bacon
> Onions
> Pineapple

Go to the Coloring Multiples in Pascal's Triangle feature on the Interactiviate disk. Use this to help determine the different combinations of pizza that have 2 toppings.

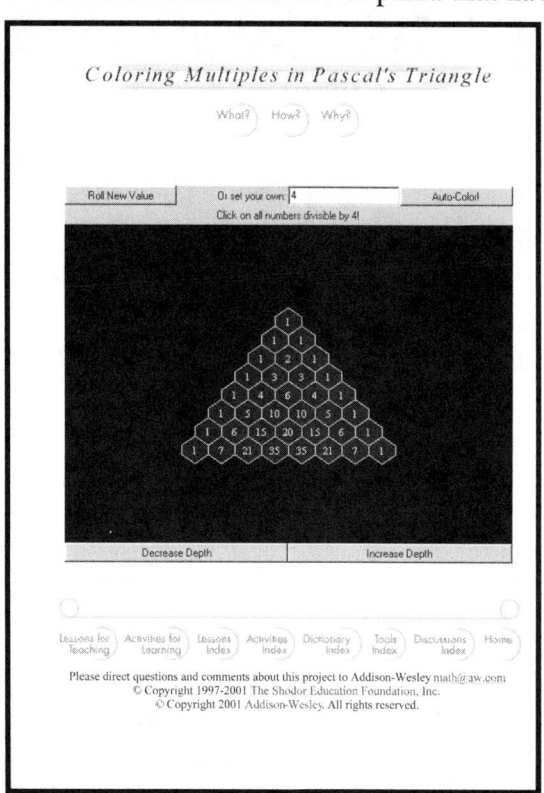

Chapter 2: Sets and Whole-Number Operations and Properties

Part A Summary Questions:
1. What are the different combinations?

2. How can you use the combinations that have only two toppings to find all combinations that have 5 toppings?

Suppose the restaurant offered 15 toppings. Use the Coloring Multiples in Pascal's Triangle feature on the Interactiviate disk and click on "Increase Depth" until you find the line corresponding to this situation.

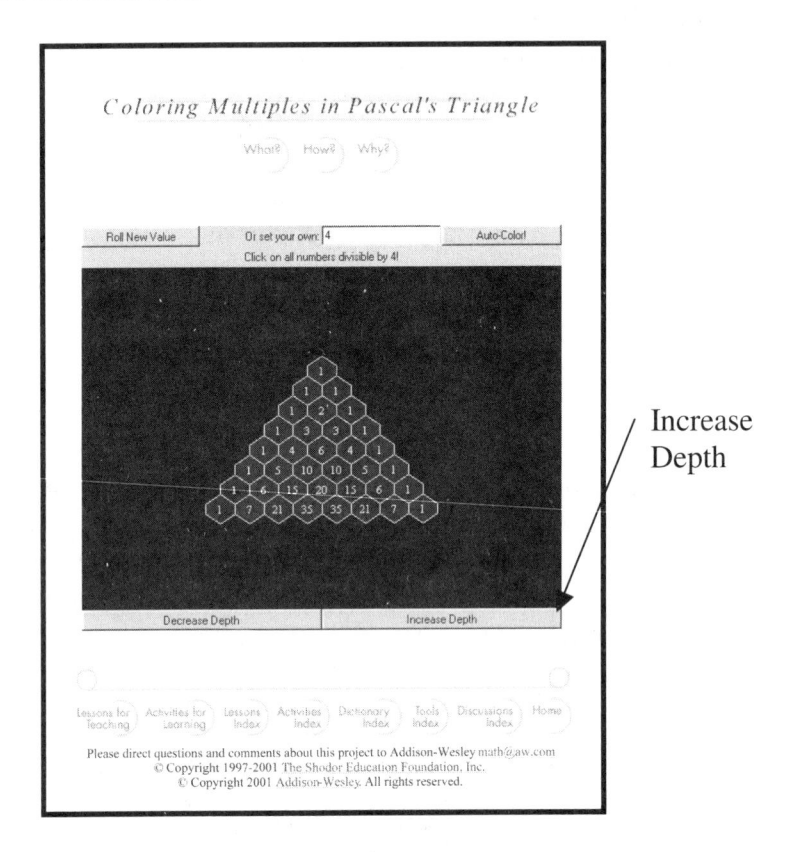

Part B Summary Questions:
1. How many combinations of pizza could be made that have 2 toppings?

2. How many combinations of pizza could be made that have 13 toppings?

3. How can you use the combinations that have only 2 toppings to find all combinations that have 13 toppings?

4. A pizza that has only 12 of the 15 toppings has more ways it can be made compared to a pizza that has 13 of the 15 toppings. Why does this happen?

TECHNOLOGY ACTIVITY 2.3

Repeated Subtraction

This activity can be performed with spreadsheet software such as Excel® in order to draw a conclusion. This activity can also be done using any standard calculator if this software is not available.

If you are using Excel®, enter the number 247 in A1. In Cell A2 type "=A1-7" (without the quotation marks) and hit enter. The number 240 should be calculated in this cell. Click on Cell A2 and copy it to the cells below A2 until Cell A40.

	A
1	247
2	240
3	233
4	226
5	219
6	
7	
8	
9	
10	

Part A Summary Questions:
1. After the first value 247, how many more positive whole numbers appear on your list?

2. What is the smallest whole number? Remember, whole numbers cannot be negative.

Perform this repeated subtraction process with 248, 249, 250, 251, 252, 253, 254, and 255. You only need to change the entry in A1. The values in the cells below A1 will be regenerated.

Part B Summary Questions:
1. What is the smallest whole number on the list for each of the eight suggested values?

2. What kind of restrictions, if any, would be placed on the smallest whole number?

3. How do the results relate to the division algorithm studied in Chapter 2 of your text?

44 Chapter 2: Sets and Whole-Number Operations and Properties

TECHNOLOGY ACTIVITY 2.4

Sums of Odds and Evens

This activity can be performed with spreadsheet software such as Excel® in order to draw a conclusion. A standard calculator can be used if this software is not available.

If you are using Excel®, label Column A "Term #" and enter the numbers 1 through 20 below. Label Column B "Odd #" and in Cell B2 type "=2*A2-1" (without the quotation marks) and hit enter. The number 1 should be calculated in this cell. Click on Cell B2 and copy it to the remaining cells in Column B (as many as you labeled in Column A). The first 20 odd natural numbers should be calculated. Label Column C "Sum" and in Cell C2 enter 1. In Cell C3 type "=C2+B3" (without quotation marks) and hit enter. Click on Cell C2 and copy it to the remaining cells in Column C (as many as you labeled in Column A). On the spreadsheet, the entry you placed in C2 represents the sum of the first odd natural number. The formulas you generated yield 4 as the sum of the first two odd natural numbers, and so on.

	A	B	C
1	Term #	Odd #	Sum
2	1	1	1
3	2	3	4
4	3	5	
5	4		

Part A Summary Questions:
1. What patterns did you find in the sums column? What patterns did you find between the columns?

2. What strategies could you use to determine the sum of the first 100 odd natural numbers without actually adding them?

To determine a pattern for the sum of even natural numbers, change the label Column B to "Even #". In Cell B2 type "=2*A2" (without quotation marks) and hit enter. The number 2 should be calculated in this cell. Click on Cell B2 and copy it to the remaining cells in Column B. The first 20 even natural numbers should be calculated. In Cell C2 enter 2. The cells below C2 should be recalculated.

	A	B	C
1	Term #	Even #	Sum
2	1	2	2
3	2	4	6
4	3	6	
5	4		

Part B Summary Questions:
1. What patterns did you find in the sums column? What patterns did you find between the columns?

2. What strategies could you use to determine the sum of the first 100 even natural numbers without actually adding them?

TECHNOLOGY ACTIVITY 2.5

Playing with Numbers

Some calculators use a series of bars to represent digits. Each representation for the digits zero through nine can be made from seven bars. The representation for "8" used all seven bars.

$$0\ 1\ 2\ 3\ 4\ 5\ 6\ 7\ 8\ 9$$

If you turn these digits upside down, (with some imagination) you can make out letters of the alphabet.

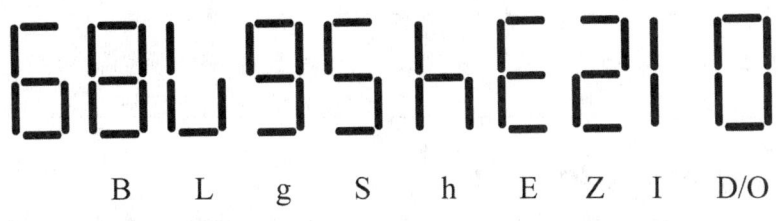

```
B   L   g   S   h   E   Z   I   D/O
```

Words and names can be represented on calculators that use this configuration to represent the digits. For example when 10134 is entered into such a calculator, it looks like (again, with some imagination) the name Heidi when viewed upside down.

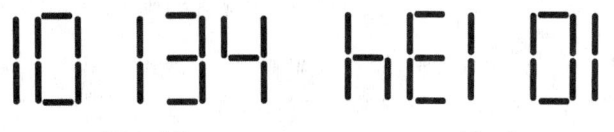

right side up   upside down

Summary Questions:
1. Perform the following operations. What words/names are represented when the calculator is turned upside down?

$$6^2 \cdot 61 \cdot 173 \quad \text{and} \quad \frac{34 \cdot 681}{3}$$

2. What problem that deals with operations of whole numbers gives a result of "BIG" when the calculator is turned upside down? There are several correct answers.

3. What problem that deals with operations of whole numbers gives a result of "LOOSE" when the calculator is turned upside down? There are several correct answers.

4. If you are dealing with operations on whole numbers, could you represent a word that ends with the letter "o"? Explain.

Create a word that is made of letters b, d, e, g, h, i, l, s, or z. Give this word to your partner to make up a problem that involves operations on whole numbers.

Chapter 2: Sets and Whole-Number Operations and Properties

TECHNOLOGY ACTIVITY 2.6

What Day Was That?

You are to determine what day of the week each member of your group was born on. You will need the month, day, and four-digit year. Perform the following calculations for each member of your group. In the division steps, you will want to write down the quotient only (no remainder). So for example if you were born in January (month = 1), the result for a will be 1.

1.	$a = \dfrac{14 - \text{month}}{12}$	
2.	$b = \text{year} - a$	
3.	$c = \text{month} + 12a - 2$	
4.	$d = \text{day}$	
5.	$e = \dfrac{b}{4}$	
6.	$f = -\dfrac{b}{100}$	
7.	$g = \dfrac{b}{400}$	
8.	$h = \dfrac{31c}{12}$	
9.	Sum together the shaded boxes. Remember that the number in step 6 is negative.	

Go to the Clock Arithmetic feature on the Interactiviate disk.

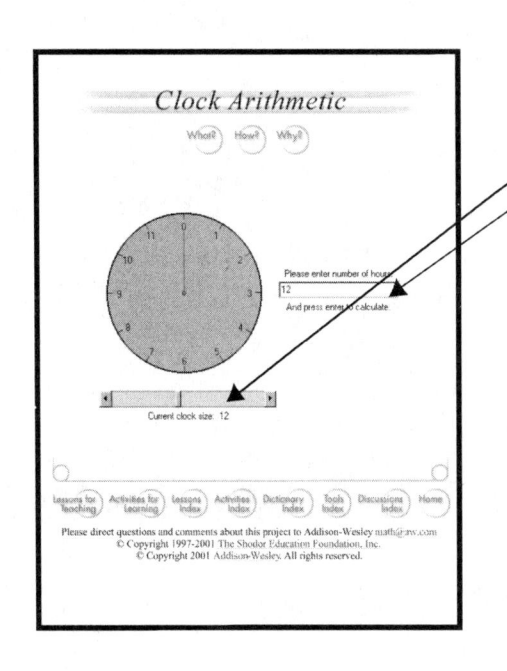

1. Adjust the clock size to 7.
2. Enter in the sum you found and hit enter.
3. The answer will correspond to the day of your birth.
   - 0 will imply Sunday
   - 1 will imply Monday
   - 2 will imply Tuesday
   - 3 will imply Wednesday
   - 4 will imply Thursday
   - 5 will imply Friday
   - 6 will imply Saturday

Summary Questions:
1. What is the significance of changing the clock from 12 to 7?

2. What is the significance of using a clock to determine the day of the week?

3. What are the numbers 0, 1, 2, 3, 4, 5, and 6 meaning in terms of your sum and 7?

4. In looking at the calculations that are performed in order to arrive at your sum, what is the significance of each of the steps?

Hint: The common rule regarding leap years is that years evenly divisible by 4 are leap years, with the exception of centurial years that are not evenly divisible by 400. Years such as 1700, 1800, and 1900 are not leap years. Years such as 1600 and 2000 are leap years.

CHAPTER 3: ESTIMATION AND COMPUTATION

INVESTIGATION 3.1

Planning a Trip

Use a map of the United States together with the data in the mileage chart to plan the trips described below. Do all calculations mentally. Distances given are approximations. If a map is not available, you can visit http://wps.aw.com/aw_odaffer_mathematic_2 to download a map with the cities below indicated.

		1.	2.	3.	4.	5.	6.	7.	8.	9.	10.	11.	12.	13.	14.
1.	Atlanta, GA	0	1500	700	825	1400	730	525	825	1100	480	830	750	1800	2483
2.	Cheyenne, WY		0	980	900	100	1250	1080	680	880	1400	700	1800	950	1200
3.	Chicago, IL			0	900	1000	280	190	550	400	900	825	785	1750	2200
4.	Dallas, TX				0	780	1200	900	500	950	500	200	1450	1000	1800
5.	Denver, CO					0	1300	1000	600	920	1300	600	1700	800	1250
6.	Detroit, MI						0	300	770	700	1100	990	600	200	2400
7.	Indianapolis, IN							0	500	600	800	750	650	1700	2300
8.	Kansas City, MO								0	450	800	350	1200	1200	1900
9.	Minneapolis, MN									0	1350	800	1200	1700	2000
10.	New Orleans, LA										0	700	1200	1500	2300
11.	Oklahoma City, OK											0	1400	1000	1700
12.	Philadelphia, PA												0	2400	2900
13.	Phoenix, AZ													0	750
14.	San Francisco, CA														0

Trip A: Plan a trip from San Francisco to New Orleans. What is the total distance?

Trip B: Can you find a different route from San Francisco to New Orleans? What is this total distance? How much more/less (in miles) is the second trip than the first?

Trip C: Plan a trip that will be about 2500 miles and passes through at least three of the cities in the chart. How much more or less is this trip than a direct route?

Summary Questions:
1. How did you use mental math to find the total distances for the two trips from San Francisco to New Orleans?

2. Describe the mental calculations you did to build a trip of about 2500 miles. Could you have done the mental calculations in a different way? Explain.

3. Compare your description of the mental calculations performed with those of a classmate. Did he/she perform the mental calculations using the same method(s) you did? Explain.

Chapter 3: Estimation and Computation

INVESTIGATION 3.2

Compatible Numbers, Compensation, and Lattice Multiplication in Other Bases

Consider the following sums in bases other than ten.

$$4_{six} + 2_{six} = 10_{six} \qquad 3_{seven} + 4_{seven} = 10_{seven} \qquad 5_{eight} + 3_{eight} = 10_{eight}$$

$$1_{two} + 1_{two} = 10_{two} \qquad 7_{nine} + 2_{nine} = 10_{nine}$$

Part A Summary Questions:
1. What do the above examples illustrate about addition of compatible numbers in bases other than ten?

2. What are the following sums?

   A. 34_{six}
      $+22_{six}$

   B. 42_{seven}
      $+25_{seven}$

Now consider the following sums in bases other than ten.

$$4_{six} + 3_{six} = 11_{six} \qquad 4_{seven} + 5_{seven} = 12_{seven} \qquad 6_{eight} + 5_{eight} = 13_{eight}$$

$$2_{three} + 2_{three} = 11_{three} \qquad 7_{nine} + 6_{nine} = 14_{nine}$$

Part B Summary Question:
How can you use *compensation* (as described on pages 129-130 in your text) to calculate the above sums mentally?

For finding products of single digit numbers in other bases mentally, a convenient method is to "multiply in base-ten and convert". The division of the base-ten product and the base can easily be performed mentally. The conversion will be the quotient followed by the remainder.

Consider the following products in bases other than ten.

$$4_{six} \cdot 3_{six} = 20_{six} \qquad 4_{seven} \cdot 5_{seven} = 26_{seven} \qquad 6_{eight} \cdot 5_{eight} = 36_{eight}$$

$$2_{three} \cdot 2_{three} = 11_{three} \qquad 7_{nine} \cdot 6_{nine} = 46_{nine}$$

Part C Summary Question:
Why does this "multiply in base-ten and convert" method *work*? Explain.

On pages 182 and 183, lattice multiplication is described. In such a method, the order in which you perform the single-digit multiplication is not critical. Although multiplication in other bases works the same way as the standard algorithm outlined in Example 3.22 on pages 166-167, it may be easier to use lattice multiplication to find "larger" products in other bases. An example would be $65_{eight} \cdot 105_{eight} = 7111_{eight}$.

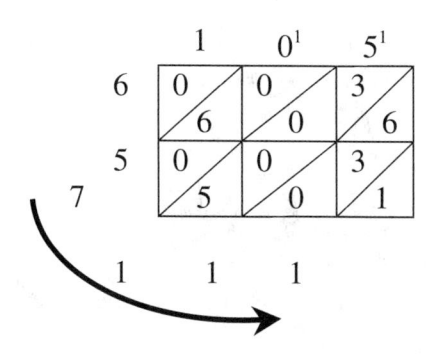

Show that $65_{eight} \cdot 105_{eight} = 7111_{eight}$ using the standard algorithm for multiplication.

Part D Summary Questions:
1. Which method seems easier to perform and why?

2. Try the "multiply in base-ten and convert" method on this above product. Do you get the correct answer? Why or why not? Explain

3. What are the following products using the lattice method. Use compatible numbers and compensation in your addition calculations.

   A. 35_{six}
      $\times 21_{six}$

   B. 641_{seven}
      $\times 65_{seven}$

   Discuss with a classmate where "multiply in base-ten and convert", compatible numbers and compensation were used.

4. Perform a multiplication in base-ten, say $62 \cdot 35 = 2170$, using lattice multiplication and the standard algorithm for multiplication. Compare the two approaches. Why does lattice multiplication *work*?

INVESTIGATION 3.3

A Weighty Problem (or Two)

A traditional problem is you are given 3 items that look alike; but one of the items weighs more than the other two. How can you use the kind of scale pictured below to determine the heaviest item in one weighing?

The answer is that you take two of the items and place one on each side and interpret the result.

Part A Summary Question:
Why does this weighing provide the solution to the problem? How do you interpret the results of the weighing?

A variation on the traditional weighing problem is to consider ten bags. Nine of these bags have the same amount of "fools gold" pieces in them. One bag, however, is filled with real gold. This bag has the same number of pieces of real gold as "fools gold" and between all ten bags each piece looks the same as any other piece. Suppose the "fools gold" pieces each weigh 1 pound and the real gold pieces each weigh 2 pounds. Can you use the kind of scale below to determine which bag has the real gold in one weighing?

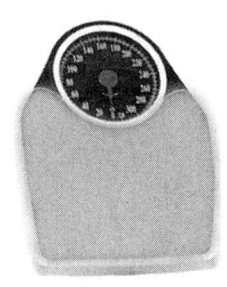

The answer is to line up the bags and label them 1 through 10. From bag 1 take one piece. From 2 two take two pieces and so on until you take ten pieces from bag 10. Weigh all of these pieces together.

Part B Summary Questions:
1. How do you interpret the results of the weighing? Why does this weighing provide the solution to the problem?
2. Can this procedure be expanded to consider 20 bags with the same conditions (one bag of gold and all bags/pieces look alike)? How would you change your interpretation of the combined weight of the pieces?

INVESTIGATION 3.4

Looking a Gift Horse in the Mouth

Suppose a relative gave you a gift certificate from an online company for $200 to spend on yourself. You can order any of the items from the catalog list below. Any money not spent on items in the catalog cannot be kept, so a goal is to spend as much of the $200 as possible. Suppose there is a shipping charge of $8 for all orders between $100 and $200 (inclusive) and a charge of $4 for all orders between $1 and $99 (inclusive). Sales tax is not considered and a "2 for" price cannot be split into two single prices. Assume all items are for males as well as females.

A. Develop two plans for spending the money.

B. Determine how much money would be left over for each plan.

C. Tell which plan you would choose and why.

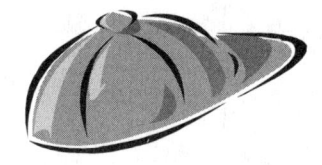

Item	Cost
Polo shirts	$30 each
Color T-Shirts	$14 each or 2 for $20
Hawaiian Shirts	$39 each
Rain Coats	$75 each
Rugby Shirts	2 for $45
Sweatshirts	$24 each

Item	Cost
Workout Shorts	$21 each
Hiking Pants	$18 each
Wind Breakers	$50 each
Baseball Hats	2 for $30
Leather Jackets	$120 each
Hiking Boots	$75 each

Summary Questions:

1. Where and how did you use addition and subtraction to complete the task above?

2. Did you do all calculations with pencil and paper? Did you do any mentally? Did you find a need for a calculator? If so, when did you find the need for a calculator?

3. Did you consider the $4 shipping charge in either of your two plans for spending? Why or why not?

Chapter 3: Estimation and Computation

INVESTIGATION 3.5

Walk-a-Thon

The chart below shows the results of a walk-a-thon conducted by a service organizer at a certain university. Some of the data was deleted by either an unreliable computer or an unreliable computer operator.

A. Complete the table.

B. Find the total amount of money earned from the walk-a-thon by adding all of the entries in the last column.

Name	Amount Pledged per Kilometer	Number of Kilometers Walked	Total Earned
Katerina Kucera	$3	18	$ 54
Dean Moore	$4		$ 96
Scott Hochwald		24	$120
Frank Capek	$6	19	
Joe Vetere		32	$224
Faiz Al-Rubaee	$2		$ 86
Nicole Pekarek	$5	36	
John Allen		23	$276
Sami Malhas	$10		$420
		TOTAL	

Summary Questions:
1. Which operations did you use to complete each row?

2. How did you decide which operations to use?

3. Which values did you calculate mentally? Which values did you calculate with pencil and paper? Which values did you calculate with a calculator? Explain why you performed each calculation in the manner you did.

INVESTIGATION 3.6

A Cross to Bear

Consider the following arrangement of the numerals 1, 2, 3, 4, and 5.

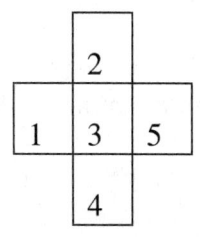

```
    2
1   3   5
    4
```

If you sum the vertical values you get the same as the sum of the horizontal values, which is 9. Notice that the center value is both a vertical and horizontal number.

Another possible variation is

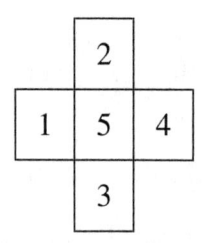

```
    2
1   5   4
    3
```

and any version that has 5 in the center is considered the same arrangement.

Summary Questions:
1. Besides 3 and 5, what other numeral could be used as a center value?

2. Consider the numerals 3, 5, 7, 8, and 9. Which of the numerals could be used as a center value in the type of arrangement above?

3. How can you determine which numeral will yield the desired result without actually investigating all of the possibilities? Explain.

Choose five natural numbers randomly (between 1 and 10) and give them to a classmate to determine which (if any) of the numerals can be used as center values in the cross-like arrangement. Is it possible to choose five natural numbers (1 and 10) that would yield no cross-like arrangements?

Chapter 3: Estimation and Computation

INVESTIGATION 3.7

Egyptian and Russian Peasant Multiplication

The Egyptian method of multiplication is sometimes referred to as the duplication method. In this method, you start generating powers of two (starting with the 0th power) until it exceeds one of the chosen factors. You then look at the powers of two and determine a combination of terms to sum to be the chosen factor. Products are found across the rows and then summed. For example, if you wish to multiply 28 and 37 then

Powers of 2	Other factor	product
1	37	
2	37	
4	37	148
8	37	296
16	37	592

$148 + 296 + 592 = 1036$.

In this method, there may be more than one way to sum the powers of two to achieve the chosen factor. Also, the powers of 2 may be used more than once.

Part A Summary Questions:
1. What values would you sum to find $25 \cdot 100$ by the Egyptian method?

2. Which factor should be chosen in the Other Factor column in order to perform the least number of *power steps*? Why?

3. Why does this method *work*?

Another method of multiplication is variation on the Egyptian method. It is called the Russian peasant method (sometimes referred to as duplation and mediation). In this process, you double one of the factors and half the other (ignoring the remainder). You then look for odd numbers in the half column and add up the corresponding values in the double column. For example, if you wish to multiply 28 and 37 then

Half	Double
28	37
14	74
7	148
3	296
1	592

$148 + 296 + 592 = 1036$.

Part B Summary Questions:
1. What values would you sum to find $25 \cdot 100$ by the Russian peasant method?

2. Which factor should be chosen in the double column in order to perform the least number of *halving steps*? Why?

3. Why does this method *work*?

INVESTIGATION 3.8

A Couple Mental Multiplications

Multiplying by 10, 100, 1000, or any power of 10 is fairly easy. In the final answer, one basically "tacks on" the number of zeros that are indicated by the power of 10.

Part A Summary Questions:
1. What is the product of 13572 and 1000 by the standard algorithm for multiplication as outlined on pages 166-167 in you text?

2. Represent 13572 in it's expanded notation. Use the distributive property to determine the product of 13572 and 1000, where $1000 = 10^3$. What reasons justify each step? See page 156 in your text for the types of reasons required.

Multiplying by 5 can be performed mentally by first "tacking on" a zero and then dividing by 2 (cutting in half).

Part B Summary Questions:
1. What are the results of the following using this method?

   A. $5 \cdot 17$ B. $120 \cdot 5$ C. $162 \cdot 5$

2. What is a justification for this procedure?

The above two procedures can be extended to multiplying by 50, 500, 5000, etc.

Part C Summary Questions:
1. What would be the procedure for multiplying by 50, 500, 5000, etc mentally?

2. Which numeration system studied in Chapter 2 could have made use of such an algorithm and why?

58   Chapter 3: Estimation and Computation

MANIPULATIVE ACTIVITY 3.1

Chip Trading Addition

For this activity you will need three different colors (thirty of each color) of PopCubes® or chips. Visit http://wps.aw.com/aw_odaffer_mathematic_2 to download printable red, blue, and green chips if PopCubes® are not available.

Consider the following addition exercises.

1. $67 + 88$ 2. $45 + 76$ 3. $39 + 28$

4. $135 + 546$ 5. $243 + 658$ 6. $667 + 55$

Choose one color to represent hundreds, another color represent tens, and the third color represent ones.

A. Show both numbers using PopCubes® or colored chips.

B. Combine groups and regroup as needed to find the total.

C. Write an addition equation in vertical form to record you work.

Example of $369 + 244$ using chips:

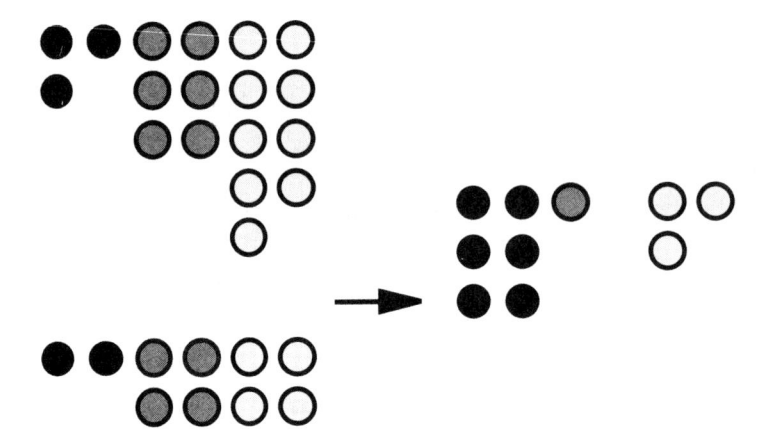

Summary Questions:
1. Why should the PopCubes® or chips be different colors?

2. Refer to page 148 in your text for the above example performed with base-ten blocks. How are PopCubes® or chips similar to base-ten blocks for doing addition calculations? How are they different?

3. Thirty of each color was chosen to be a convenient number (ten for each digit representation in each addend and ten for each digit representation in the sum). Consider the above example. What is the minimum number of each color PopCube® or chip needed to perform problems that involve at most three digits?

MANIPULATIVE ACTIVITY 3.2

Chip Trading Subtraction

For this activity you will need three different colors (thirty of each color) of PopCubes® or chips. Visit http://wps.aw.com/aw_odaffer_mathematic_2 to download printable red, blue, and green chips if PopCubes® are not available.

Consider the following subtraction exercises.

1. 81 – 35
2. 75 – 18
3. 64 – 34
4. 135 – 63
5. 243 – 138
6. 321 – 168

Choose one color to represent hundreds, another color represent tens, and the third color represent ones.

A. Show the first number using PopCubes® or colored chips.

B. Take away the chips representing the second number. Regroup as needed to find the amount left.

C. Write a subtraction equation in vertical form to record you work.

Example of 245 – 18 using chips:

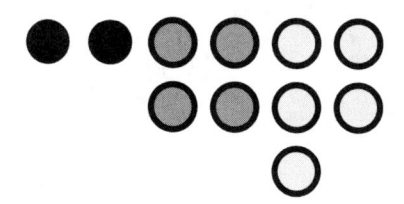

●● ◐◐◐◐   Regroup 1 tens for 10 ones.   ●● ◯◯◯
◯◯◯◯   Take away 8 ones.   ◯◯
◯   Take away 1 ten.   ◯◯
                                          ◯

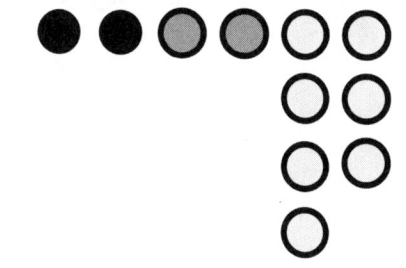

Summary Question:
Refer to page 152 in your text for the above example, performed with base-ten blocks. How are PopCubes® or chips similar to base-ten blocks for doing subtraction calculations? How are they different?

Create a subtraction problem using PopCubes® or chips in which regrouping must be performed. Show the first number and the difference to a classmate (both represented in PopCubes® or chips) and have them determine your subtraction problem.

MANIPULATIVE ACTIVITY 3.3

Finger Multiplication

A common method to multiply by nines is to hold you hands in front of you (palms down) and your fingers and thumbs will be labeled as follows.

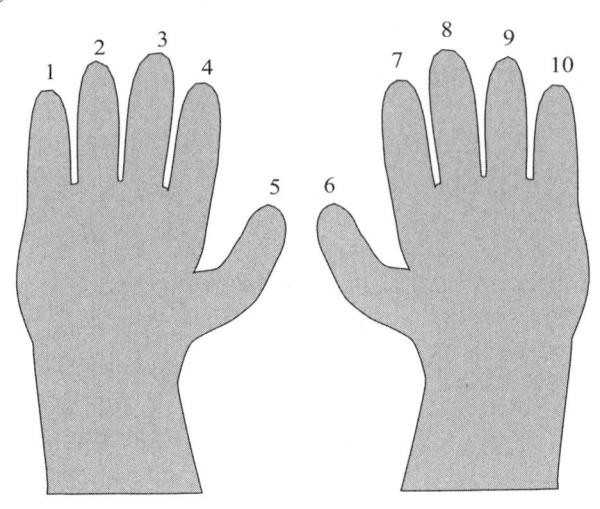

If you want to multiply 7×9, for example, fold the finger labeled 7 down. Read the product as the number of fingers/thumbs to the left of the folded finger as the tens digit followed by the number of fingers/thumbs to the right of the folded finder as the ones digit. This method will work for multiplying nine by one through ten.

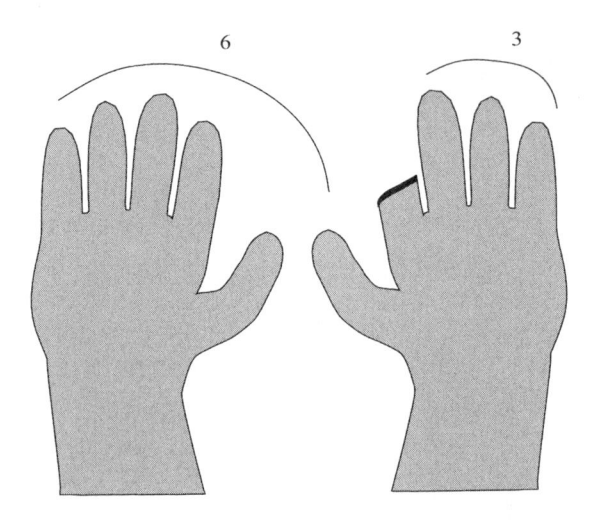

Part A Summary Questions:
1. Why does this method work?

2 How would you interpret the product 1×9 and 10×9 using the above method?

Rules for 6, 7, 8, 9, and 10

A. Hold up your hands. Your palms should be facing you and your thumbs should be up (as shown below).

B. Match the problem to the numbered fingers.

C. Multiply the number of fingers that touch and above by ten.

D. Multiply the number of fingers below the touching fingers on one hand by the other.

E. Add these two products together.

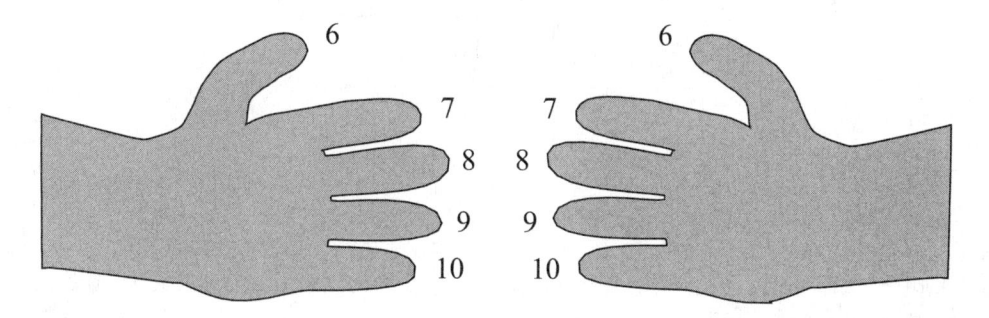

Part B Summary Questions:

1. How would you find the product 7×8 using the above method? Explain by drawing the hands and interpreting the results.

2. Although 8×7 will yield the same product as 7×8 by the Commutative Property of Multiplication, why will the products be the same using the above method?

Rules for 11, 12, 13, 14, and 15

A. Hold up your hands. Your palms should be facing you and your thumbs should be up (as shown below).

B. Match the problem to the numbered fingers.

C. Start with 100 in reserve.

D. Multiply the number of fingers that touch and above by ten.

E. Multiply the number of touching fingers and above on one hand by the other.

F. Add the two products and the 100 together.

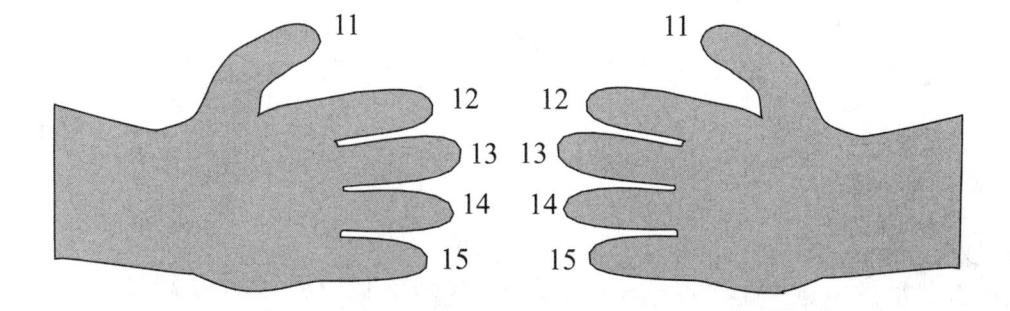

62   Chapter 3: Estimation and Computation

Fill out the following multiplication table using the hand procedure described.

×	11	12	13	14	15
11					
12					
13					
14					
15					

Part C Summary Question:
Why does this procedure work in general? Hint: Start with a product such 14×12. Find its product by breaking apart the numbers according to the place value of the digits. See Example 3.23 on page 167.

Fill out the following table. You may use a calculator.

×	16	17	18	19	20
16					
17					
18					
19					
20					

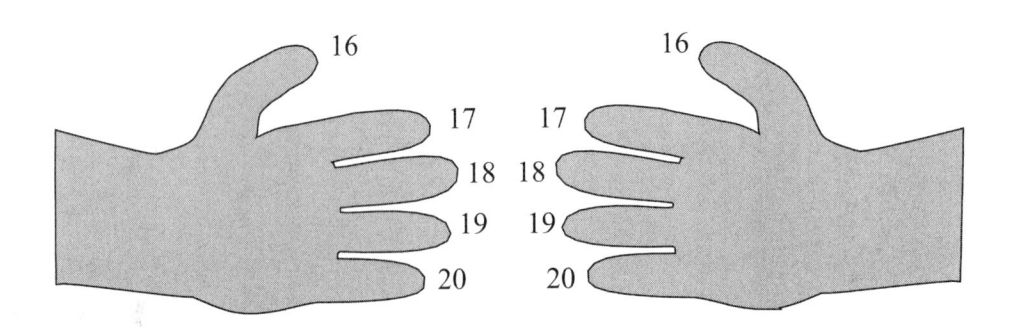

Part D Summary Question:
Using the diagram above, what are the "Rules for 16, 17, 18, 19, and 20"?

MANIPULATIVE ACTIVITY 3.4

Race to 500 Game

For this activity, you will need one set of cards numbered 0 through 9. These cards are available at http://wps.aw.com/aw_odaffer_mathematic_2 for download. Perform the following four steps.

A. The first player shuffles the cards. Without looking, the first player takes the top four cards and arranges the four digits to make a two-digit plus two-digit addition problem. The player calculates mentally to find the sum and writes it down.

B. The second player reshuffles the deck and repeats the process described in A.

C. Players alternate taking turns, mentally adding the total from each turn to their previous total.

D. The game ends when one of the players has a grand total that exceeds 400 and both players have had the same number of turns. The player closest to 500 wins.

The following table may be helpful in record keeping in order to answer the summary questions. Remember, all calculations would be performed mentally.

Card Problem	Sum	Grand Total	
			In this initial turn the Grand Total will be the same as the sum of the card problem.
			The previous Grand Total plus the sum of the second card problem will be your new Grand Total.

Summary Questions:

1. Give an example of a mental calculation you did that was difficult for you. Why was it difficult?

2. Give an example of a mental calculation that was easy for you. Why was it easy?

3. Repeat the game with a variation using three-digit numbers and racing to 5000. The game ends when one of the players has a grand total that exceeds 4000 and both players have had the same number of turns. The player closest to 5000 wins

MANIPULATIVE ACTIVITY 3.5

Race to 0 Game

For this activity, you will need one set of cards numbered 0 through 9. These cards are available at http://wps.aw.com/aw_odaffer_mathematic_2 for download. Perform the following four steps. Each player starts with 500.

A. The first player shuffles the cards. Without looking, the first player takes the top four cards and arranges the four digits to make a two-digit minus two-digit problem. If the second two-digit number is greater than the first, then switch the two two-digit numbers. The player calculates mentally to find the difference and writes it down.

B. The second player reshuffles the deck and repeats the process described in A.

C. Players alternate taking turns, mentally subtracting the difference from each turn from their previous difference.

D. The game ends when one of the players has a less than 100 and both players have had the same number of turns. The player closest to 0 wins.

The following table may be helpful in record keeping in order to answer the summary questions. Remember, all calculations would be performed mentally.

Card Problem	Difference	Overall Difference	
			In this initial turn the Overall Difference will be 500 less the difference found in the card problem.
			The previous Overall Difference less the difference of the second card problem will be your new Overall Difference.

Summary Questions:
1. Give an example of a mental calculation you did that was difficult for you. Why was it difficult?

2. Give an example of a mental calculation that was easy for you. Why was it easy?

3. Repeat the game with a variation using three-digit numbers and racing to 0. Both players start with 5000. The game ends when one of the players has an Overall Difference that is less than 1000 and both players have had the same number of turns. The player closest to 0 wins.

MANIPULATIVE ACTIVITY 3.6

Five Digit Challenge

For this activity, you will need one set of cards numbered 0 through 9. These cards are available at http://wps.aw.com/aw_odaffer_mathematic_2 for download. Perform the following steps.

A. Shuffle the cards and deal five cards to each of the two players.

B. Use as many of the five digits, once only, as you want to get the best possible answer for each of the statements below. Some may be impossible.

C. After both players have written their answers, decide which answer to each statement is better.

D. Discuss the strategy you used at each step with your partner in order to get the best possible result with your cards.

	Player 1	Player 2
1. Number closest to 3000		
2. Number closest to 5000		
3. Number that rounds to x00, where x is an even number		
4. Number that rounds to x00, where x is an odd number		
5. Number closer to 100 than 200		
6. Number closer to 3000 than 4000		
7. Number that rounds to x000, where x is an even number		
8. Number that rounds to x000, where x is an odd number		
9. Number closest to 2500		
10. Largest number divisible by 2		

Summary Questions:
1. Were there any of the items above impossible for you to complete? If so, why?

2. How do you decide if a number between 3000 and 4000 is closer to 3000 or 4000?

Have both you and your partner write two statements like the ones in the table and complete these statements with your cards.

66   Chapter 3: Estimation and Computation

MANIPULATIVE ACTIVITY 3.7

Other Base Blocks

For this activity you will need Base-Ten blocks and scissors. If you wish, visit http://wps.aw.com/aw_odaffer_mathematic_2 to download printable Base-Ten blocks and Unit blocks. In the process of this activity, you will be creating the other base blocks.

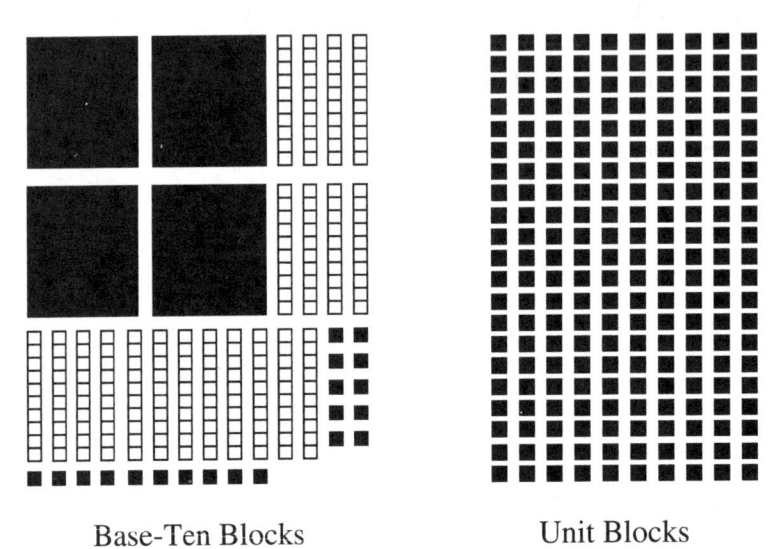

Base-Ten Blocks   Unit Blocks

Using Base-Ten blocks perform the following operations.

1. $157 + 254$ (Refer to pages 146-149 in your text.)

2. $304 - 257$ (Refer to pages 152-153 in your text.)

3. $27 \cdot 13$ (Refer to page 165 in your text.)

4. $132 \div 16$ (Refer to pages 171-172 and 174-177 in your text.)

Next create Base-Eight blocks. You will need to cut down the blue and yellow figures.

Summary Questions:
1. What size did you make the blue and yellow figures and why?

2. Using your Base-Eight blocks what are the following?

   A. $157_{eight} + 254_{eight}$ B. $304_{eight} - 257_{eight}$

   C. $27_{eight} \cdot 13_{eight}$ D. $132_{eight} \div 16_{eight}$

Choose a base smaller than eight. Cut your blocks down to size and create appropriate addition, subtraction, multiplication, and division problems (one of each type). Give the blocks and the four problems to a classmate to perform.

TECHNOLOGY ACTIVITY 3.1

Patterns Through Calculations

Using a calculator, simplify $1^7 + 7^7 + 4^7 + 1^7 + 7^7 + 2^7 + 5^7$.

Part A Summary Questions:
1. What do you notice about the sum?

2. Is this numeral therefore a base-seven numeral? Explain.

Using a calculator, simplify and record your results.

11^0	
11^1	
11^2	
11^3	
11^4	

Part B Summary Questions:
1. What is the pattern formed in these problems and their results?

2. If you raise 11 to the next power in the pattern, what is the result? Does this result fit your pattern? Explain.

Using a calculator, simplify and record your results.

$10 - 9$	
$100 - 89$	
$1000 - 789$	
$10000 - 6789$	
$100000 - 56789$	

Part C Summary Questions:
1. What is the pattern formed in the subtraction problems and the resulting differences?

2. What are the next four lines in this pattern?

3. What are the next two lines? What do you notice about them? Explain.

TECHNOLOGY ACTIVITY 3.2

Sums and Differences of Whole Numbers

Use any type of calculator for this activity. You will be using the digits

$$0\ 1\ 2\ 3\ 4\ 7\ 8 \text{ and } 9.$$

A. Place one digit in each box to create a difference as close to 5000 as possible. Use each digit only once.

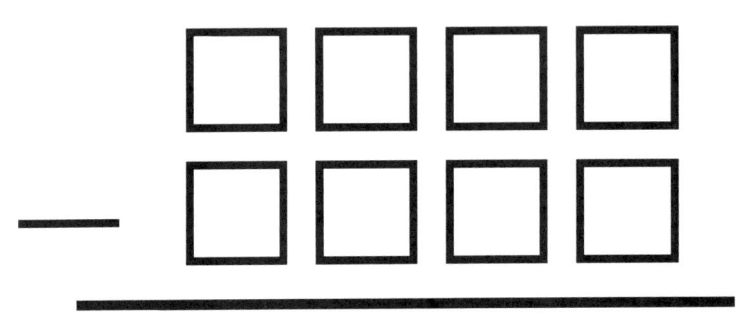

```
  ☐ ☐ ☐ ☐
− ☐ ☐ ☐ ☐
──────────
```

B. Place one digit in each box to create a sum as close to 8500 as possible. Use each digit only once.

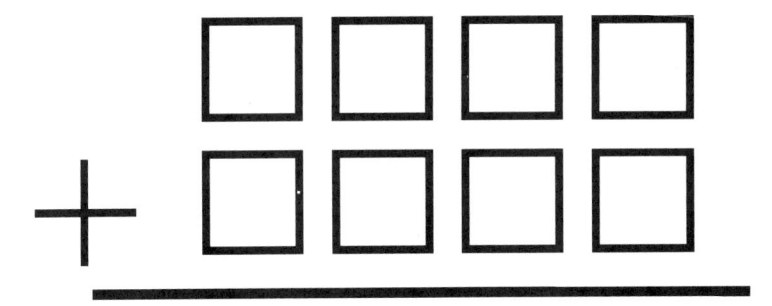

```
  ☐ ☐ ☐ ☐
+ ☐ ☐ ☐ ☐
──────────
```

Summary Questions:
1. What strategies did you use to solve each problem?

2. How did you use whole-number computation and estimation skills?

3 What assurance do you have that you actually solved the problem?

TECHNOLOGY ACTIVITY 3.3

Expense Report Errors

Use any type of calculator for this activity.

Adam was helping his mother with the end-of-the-month reports for the local animal shelter. Adam was checking the calculations on the form showing expenses for the dogs and cats housed in the shelter. His mother felt that since she used her calculator to make the entries, there was no need to check for errors. Adam took a look at the form, made a quick estimate, and told his mother that she must have made an error because the total expenses were well off the mark. The worksheet is below.

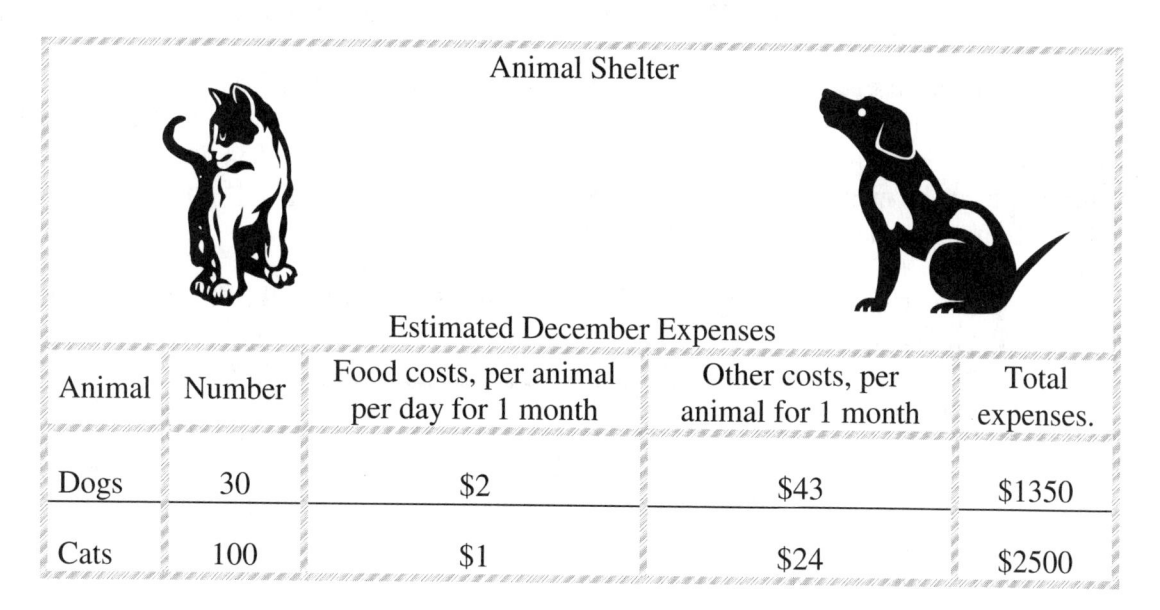

Animal Shelter

Estimated December Expenses

Animal	Number	Food costs, per animal per day for 1 month	Other costs, per animal for 1 month	Total expenses.
Dogs	30	$2	$43	$1350
Cats	100	$1	$24	$2500

Summary Questions:

1. How did Adam determine that the calculations were well off the mark?

2. What do you think Adam's mother did to calculate the total expenses?

3. What values should be in the "total expenses" column? How did you determine them?

TECHNOLOGY ACTIVITY 3.4

Using Caesar Cipher to Encrypt a Message

In this activity, you will be using the correspondence between the alphabet and the first 26 whole numbers to encrypt messages. That is

A	B	C	D	E	F	G	H	I	J	K	L	M
0	1	2	3	4	5	6	7	8	9	10	11	12

N	O	P	Q	R	S	T	U	V	W	X	Y	Z
13	14	15	16	17	18	19	20	21	22	23	24	25

.

So if you wanted to encrypt the message "hi", it would numerically be interpreted as "7 8". To further encrypt it you could pick a multiplier and/or a constant. If you chose a multiplier of 1 or a constant of 0, then there would be no change. If you choose 2 as a multiplier, then the message would be encrypted as "14 16", or "OQ". If you choose 2 as a constant, then the message would be encrypted as "9 10", or "JK".

Go to the Caesar Cipher feature on the Interactiviate disk and type in the message "hi" and verify the above encryptions.

Summary Questions:
1. Using a multiplier of 2 and a constant of 3, encrypt "ABCD". Judging from the encryption, does Caesar Cipher multiply first or add the constant first.

2. Why would it not be a good idea to use a multiplier of zero?

3. Use a multiplier of 10 on the message "ABCD". According to the description above, the "0 1 2 3" would become "0 10 20 30". How does Caesar Cipher interpret the 30 and why?

Make up a phrase and an encryption rule that involves both a multiplier and a constant. Each must have a value between 0 and 25, inclusive. Have a classmate encrypt the message by hand and verify their answer using Caesar Cipher. If you messages have spaces between words, the spaces will not be encrypted and the spacing will not appear in the encryption. If you encrypt "HERE I GO", the encryption will have seven letters and you would ignore what might appear to be spaces.

Chapter 3: Estimation and Computation

TECHNOLOGY ACTIVITY 3.5

Using Caesar Cipher II to Determine Encryption Rules

In this activity, you will be using the correspondence between the alphabet and the first 26 whole numbers to encrypt messages. That is,

A	B	C	D	E	F	G	H	I	J	K	L	M
0	1	2	3	4	5	6	7	8	9	10	11	12

N	O	P	Q	R	S	T	U	V	W	X	Y	Z
13	14	15	16	17	18	19	20	21	22	23	24	25

So if you had an encrypted message that read "OQ", it could have been the message "HI" with the encryption rule of a multiplier of 2 and a constant of 0.

In this activity you will be encrypting a message and determining the encryption rule used by Caesar Cipher II. In the encryption process, spaces are ignored (although you can type then in the text box) and the values for the multiplier and constant are each between 0 and 25 (inclusive). When the corresponding value of a letter exceeds 25 when encrypted, it starts back at 0. If L were to be encrypted with a multiplier of 3, the software would return the letter H $(11 \cdot 3 - 26 = 7)$ when encrypted.

Go to the Caesar Cipher II feature on the Interactiviate disk and type in the text box "I WILL BE AN ENCRYPTED MESSAGE".

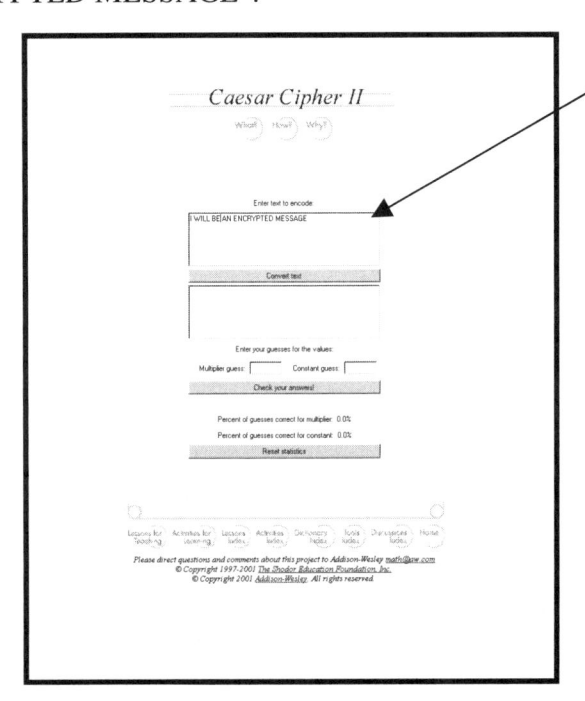

Click on the "Convert text" button and the encrypted text will appear. It may be helpful to use the following table to determine the encryption rule.

Original message	Numeric equivalent	Numeric equivalent	Encrypted message
I	8		
W	22		
I	8		
L	11		
L	11		
B	1		
E	4		
A	0		
N	13		
E	4		
N	13		
C	2		
R	17		
Y	24		
P	15		
T	19		
E	4		
D	3		
M	12		
E	4		
S	18		
S	18		
A	0		
G	6		
E	4		

Make your guesses as to the multiplier and the constant and click on the "Check your answers!" button. Adjust your answers until you find the correct multiplier and constant. Repeat the exercise at least two more times.

Summary Questions:
1. What methods did you use in order to arrive at the correct rule?

2. Once a correct multiplier is found, what letter of the original message could be used to quickly determine the constant? Explain.

3. Suppose you were to type the alphabet as the text to be encrypted. After clicking on the "Convert text" button, the encryption is "PALWHSDOZKVGRCNYPUFQBMXITE". What would this encryption indicate about your text? Explain.

CHAPTER 4:   NUMBER THEORY

INVESTIGATION 4.1

Divisibility

Refer to the *Definition of Divisibility* on page 194. In this definition, there are restrictions on variables (such as being whole numbers). Also in this definition "there is a whole number" indicates the existence of the value, x. It does not however require that this value is unique.

Part A Summary Questions:
1. Is it true that $a|0$? Use examples and then give a justification for your response.

2. Suppose the restriction $a \neq 0$ is not stated. Under what condition would $0|b$? Give a justification for your response.

Refer to the *Definition of Divisibility* as well as the examples, theorem, and justification of *Divisibility of Sums* on page 194. Determine the validity of the following by using examples to explore the following statements.

A. For natural numbers a, b, and c, if $a|b$ and $a|c$, then $a|(b-c)$.

B. For natural numbers a, b, and c, if $a|b$ and $a \nmid c$, then $a \nmid (b+c)$.

C. For natural numbers a, b, and c, if $a \nmid b$ and $a \nmid c$, then $a \nmid (b+c)$.

Part B Summary Questions:
1. What examples for a, b, and c did you use to help determine the validity of statement A? Do your examples indicate that the statement is valid or invalid?

2. What examples for a, b, and c did you use to help determine the validity of statement B? Do your examples indicate that the statement is valid or invalid?

3. What examples for a, b, and c did you use to help determine the validity of statement C? Do your examples indicate that the statement is valid or invalid?

4. Which of the above statements (A, B, and/or C) would be valid if bc were substituted for $b+c$ and $b-c$? Give a justification for your response.

INVESTIGATION 4.2

GCF and LCM

Which of the problems, A or B, involves the concept of the greatest common factor (GCF)? Which involves the concept of the least common multiple (LCM)?

A. What is the shortest length of rope that can be cut into either 24 ft pieces or 30 ft pieces?

B. A swimming instructor wants to form small groups selected from 28 students in the morning and from 42 students in the afternoon, with the same number in each group. What is the largest group size possible?

Summary Questions:
1. What is the basic clue in Problem A that helped you decide whether it embodied the idea of GCF or LCM?

2. What is the basic clue in Problem B that helped you decide whether it embodied the idea of GCF or LCM?

3. How do the ideas of GCF and LCM compare? Use the situations above, Problem A or B, to discuss.

4. How would you change Problem A so that the situation embodies the other idea of LCM or GCF? Write the problem.

5. How would you change Problem B so that the situation embodies the other idea of LCM or GCF? Write the problem.

INVESTIGATION 4.3

Sums of Odd Numbers

Consider the first five rows of the following pattern. Find the sum (either by hand or with a calculator) in each row and determine the values to be added in Row 6.

		Sum
Row 1	1	
Row 2	3 + 5	
Row 3	7 + 9 + 11	
Row 4	13 + 15 + 17 + 19	
Row 5	21 + 23 + 25 + 27 + 29	

Part A Summary Questions:
1. How did you determine the values to be added in Row 6?

2. What will be the sum for Row 6? For Row 7?

3. What will be the sum for Row n? Explain your reasoning.

Using the calculations from above, determine the following.

Row 1	1	Sum in Row 1	1
Row 2	3 + 5	Sum of Rows 1 and 2	9
Row 3	7 + 9 + 11	Sum of Rows 1, 2, and 3	
Row 4	13 + 15 + 17 + 19	Sum of Rows 1, 2, 3 and 4	
Row 5	21 + 23 + 25 + 27 + 29	Sum of Rows 1, 2, 3, 4 and 5	

Part B Summary Questions:
1. What will be the sum for Rows 1 through 6? For Rows 1 through 7?

2. What will be the sum for Rows 1 through n? Explain your reasoning.

78 Chapter 4: Number Theory

INVESTIGATION 4.4

Divisibility Tests

On page 199, divisibility tests for 7 and 11 are given along with examples. As well as being involved tests, their justifications are equally as involved. For an arbitrary four-digit number, *abcd*, fill in the blanks to complete the tests' justifications.

Eleven: For *abcd*, we need to conclude the difference between $a+c$ and $b+d$ needs to be divisible by 11.

$$abcd = a \times 1000 + b \times 100 + c \times 10 + d$$
$$= a \times (\underline{}) + b \times (\underline{}) + c \times (\underline{}) + d$$
$$= 1001a - a + 99b + b + 11c - c + \underline{}$$
$$= \underline{}$$
$$= 11 \times (91a + 9b + c) + [(b+d) - (a+b)]$$

Since we know 11 divides $11 \times (91a + 9b + c)$, we need only show that 11 divides $(b+d) - (a+b)$. Although this represents the difference between $b+d$ and $a+c$, this still verifies the result because of the last line could have been stated

$$= 11 \times (91a + 9b + c) - [(a+b) - (b+d)].$$

In practice, with this test we take the larger sum (formed from either the even-powered places or odd-powered places) minus the smaller sum.

Seven: For *abcd*, we need to conclude the difference between *abc* (the three-digit number) and $2d$ needs to be divisible by 7.

$$abcd = a \times 1000 + b \times 100 + c \times 10 + d$$
$$= a \times (\underline{}) + b \times (\underline{}) + c \times (\underline{}) + d \times (\underline{})$$
$$= 700a + 300a + 70b + 30b + 7c + 3c + 7d - 6d$$
$$= \underline{}$$
$$= 7 \times (100a + 10b + c + d) + 3 \times [100a + 10b + c - 2d]$$
$$= 7 \times (100a + 10b + c + d) + 3 \times [abc - 2d]$$

Summary Questions:
1. Why are the justifications for divisibility tests valuable?

2. How do you think these tests were discovered?

3. Do you think there are other divisibility tests beyond 11? Why or why not?

INVESTIGATION 4.5

Three Short Problems

The Teacher's Age Old Riddle

A teacher told a group of students that her age is divisible by each of the first 6 natural numbers. How old is the teacher?

Part A Summary Questions:
1. What strategies did you use to arrive at your answer?

2. Which (if any) of the natural numbers can be removed from the teacher's statement and the answer to the question remain the same?

3. Is your answer to the age of the teacher the only possible answer?

The Student's Conclusion

A student determined that 2 was not a factor of a given number. His conclusion was that no even number could possibly be a factor of that number.

Part B Summary Question:
Is the student's logic correct? Explain.

Repeated Addition

Begin with the number 1 and repeatedly add 3. You can do this on certain calculators (graphing calculators, for instance) you can type first type "1" and then hit enter. After the 1 appears on the right-hand side of your screen, you can type "+ 3" and then hit enter. "Ans+3" will appear on the left-hand side of the screen and "4" will appear on the right. Keep on pressing enter to display the terms of the sequence formed.

Part C Summary Questions:
1. Does the number 91 appear on your screen?

2. Without generating any additional values, would 333 appear on your screen? Why or why not?

3. Without generating any additional values, would 37,036 appear on your screen? Why or why not?

80   Chapter 4: Number Theory

INVESTIGATION 4.6

Factor Rainbows

Consider the whole number 24. The factors are 1, 2, 3, 4, 6, 8, 12, and 24.

The factors can be "linked up" as follows.

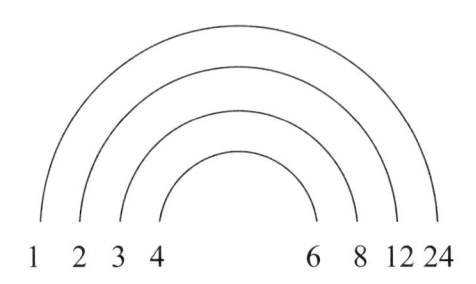

1 2 3 4   6 8 12 24

Factors on the ends of each "band" multiply to be the original number.

Part A Summary Questions:
1. What would the factor rainbow look like for 96?

2. What would the factor rainbow look like for 36?

3. What would the factor rainbow look like for a prime number?

Every natural number greater than 1 can be expressed as $p_1^{q_1} p_2^{q_2} p_3^{q_3} ... p_n^{q_n}$ where the p's represent distinct prime factors and the q's represent how many of the individual p's the factorization has. In the case of 288, the prime factorization is $2^5 \cdot 3^2$. Thus $p_1 = 2$, $q_1 = 5$, $p_2 = 3$ and $q_2 = 2$. By looking at the prime factorization of a number, one can determine how many factors it has. You will need to find the product of $(q_1 + 1)(q_2 + 1)(q_3 + 1)...(q_n + 1)$. In the case of 288, there should be $(5+1)(2+1) = 6 \cdot 3 = 18$ factors.

Part B Summary Questions:
1. What would the factor rainbow look like for 288?

2. Under what conditions would you have an odd number of factors of a given number? Justify your response by looking at the general prime factorization, $p_1^{q_1} p_2^{q_2} p_3^{q_3} ... p_n^{q_n}$.

3. The prime factorization of 373,248 is $2^9 \cdot 3^6$. Since it will have $(9+1)(6+1) = 10 \cdot 7$ or 70 factors, an organized method of finding these factors may be helpful. How can the following table (on the next page) be used to find the 70 factors?

	0	1	2	3	4	5	6	7	8	9
0										
1										
2										
3										
4										
5										
6										

Distribute the cells among your group to calculate the 70 factors. Organize the 70 factors in order and make sure the factors "link up".

INVESTIGATION 4.7

Same Numbers, Same Operations, Different Results

Consider the numbers 5, 4, 3, 2, and 1 (in that order) along with the four basic operations (addition, subtraction, multiplication, and division). With these five numbers it is possible to insert the four basic operations in 24 different ways. Consider the following.

$$5 + 4 - 3 \cdot 2 \div 1$$

If we performed operations from left to right (**not** following orders of operations), the result would be $5 + 4 - 3 \cdot 2 \div 1 = 9 - 3 \cdot 2 \div 1 = 6 \cdot 2 \div 1 = 12 \div 1 = 12$. Using a table, such as the one below, fill in systematically the 24 combinations of the four basic operations. You do not need to calculate the result.

5		4		3		2		1	Result
5	+	4	−	3	·	2	÷	1	
5		4		3		2		1	
5		4		3		2		1	
5		4		3		2		1	
5		4		3		2		1	
5		4		3		2		1	
5		4		3		2		1	
5		4		3		2		1	
5		4		3		2		1	
5		4		3		2		1	
5		4		3		2		1	
5		4		3		2		1	
5		4		3		2		1	
5		4		3		2		1	
5		4		3		2		1	
5		4		3		2		1	
5		4		3		2		1	
5		4		3		2		1	
5		4		3		2		1	
5		4		3		2		1	
5		4		3		2		1	
5		4		3		2		1	
5		4		3		2		1	
5		4		3		2		1	

Summary Question:
Using divisibility tests, which of the combinations will not result in a whole number? Explain what strategies you used to determine your results.

MANIPULATIVE ACTIVITY 4.1

Factors of 2 through 50

For this activity you will need a set of PopCubes® to find factors of 2 through 50. If PopCubes® are not available, unit blocks are available for download at http://wps.aw.com/aw_odaffer_mathematic_2. For each value of 2 though 50, create as many possible rectangles for each value. Record the length and width of each of these rectangles as factors. For example, 10 PopCubes® can be expressed as a 1×10 rectangle and a 2×5 rectangle. 10×1 and 5×2 rectangles are rotations of the others and do not yield any new factors. You may choose to keep tract of the factors in the table below.

Number of Cubes	Factors
2	
3	
4	
5	
6	
7	
8	
9	
10	1, 2, 5, 10
11	
12	
13	
14	
15	
16	
17	
18	
19	
20	
21	
22	
23	
24	
25	

26	
27	
28	
29	
30	
31	
32	
33	
34	
35	
36	
37	
38	
39	
40	
41	
42	
43	
44	
45	
46	
47	
48	
49	
50	

Summary Question:
How would you write a definition of a prime number and a composite number that uses the idea of multiple-row rectangles? Your definition should also insure that the number 1 is not a prime number.

MANIPULATIVE ACTIVITY 4.2

Colored Rods

For this exercise you need colored rods. If they are not available, printable colored rods are available at http://wps.aw.com/aw_odaffer_mathematic_2.

To show that 2 is a factor of 6 using colored rods, you weed need to show that 6 (dark green) can be represented by a certain number of 2's (red's).

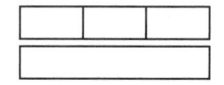

The non-colored diagram above shows that a "train" of length 6 can be represented by three lengths of 2.

Part A Summary Questions:
1. Do colored rods show that $3|9$? Why or why not?

2. Do colored rods show that $3|10$? Why or why not?

3. Do colored rods show that $3|12$? How did you create 12? Are there other ways?

4. Can colored rods be used to show that $\text{LCM}(4,6) = 12$? If so explain how and provide a diagram.

5. Can colored rods be used to show that $\text{GCF}(4,6) = 2$? If so explain how and provide a diagram.

Use colored rods to show that $2|10$ and $2\nmid 9$. Refer to the *Definition of Even and Odd Numbers* on page 195 of your text. Give a definition of even natural numbers and odd natural numbers in terms of colored rods.

Part B Summary Questions:
1. How could you use colored rods to suggest that the sum of two even natural numbers is an even natural number?

2. How could you use colored rods to suggest that the sum of an even natural number and an odd natural number is an odd natural number?

MANIPULATIVE ACTIVITY 4.3

Prime Factor Game

On pieces of paper write each of the prime numbers 2, 3, 5, and 7 down five times (twenty pieces total). Also draw the three Venn Diagrams on separate pieces of paper as shown below. Downloads for the prime number pieces as well as the Venn diagrams are available at the web site, http://wps.aw.com/aw_odaffer_mathematic_2.

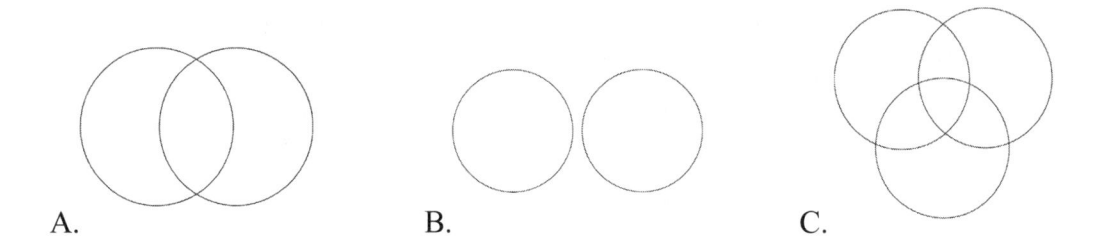

A. B. C.

For each of the Venn diagrams, randomly place prime numbers in the sections. Place at least seven numbers each time. For <u>each</u> Venn diagram,

A. Determine the number that is represented by the product of the factors in each circle.

B. Determine the number that is represented by the product of the numbers in the union.

C. Determine the number that is represented by the product of the numbers in the intersection of the circles.

Summary Questions:
1. Were you able to perform Parts A through C for each diagram? If not, which parts could you not perform and why.

2. What is the relationship between the product of the factors in the intersection/union and GCF/LCM?

3. The composite number $24 = 2^3 \cdot 3$ has four prime factors that are not necessarily distinct. Suppose a number a has 10 prime factors that are not necessarily distinct. Let the $\text{LCM}(a,b)$ have 16 prime factors that are not necessarily distinct and the $\text{GCF}(a,b)$ have 2 prime factors that are not necessarily distinct. How many prime factors does b have that are not necessarily distinct? Explain.

MANIPULATIVE ACTIVITY 4.4

Pick's Theorem

A lattice polygon is formed by connecting dots in a lattice, where points are equally spaced. According to Pick's Theorem, the area of the polygon formed will be

$$A = \frac{B}{2} + I - 1,$$

where B represents the number of dots on the perimeter and I represents the number of dots in the interior. For example, consider the following square.

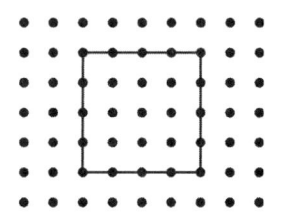

There are 16 points on the boundary and 9 points in the interior. According to the formula, this square should have an area of $\frac{16}{2} + 9 - 1 = 8 + 9 - 1 = 17 - 1 = 16$ square units.

Consider the Figures A through F. For each one, calculate the area according to Pick's Theorem. Verify each area found by first drawing each figure on a separate piece of paper. An enlarged lattice is available at http://wps.aw.com/aw_odaffer_mathematic_2. Arrange pieces of each figure to form rectangular figures. Be sure to cut through the center of the dots to make the pieces fit together. You will need to make additional cuts to each cutout in order to arrange them into rectangular figures.

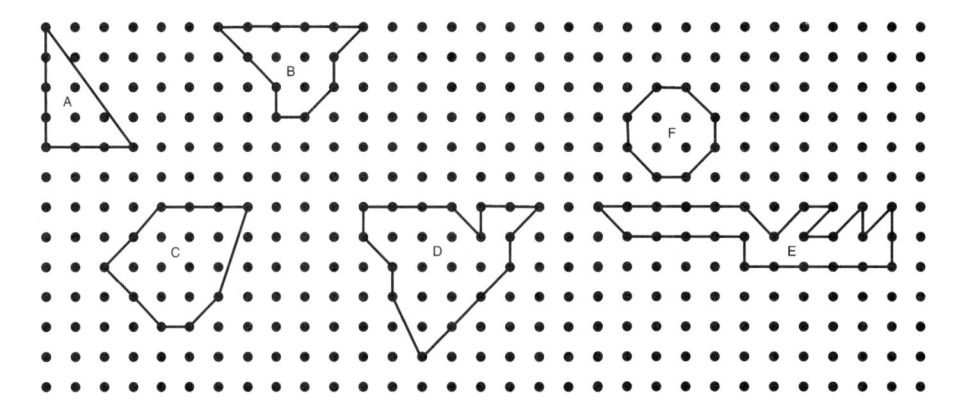

Summary Questions:
1. What determines whether the area of the figure is a natural number or not?

2. Which figures can be cut out and arranged into more than one type of rectangle? A 2×3 and a 3×2 are considered the same type of rectangle.

TECHNOLOGY ACTIVITY 4.1

Five Factors

For this activity you will need to use a spreadsheet program such as Excel®. If a spreadsheet program is not available, a calculator can be used.

Determine a value of x that makes the following equation true.

$$(x-2)(x-1)(x)(x+1)(x+2) = 360{,}360$$

In Cell A1, enter a value of x such as 5. Cell B1 will represent $x-2$. Enter "=A1-2" in Cell B1. Quotation marks should not be included in any of the entries. Cell C1 will represent $x-1$. Enter "=A1-1" in Cell C1. Cell D1 will represent x. Enter "=A1" in Cell D1. Cell E1 will represent $x+1$. Enter "=A1+1" in Cell E1. Cell F1 will represent $x+2$. Enter "=A1+2" in Cell F1. Cell G1 will represent the product of $(x-2)(x-1)(x)(x+1)(x+2)$. Enter "=Product(B1:F1)" You should get the screen below. Change the values in Cell A1 until you find the desired product.

	A	B	C	D	E	F	G	H
1	5	3	4	5	6	7	2520	
2								
3								

Summary Questions:
1. What strategies did you use in finding the value of x that solves the equation?

2. Are you sure there is only one value of x that solves this problem? Give a convincing argument.

3. If all factors are to be whole numbers, what is the smallest value of x that can be used?

4. If x is a whole number will the product $(x-2)(x-1)(x)(x+1)(x+2)$ always be a whole number? Explain.

5. Change the value of x (Cell A1) so that you calculate the product of $(x-2)(x-1)(x)(x+1)(x+2)$ for several values. What do you notice about the last digit of the product? Justify why this is always the case if x is a whole number.

88   Chapter 4: Number Theory

TECHNOLOGY ACTIVITY 4.2

A Bigger Cross to Bear

For this activity you will need to use a spreadsheet program such as Excel®. If a spreadsheet program is not available, any standard calculator can be used.

Consider the arrangement of the numerals 2, 3, 4, 5, 6, 7, 8, 9, and 10.

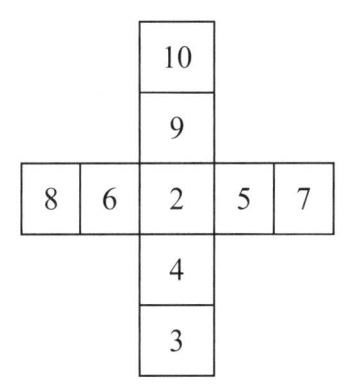

		10		
		9		
8	6	2	5	7
		4		
		3		

If you sum the vertical values you get the same as the sum of the horizontal values, which is 28. In such an arrangement, you are concerned about which number can be placed in the center to yield such an arrangement. It would be rather tedious to try all combinations of center values, so in order to determine which numbers can *potentially* be placed as a center number set up you spreadsheet as follows:

	A	B	C	D	E
1					
2	2		52	13	
3	3		51	12.75	
4	4		50	12.5	
5	5		49	12.25	
6	6		48	12	
7	7		47	11.75	
8	8		46	11.5	
9	9		45	11.25	
10	10		44	11	
11					
12					
13		54			
14					

In Column A, the 2 through 10 are placed in Cells A2 through A10. Cell A13 is the sum of Cells A2 through A10. Cell C2 is the difference between the sum and Cell A2 (=(A13-A2)). Cell C3 is the difference between the sum and Cell A3 (=(A13-A3)). This is continued down to Cell C10 (=(A13-A10)). Cell D2 is the quotient of Cell C2 and 4 (=C2/4). Cell D3 is the quotient of Cell C3 and 4 (=C3/4). This is continued down to Cell D10 (=C10/4).

In order to determine which numerals can potentially be used, you look for differences (cells in Column C) that are divisible by 4. By looking for whole numerals in Column D, you can easily spot the center values.

Part A Summary Questions:
1. Besides 2, what two other numerals in the list could be used as a center values?

2. Once you've determined the center value, how can you use the values in Column C to determine which four numerals should be horizontal values or vertical values?

3. What are arrangements for the center values you found in Question 1? Answers may vary as to how numerals are arranged on the horizontal and vertical parts.

Change the Cell C5 entry to 11. The spreadsheet should recalculate the values.

Part B Summary Questions:
1. How many center values are there for these numerals?

2. Why does this procedure *work*?

3. Now if you change 10 to 100 and recalculate, you will get the following.

	A	B	C	D	E
1					
2	2		148	37	
3	3		147	36.75	
4	4		146	36.5	
5	11		139	34.75	
6	6		144	36	
7	7		143	35.75	
8	8		142	35.5	
9	9		141	35.25	
10	100		50	12.5	
11					
12					
13		150			
14					

Does this mean that 2 and 6 are center values? Explain.

TECHNOLOGY ACTIVITY 4.3

Square Patterns

Using a calculator, find the following.

A.

1^2	
11^2	
111^2	
1111^2	
11111^2	

B.

9^2	
99^2	
999^2	
9999^2	
99999^2	

C.

1^2	
11^2	
101^2	
1001^2	
10001^2	

Summary Questions:
1. What is the pattern formed in squaring Problem A and what are the next three lines?

2. What is the pattern formed in squaring Problem B and what are the next three lines?

3. What is the pattern formed in squaring Problem C and what are the next three lines?

4. Which of the above squaring patterns will "stop" at some point? Continue the pattern and determine where it stops. Why did the pattern stop?

TECHNOLOGY ACTIVITY 4.4

Ulam's Algorithm

Ulam's Theorem is a conjecture that remains unproven. Using a calculator, generate the sequence of numbers using the following Algorithm.

Start with any natural number.

- ❑ If the number is even, divide it by 2.
- ❑ If the number is odd, multiply it by 3, add 1, and then divide the result by 2.

Repeat this process with the new number generated. Ulam's Theorem suggests that if this process is applied repeatedly, you will eventually arrive at 1.

For example, if you choose 6 as your starting number, the sequence would be

$$3 \to 5 \to 8 \to 4 \to 2 \to 1.$$

A. Carry out Ulam's algorithm using the following six starting values and record the number of steps required to reach 1.

Starting value	Sequence	Number of terms in sequence
12		
17		
32		
64		
69		
80		

B. Carry out Ulam's algorithm using three other two-digit numbers.

Starting value	Sequence	Number of terms in sequence

Chapter 4: Number Theory

Summary Questions:

1. Why is 1 considered to be the final number? What would happen if we continue the sequence after 1 is reached?

2. How are we guaranteed that when an odd number is generated (or the original number) the result will be a natural number once applying the algorithm?

3. How could you predict the number of steps required to reach 1 when 128 is the starting number? What generalizations can you make from this?

4. What are the required steps to reach 1 for each of the first 100 natural numbers? You can determine the number of steps required for certain numbers like 34. It will require one more step than 17 since 34 is twice 17. Examine the data you generated by considering various categories of numbers (primes, composites, perfect squares, powers) and looking at the number of steps required for such numbers or by grouping together starting numbers according to the number of steps required. For example 6, 20, 21, and 64 are the only starting numbers that require exactly 6 steps. The table below may be helpful.

1	2	3	4	5	**6** 6 steps	7	8	9	10
11	12	13	14	15	16	17	18	19	20
21	22	23	24	25	26	27	28	29	30
31	32	33	34	35	36	37	38	39	40
41	42	43	44	45	46	47	48	49	50
51	52	53	54	55	56	57	58	59	60
61	62	63	64	65	66	67	68	69	70
71	72	73	74	75	76	77	78	79	80
81	82	83	84	85	86	87	88	89	90
91	92	93	94	95	96	97	98	99	100

5. What observations can you make about patterns you see between the steps required to reach 1 and the starting number? Identify three or more observations.

TECHNOLOGY ACTIVITY 4.5

Using Coloring Multiples in Pascal's Triangle

Go to the Coloring Multiples in Pascal's Triangle feature on the Interactiviate disk. Click on the "Increase Depth" button until you have 16 rows (the row will start 1 15 105 etc.).

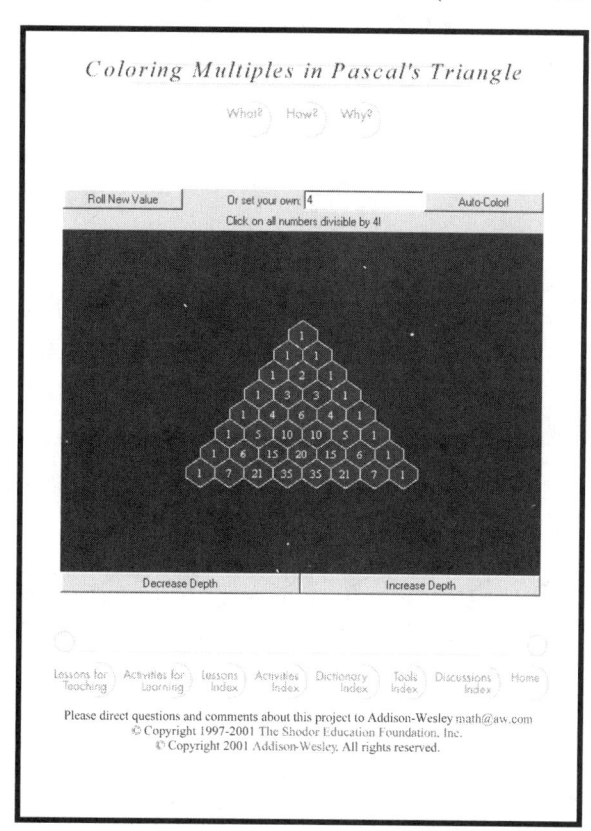

Count or use some other method of determining how many cells are in the 16 rows.

Part A Summary Questions:
1. What kind of numbers are you adding up?

2. If you had 100 rows of Pascal's triangle, how would you determine the number of cells in the drawing?

The "Roll New Value" button randomly generates natural numbers between 2 and 10 (inclusive). You can either try to determine which cells should be highlighted for a given value or press the "Auto Color" button to have the software do it for you.

Part B Summary Questions:
1. How many cells are divisible by 2? By 3? Describe any patterns you see in the coloring of the cells.

94   Chapter 4: Number Theory

2. Without coloring in the cells divisible by 6, how many cells would you expect to be divisible by 6? Use the software to determine how many cells are divisible by 6. Is your guess correct, too high, or too low? Explain and describe any common features between the colorings of cells divisible by 2 or 3.

Using the drawing below, color in all cells that are divisible by 2, 3, 4, 5, 6, 7, 8, 9, or 10. You only need the one drawing and for a printable version you may visit http://wps.aw.com/aw_odaffer_mathematic_2.

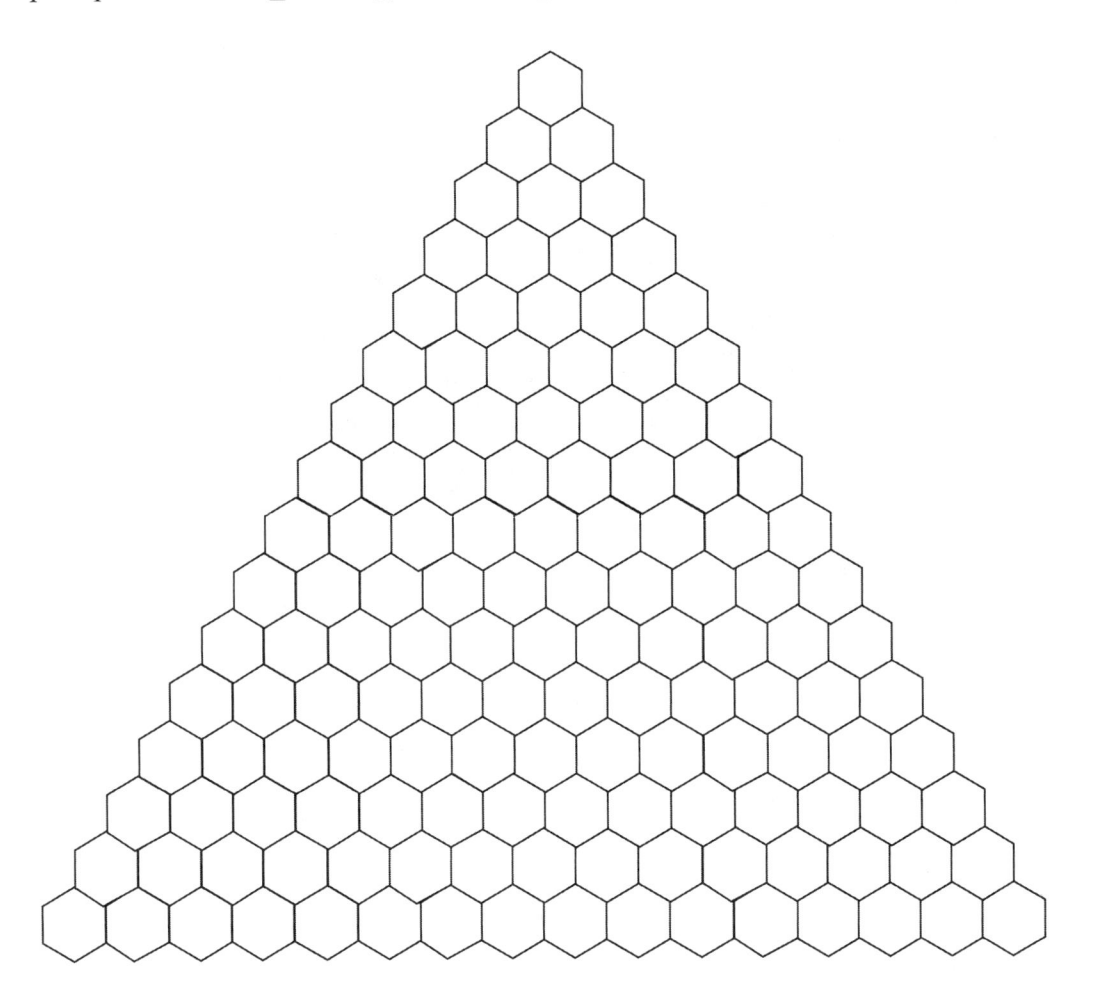

Part C Summary Questions:
1. How many cells are not colored in? What number appears in most of these cells? What numbers appear in the remaining uncolored cells?

2. If you are to use a different color as you progress from 2 to 10, how many different colors will you need? Once a cell is colored it does not get colored again.

TECHNOLOGY ACTIVITY 4.6

Using Coloring Remainders in Pascal's Triangle

Go to the Coloring Remainders in Pascal's Triangle feature on the Interactiviate disk. Click on the "Increase Depth" button until you have 16 rows (the row will start 1 15 105 etc.).

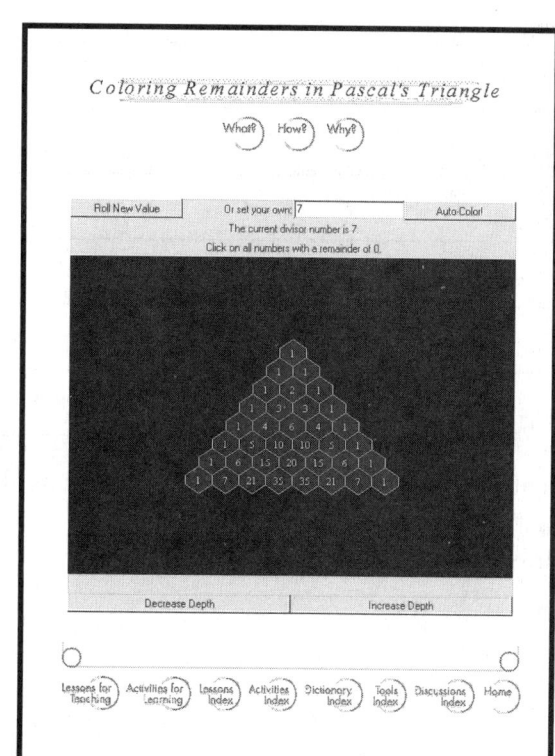

The "Roll New Value" button randomly generates natural numbers between 2 and 10 (inclusive).

Summary Questions:

1. How many different colors are used for each of the values 2 through 10 (inclusive)? Discuss.

Number	Number of colors
2	
3	
4	
5	
6	

Number	Number of colors
7	
8	
9	
10	

96 Chapter 4: Number Theory

2. By using values 2 through 10 (inclusive), what do the different colors indicate?

Color	
Green	
Yellow/Green	
Yellow	
Purple (lavender)	
Blue (blue/gray)	
Red	
Pink	
Dark Red (Brick)	

3. Which color consistently appears in an "upside down" triangular shape? What does this color correspond to? Explain using *Theorem: Divisibility of Sums* on page 194 of your text to explain this triangular shape.

TECHNOLOGY ACTIVITY 4.7

Playing with Numbers II

Refer to TECHNOLOGY ACTIVITY 2.5. To represent the word IS upside down on a calculator as the product of two natural numbers, we can find $1 \cdot 51$ or $3 \cdot 17$. Switching the order does not yield a different combination.

Determine the number that must be viewed by turning the calculator upside down in order to obtain each of the following.

A. HILL

B. LIE

C. BILL

D. OIL

E. SIDE

F. SHELL

G. SHELLS

Summary Questions:
1. Of the above words, which can be expressed as a product in only one way? How can you tell?

2. Of the above words, which can be expressed as a product in only two ways? How can you tell?

3. Of the above words, which can be expressed as a product in three or more ways? How can you tell?

CHAPTER 5: UNDERSTANDING INTEGER OPERATIONS AND PROPERTIES

INVESTIGATION 5.1

Whole Numbers and Integers

Student A said: There are more integers than whole numbers because the positive integers and zero are the whole numbers and the negative integers are extra.

Student B said: There are just as many integers as whole numbers - just look at the way they are matched below. If you give me any integer, I can always match it with an unused whole number. If an integer is positive, match it with its whole number double. If it's negative, match it with one less than the double of its absolute value. So how can you say there are more integers than whole numbers?

0	−1	1	−2	2	−3	3	−4	4	−5	•	•	•
↓	↓	↓	↓	↓	↓	↓	↓	↓	↓	↓	↓	↓
0	1	2	3	4	5	6	7	8	9	•	•	•

In a small group, discuss the merits of each student's reasoning.

Summary Questions:

1. Do you think there are more positive integers than whole numbers, more whole numbers than positive integers, or the same number of each? Explain. Do you think there are more integers than positive integers? Explain. Because of your answers to these questions, do you agree with Student A?

2. Looking at Student B's matching; do you think there could be extra integers that wouldn't have a matching whole umber? Explain. Do you think there could be extra whole numbers that wouldn't be matched with an integers? Explain. Because of your answers to these questions, do you agree with Student B?

3. After analyzing Questions 1 and 2, which student, if either, do you think is correct? Explain your reasoning.

4. Do you think Student B would say that there are the same number of integers as there are positive integers, even though the positive integers are a proper subset of the integers?

5. Since the whole numbers and the integers are both *infinite* sets of numbers, perhaps we need to think differently when comparing infinite sets than we do when comparing finite sets. How might such a point of view affect your answer to Question 3, if at all?

Chapter 5: Understanding Integer Operations and Properties

INVESTIGATION 5.2

Integer Operations

Join a small group of classmates and discuss the following questions about learning integer operations.

A. Do you think the rules for addition are helpful in learning/using rules for multiplication, or are they confusing? Explain.

B. As a future teacher, how would you rate the reasons below for learning the integer operations with understanding? Respond by rating the reasons below on a scale of 0 (weak reason) to 10 (excellent reason).

  a. So one won't get the rules for addition confused with the rules for multiplication.

  b. So teachers can be better able to teach their students or children about them.

  c. So one can apply the operations to solve problems encountered in everyday life, such as combining debit and credits, evaluating change in stock prices, keeping golf scores, charting a sailing course, scoring other games, an do forth.

  d. So one will be prepared to study other areas of mathematics that require the use of integer operations.

  e. So one can have a better appreciation of how all number systems in mathematics are consistent and connected.

  f. So one will see mathematics as logically sensible rather than a "bag of tricks".

  g. So one will enjoy mathematics by being able to understand it.

Summary Questions:
1. What ways of understanding the operations used in this chapter were most meaningful to you?

2. What reasons do you think would be most persuasive in countering the following position: "They don't need to learn them with understanding, since there are no really good reasons for not simply just memorizing the rules and using them."

INVESTIGATION 5.3

Pascal and Company

Pascal's triangle is generated by 1's on the left and right sides and adding two cells to get the one below. Find the sum of the cells at each level.

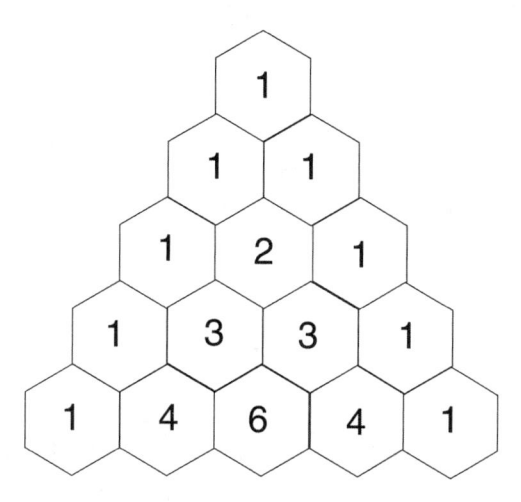

```
                1
              1   1
            1   2   1
          1   3   3   1
        1   4   6   4   1
```

Part A Summary Question:
What is the sum of the cells on the 6th level? 10th level? In general?

Consider the following variation where the values on the side are all -1. Complete the missing values by using the same procedure of adding adjacent cells to obtain the cell below.

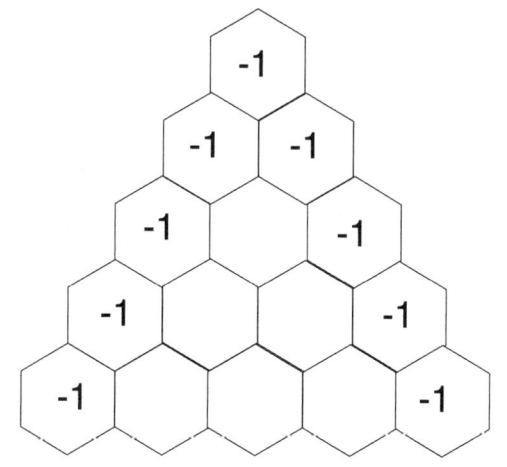

```
                -1
              -1   -1
            -1        -1
          -1             -1
        -1                  -1
```

Part B Summary Questions:
1. What is the sum of the cells on the 6th level? 10th level? In general?

2. What are the similarities and differences between Pascal's triangle and this variation? Explain why these similarities and differences occur.

102 Chapter 5: Understanding Integer Operations and Properties

The next variation has 1's on the left side and −1's on the right. The top number could be either 1 or −1. Complete the missing values by using the same procedure of adding adjacent cells to obtain the cell below.

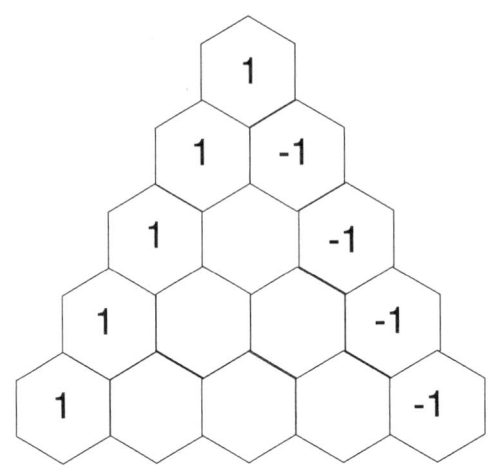

Part C Summary Questions:
1. What is the sum of the cells on the 6th level? 10th level? In general?

2. Which levels, in general, have a cell that contains zero? On these levels, how many times does it appear? Explain.

The final variation has 1's and −1's alternating on the left and right sides. The top number could be either 1 or −1. Complete the missing values by using the same procedure of adding adjacent cells to obtain the cell below.

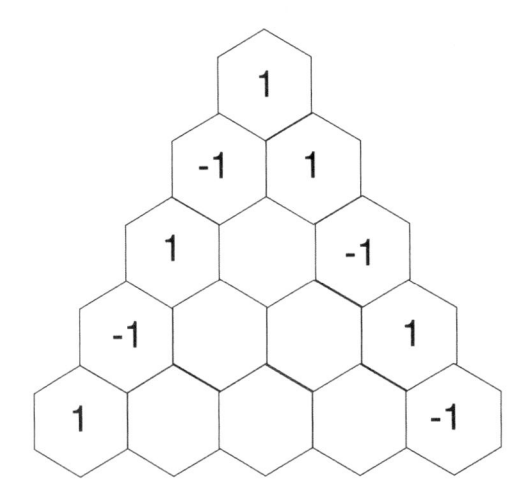

Part D Summary Questions:
1. What is the sum of the cells on the 6th level? 10th level? In general?

2. Complete at least 7 more levels and observe the pattern of zero's. Which rows, in general, have a cell that contains zero? On these levels, how many times does it appear? Explain.

INVESTIGATION 5.4

Sums and Differences of Consecutive Integer

In Investigation 1.8 sums of natural numbers were explored. In that activity one discovered that the sum of the first n natural numbers is:

$$\frac{n(n+1)}{2}.$$

For example, the sum of $1+2+3+...+49+50$ would be:

$$\frac{50(50+1)}{2} = \frac{50 \cdot 51}{2} = \frac{2550}{2} = 1275.$$

Part A Summary Questions:
1. What would the outcome of $-50-49-...-3-2-1$ be? Justify using the *Distributive Property for Opposites Over Addition* on page 269 and the *Commutative Property* on page 239 of your text.

2. In general, what would the outcome of $-n-(n-1)-...-3-2-1$ be where n is a natural number?

Consider the following.

$$(-50)+(-49)+(-48)+...+48+49+50$$

Part B Summary Questions:
1. What is the sum? Justify your response.

2. How many terms are there in the given expression?

Consider the following.

$$(-100)+(-99)+(-98)+...+48+49+50$$

Part C Summary Questions:
1 How many terms are there in the given expression?

2. What is the sum? Justify your response.

Chapter 5: Understanding Integer Operations and Properties

INVESTIGATION 5.5

Integer Towers

Consider the following arrangement

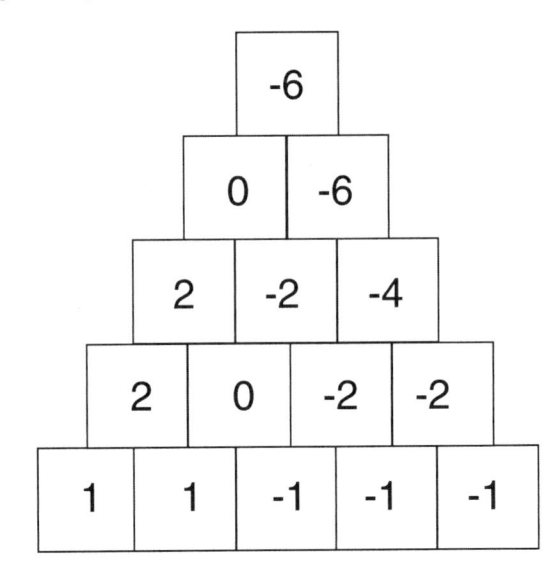

```
            -6
          0    -6
        2   -2   -4
      2   0   -2   -2
    1   1   -1   -1   -1
```

To obtain such an arrangement, you start at the bottom and add the entries in adjacent squares to obtain the number above. You continue the process until the top number is obtained.

With the bottom row having two 1's and three -1's, there are ten possible arrangements (including the one given above).

Part A Summary Question:
Do you think that in the other nine arrangements of the bottom row, the top number will be the same or will be different? Explain.

Find the other nine arrangements and determine the top number of each. If you visit http://wps.aw.com/aw_odaffer_mathematic_2, a download is available to help organize these towers. You may wish to print out two copies, one for a later part of this Investigation.

Part B Summary Questions:
1. How many different top numbers are there?

2. Why could one expect duplicate top numbers?

Now consider the same ten arrangements of the bottom numbers, but instead of adding the entries in adjacent squares, multiply them to obtain the number above.

Part C Summary Question:
What are the only top numbers that occur and why?

INVESTIGATION 5.6

Three Short Problems II

A student made the following statement:

> "When an integer is not positive, then it must be negative."

Part A Summary Questions:
1. Is the student correct? Why or why not?

2. Does $-n$ always represent a negative integer? Why or why not?

In justifying rules for integer multiplication, the distributive property, additive inverse property, and zero property for multiplication were often utilized. On pages 258-259, integer addition was employed to show that $3(-4) = -12$.

Part B Summary Question:
Using integer addition, how can you show that ab is a negative integer when b is a negative integer and a is a positive integer?

As you know, integers can be positive, negative, or zero. If we were to look at the product ab, it would be positive when both a and b are positive or both a and b are negative.

Part C Summary Questions:
1. What are all the conditions in which ab is negative?

2. What are all the conditions in which $a \div b$ is non-negative?

3. What are all the conditions in which $a + b$ is negative?

4. What are all the conditions in which $a + b$ is positive?

5. What are all the conditions in which $a - b$ is positive?

6. What are all the conditions in which $a - b$ is negative?

MANIPULATIVE ACTIVITY 5.1

Integer Addition and Subtraction Encounters

For this activity you will need 20 red counters and 20 black counters. You can visit http://wps.aw.com/aw_odaffer_mathematic_2 to download printable color counters.

In small groups perform the following:

A. Lay out a small pile of black counters and a different size pile of red counters. Write a positive integer to represent the black counter and a negative integer to represent the red counters.

B. Push the piles together, use the agreement that a black counter and a red counter cancel each other out, and remove all pairs of black-red counters. Write an integer that represents the counters that remain.

C. Use the idea that pushing piles of counters together models addition and write an integer addition sentence to record what happened with the counters.

D. Do Steps A - C several times.

E. Lay out a small pile of black or a small pile of red counters. Choose a positive or negative integer to designate the number of counters to be taken away from the pile.

F. Put as many black-red pairs of counters in the pile as needed so that the designated counters can actually be taken away. Write the integer that represents the counters that remain.

G. Use the idea that taking away counters models subtraction and write an integer subtraction sentence to record what happened with the counters.

H. Do Steps E - G several times.

Summary Question:
How would your change the directions in Steps A - C to demonstrate the sum of two negative numbers or the sum of two positive numbers?

MANIPULATIVE ACTIVITY 5.2

Number Lines and Cars

A variation of the number line model for integer addition and subtraction, presented in Chapter 5 of your text, involves the movement of cars. For this exercise you will use a number line and a car. If you visit the web site http://wps.aw.com/aw_odaffer_mathematic_2, a number line and a foldable car are available. You will need to cut out the two-sided car and fold.

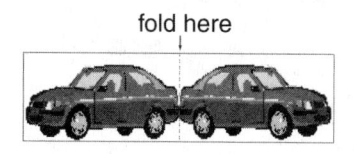

In this number line model, you always start on 0 (neutral). If your first value is positive, you drive forward. If it is negative, you back up. In subtraction, you must turn the car around (flip over) and then either drive forward or back up depending on the second value.

Consider the following examples:

$3 + (-5) = -2$

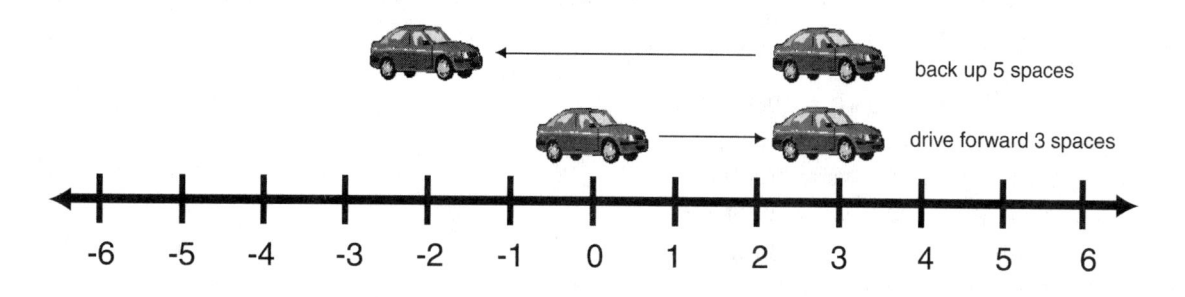

$-3 + 6 = 3$

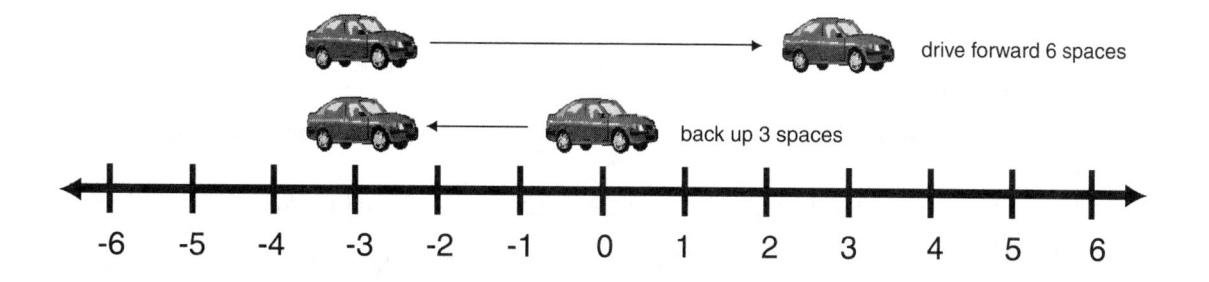

108 Chapter 5: Understanding Integer Operations and Properties

$4 - (-2) = 6$

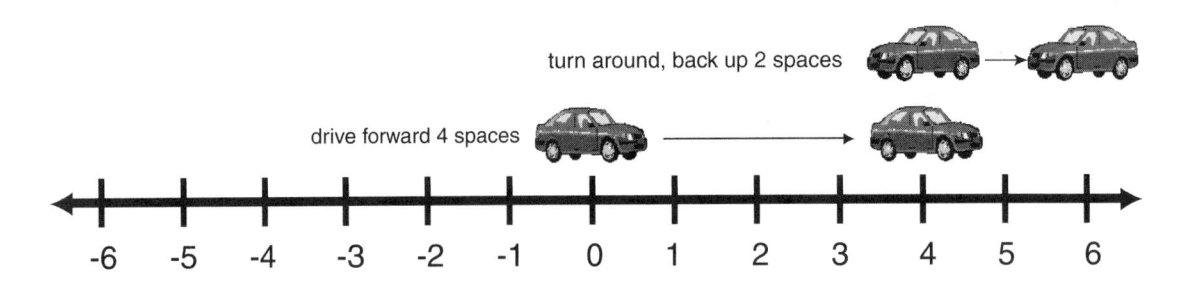

$-4 - (-5) = 1$

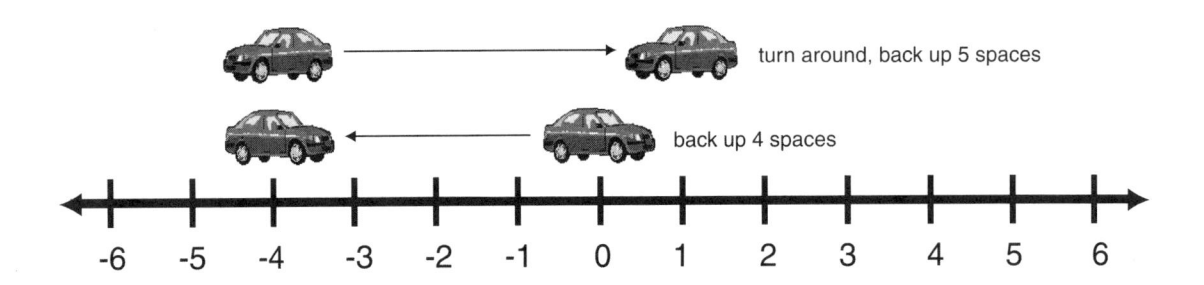

Create ten addition/subtraction problems as described below that involve integers. The results should be no less than -6 and no more than 6. Have a classmate perform the problems you created.

    A. positive + positive = positive
    B. negative + negative = negative
    C. positive + negative = positive
    D. positive + negative = negative
    E. positive − positive = positive
    F. positive − positive = negative
    G. negative − negative = negative
    H. negative − negative = positive
    I. positive − negative = positive
    J. negative − positive = negative

Summary Questions:
1. In an addition problem, what direction will the car always face when the sum is found?
2. In a subtraction problem, what direction will the car always face when the difference is found?

MANIPULATIVE ACTIVITY 5.3

Integer "Football"

For this activity, you will need to visit http://wps.aw.com/aw_odaffer_mathematic_2 to download the "football" field and integers. Cut out the twenty integers and place them in a bag.

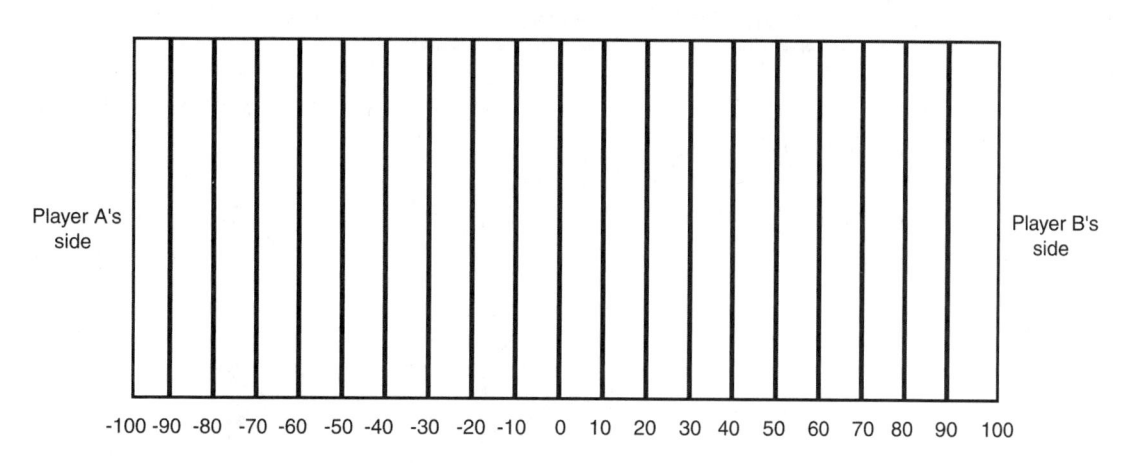

-50 -40 -30 -20 -10 -10 -10 -10 -10 0

50 40 30 20 10 10 10 10 10 0

Player A's side   Player B's side

-100 -90 -80 -70 -60 -50 -40 -30 -20 -10 0 10 20 30 40 50 60 70 80 90 100

You and a classmate will play as Player A and Player B. Player A wins if a sum of at most −100 is obtained as the game progresses. Player B wins if a sum of at least 100 is obtained as the game progresses. The game starts by placing a marker (such as a coin) on 0. Each player takes turns pulling out pieces from the bag and adding it's value to the location of the marker. The piece that is pulled out should not be returned to the bag.

Summary Questions:
1. In the game there are three possibilities. Either Player A wins, Player B wins, or neither player wins. What occurs and why when neither player wins?

2. If pieces are retuned to the bag, how many possible outcomes are there and why?

110   Chapter 5: Understanding Integer Operations and Properties

MANIPULATIVE ACTIVITY 5.4

Adding and Subtracting Integers with PopCubes®

Each PopCube® has a "tip" that can be used to link the cubes together. The "tip" can also be used to indicate positive and negative integers, depending on whether it is on the left or the right.

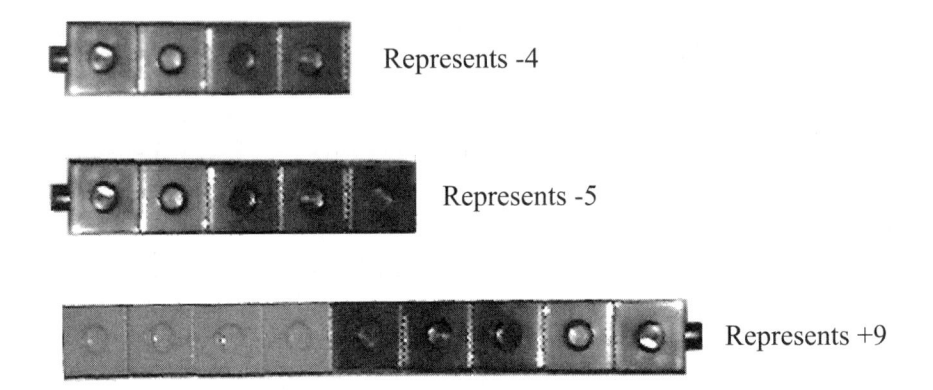

Represents -4

Represents -5

Represents +9

For addition of integers, we will need to match up the "tip" of the first addend to the "tail" of the second. The "tail" is the end that is flat.

For example, to show that $9 + (-5) = 4$, we would start with 9 and match the "tip" of 9 to the "tail" of -5.

4 cubes pointing in the positive direction

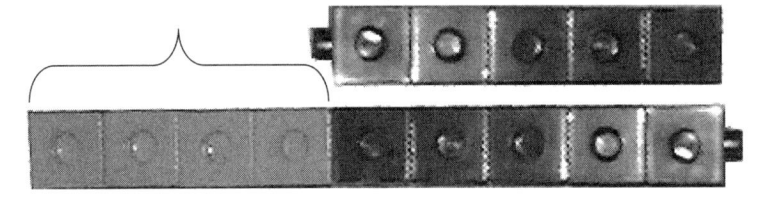

Part A Summary Questions:
1. What would the PopCubes® look like if you were asked to find $-5 + 9$? Interpret the result.

2. What would the PopCubes® look like if you were to asked to find $5 + (-9)$? Interpret the result.

3. What would the PopCubes® look like if you were to asked to find $-5 + (-4)$? Interpret the result.

For subtraction of integers using PopCubes®, you change the direction of the second value (the subtrahend) and proceed as before.

Part B Summary Questions:
1. What would the PopCubes® look like if you were asked to find $-5-9$? Interpret the result.

2. What would the PopCubes® look like if you were to asked to find $5-(-9)$? Interpret the result.

3. What would the PopCubes® look like if you were to asked to find $-5-(-4)$? Interpret the result.

4. Why do we change the direction of the second value (the subtrahend) and proceed as before?

112 Chapter 5: Understanding Integer Operations and Properties

TECHNOLOGY ACTIVITY 5.1

Sums and Differences of Integers

Use any type of calculator for this activity. You will be using the digits

1 2 3 5 7 8 and 9.

A. Place one digit in each box to create a difference as close to −1000 as possible. Use each digit only once.

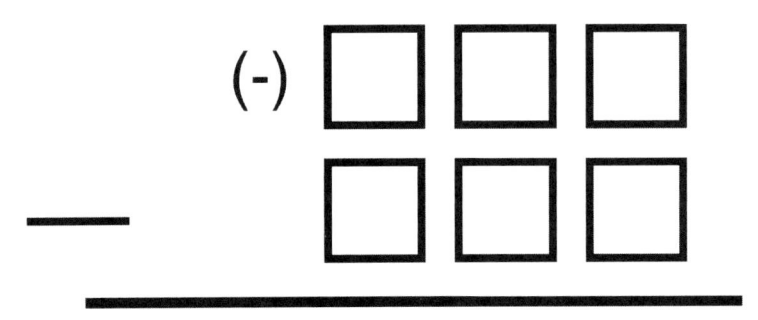

$$(-)\ \square\ \square\ \square$$
$$-\ \ \ \ \ \square\ \square\ \square$$

B. Place one digit in each box to create a sum as close to −1200 as possible. Use each digit only once.

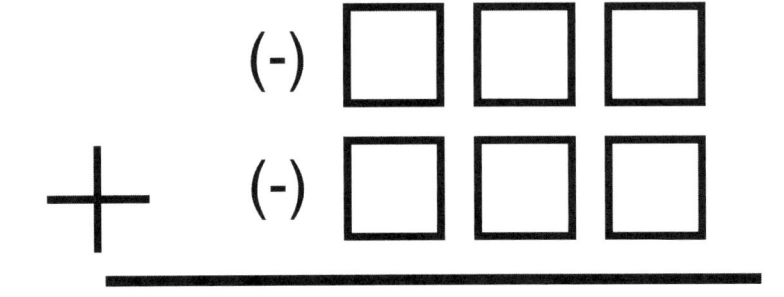

$$(-)\ \square\ \square\ \square$$
$$+\ (-)\ \square\ \square\ \square$$

Summary Questions:
1. What strategies did you use to solve each problem?

2. How did you use integer computation and estimation skills?

3 What assurance do you have that you actually solved the problem?

TECHNOLOGY ACTIVITY 5.2

A Twist on Ulam's Algorithm

In Technology Activity 4.4, Ulam's Theorem was investigated. A twist on the algorithm is instead of dividing by 2 at each step, divide by -2 and allow the initial number to be any non-zero integer. Using a calculator, generate the sequence of numbers using the following algorithm.

Start with any non-zero integer number.

- If the number is even, divide it by -2.
- If the number is odd, multiply it by 3, add 1, and then divide the result by -2.

Repeat this process with the new number generated and determine if there is an eventual stopping place.

For example, if you choose 6 as your starting number, the sequence would be

$$-3 \to 4 \to -2 \to 1.$$

Also, if you choose -6 as your starting number, the sequence would be

$$3 \to -5 \to 7 \to -11 \to 16 \to -8 \to 4 \to -2 \to 1.$$

A. Carry out the algorithm using the following six starting values and record the number of steps required to reach a stopping place.

Starting value	Sequence	Number of terms in sequence
12		
17		
32		
64		
69		
80		

B. Carry out the algorithm using the following six starting values and record the number of steps required to reach a stopping place.

Starting value	Sequence	Number of terms in sequence
−12		
−17		
−32		
−64		
−69		
−80		

Summary Questions:
1. What number (if any) was your stopping number?

2. Suppose your stopping number was 1, what would happen if you continue the process?

3. Would it make sense to have −1 as a stopping number? Why or why not?

4. What are any similarities and difference between the sequences generated by a number and its opposite?

TECHNOLOGY ACTIVITY 5.3

Sequencer and Integers

Go to the Sequencer feature on the Interactiviate disk. Sequencer will generate three types of sequences. They are arithmetic, geometric, and neither.

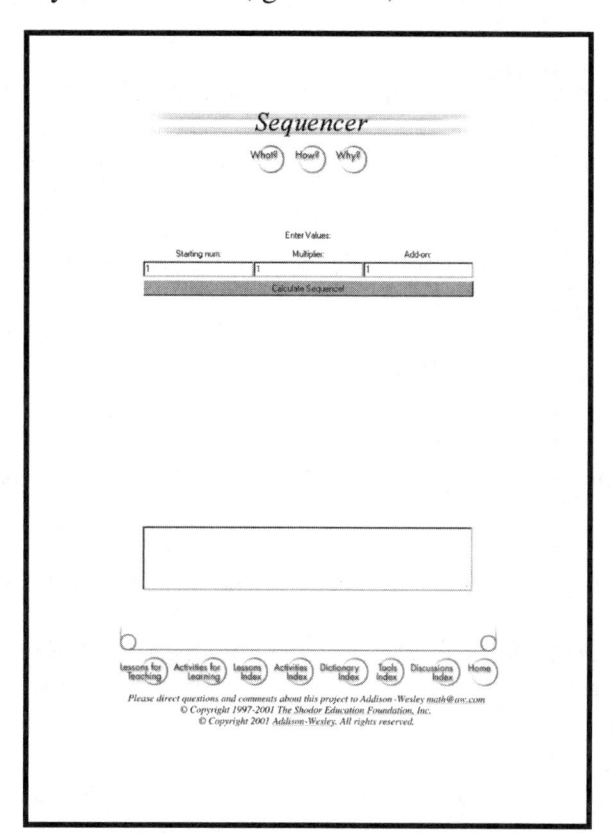

- To generate an arithmetic sequence, the multiplier should be 1. You can have any starting number and any non-zero add-on number.
    - For example, Starting number: 2 Multiplier: 1 Add-on 3
- To generate a geometric sequence, the add-on should be 0. You can have any starting number and any non-zero multiplier.
    - For example, Starting number: 2 Multiplier: 3 Add-on 0
- To generate neither a geometric or arithmetic sequence, the multiplier should not be 0 nor 1. You can have any starting number and any add-on number.
    - For example, Starting number: 1 Multiplier: 2 Add-on 3

Using Sequencer generate the first ten terms of all three types of sequences using the example values.

Chapter 5: Understanding Integer Operations and Properties

Summary Questions:
1. Given the examples, what are the similarities between these sequences and what are the differences? You may choose to include variations and similarities between the graphs that are displayed.

2. What happens to the example arithmetic sequence if you change the add-on to a negative value?

3. What kind of sequence would occur if the multiplier is 1 and the add-on is 0?

4. What effect does a negative starting number have on an arithmetic sequence if the add-on was positive?

5. After displaying the sample geometric sequence, change the multiplier to 5. What effect did this change have on the sequence?

6. Create the sequence -5, -10, -20, -40,... What are the starting number, multiplier, and add-on?

7. Create the sequence -5, -7, -9, -11,... What are the starting number, multiplier, and add-on?

8. What effect on a geometric sequence occurs when the multiplier is negative?

9. What are the next 5 terms after the ten calculated by Sequencer of the example sequence that is neither arithmetic nor geometric? Is there a way to use Sequencer to verify your results?

10. What is the general term for the example arithmetic and geometric sequences?

11. What difficulties arise in determining the general term for the sequence that is neither arithmetic nor geometric?

TECHNOLOGY ACTIVITY 5.4

Powers of Negative Integers

For this activity, you will need a calculator. Consider the following,

$$(-2)^n(-3)^m.$$

This expression will produce either a positive integer or a negative integer, depending on what whole-number exponents are used to evaluate the expression.

First evaluate this expression for $n=1$ and $m=1$. Write down the product. Next we are going to increment the exponent of one of the factors and then the other in order to observe the outcome. Find the next ten products in such a process. The table below may be helpful in keeping track of these values.

n	m	$(-2)^n(-3)^m$	Product
1	1	$(-2)^1(-3)^1$	6
1	2		
2	2		
2	3		
3	3		
3	4		
4	4		
4	5		
5	5		
5	6		
6	6		

Summary Questions:
1. What generalizations can be made regarding the expression and whether its outcome is positive or negative when evaluated?

2. If this expression can produce either positive or negative integers, why can't it produce zero?

3. If continued, would it possible that $-839,808$ would be on your table? Explain.

4. If continued, would it possible that $-559,872$ would be on your table? Explain.

5. If continued, would it possible that 1,5116,544 would be on your table? Explain.

6. How could you use powers of 6 in Questions 3-5 to help in your calculations to determine an answer?

Chapter 5: Understanding Integer Operations and Properties

TECHNOLOGY ACTIVITY 5.5

Playing with Numbers III

Refer to TECHNOLOGY ACTIVITY 2.5 and 4.7. To represent the word DIG upside down on a calculator as the sum of two integers, we can find $1234 + (-624)$. Notice that there are infinitely many ways to create a sum or difference.

Determine the number that must be viewed by turning the calculator upside down in order to obtain each of the following.

A. HIDE

B. SLIDE

C. HIGH

D. HOLE

Write four simple riddles that involve addition and/or subtraction of integers whose answer will be each of the above words when viewed upside down. The result could be the negative of the number if desired. Also, you may choose to have more than two integers to add and/or subtract. Try to make the problem correlate to the answer. For example:

> Anne is looking for treasure. She goes 1234 paces forward and 624 paces back. In the end, what should she do?

Since this problem implies $1234 + (-624)$, the result is DIG when this sum if viewed upside down on a calculator. Trade your four problems with a classmate. Work out their problem while they are working out yours.

Summary Questions:
1. Did you make any of the results negative? If so, which ones and why?

2. For each of the words, were there any common features of the questions between you and your classmates? Were there any major differences?

CHAPTER 6: RATIONAL NUMBER OPERATIONS AND PROPERTIES

INVESTIGATION 6.1

Rational Numbers as Quotients

In the systems of whole numbers and integers, there are no solutions to equations such as $5 \times n = 4$ or $17 \div 5 = q$. Rational numbers provide solutions to these equations.

A. Make up a problem situation to fit each of the given equations.

B. Use the whole number division algorithm to find the whole number quotient and remainder that solve each equation. Interpret the solutions based on your problem situations in Part A.

C. Find the rational number that solves each equation. Write each rational number solution in both fraction and decimal form. Interpret these solutions based on your problem situations in Part A.

Summary Questions:
1. What process did you use to find the fraction form of the rational number solutions? Why?

2. What process did you use to find the decimal form of the rational number solutions? Why?

3. How does your whole number quotient and remainder solution for each equation compare to its rational solution?

4. How does the process you used for finding the whole number quotient and remainder solutions compare to the process you used for finding the rational number solutions?

5. How do your interpretations in Parts B and C differ? How are they alike? Why?

6. Create two other single-operation equations involving integers that have non-integer, rational number solutions. Which operations are you able to use in these equations? Why? Which operations are you not able to use? Why?

INVESTIGATION 6.2

Adding and Subtracting Fractions

A. Draw a picture to represent the following situation and write an equation to answer the question.

Nadia's team used 5 yards of fabric on the project today and 4 yards yesterday. How much fabric have they used on the project?

B. Draw a picture to represent the following situation and write an equation to answer the question.

Nadia's team used $\frac{1}{2}$ of a yard of fabric on the project today and $\frac{2}{3}$ of a yard yesterday. How much fabric have they used on the project?

Summary Questions:
1. How are the situations in A and B alike? How are they different?

2. How are the pictures you drew for representing Situations A and B alike? How are they different?

3. How are the equations you used to answer the questions in Situations A and B alike? How are they different?

4. Write a summary comparing addition with whole numbers to addition with fractions. How are they alike? How are they different?

5. How would your responses to the previous questions change if the situations involved subtraction? Make up a whole number situation and a similar fraction situation involving subtraction in order to test your conjecture.

INVESTIGATION 6.3

Multiplying and Dividing Fractions

A. Draw a picture to represent the following situation and write an equation to answer the question.

Carol and her daughter, Ileana, picked six buckets of berries this morning. They were able to make two batches of preserves with these berries. If tomorrow they only want to make one batch of preserves, how many buckets of berries should they pick?

B. Draw a picture to represent the following situation and write an equation to answer the question.

Carol and her daughter, Ileana, picked four and one-half buckets of berries this morning. They were able to make one and one-half batches of preserves with these berries. If tomorrow they only want to make one batch of preserves, how many buckets of berries should they pick?

Summary Questions:

1. How are the situations in A and B alike? How are they different?

2. How are the pictures you drew for representing Situations A and B alike? How are they different?

3. How are the equations you used to answer the questions in Situations A and B alike? How are they different?

4. Write a summary comparing your processes for solving the two problems. How are they alike? How are they different?

5. Consider the following situations:

   Alex had 3 boxes of candy that each held 4 ounces. How many ounces of candy did he have?

   Create a similar situation that involves fractions. Draw a picture and write equations for each situation, and answer the summary questions above.

6. Write a summary comparing multiplication and division with whole numbers to multiplication and division with fractions. How are they alike? How are they different?

INVESTIGATION 6.4

Comparing Fractions

Create a set of examples to explore the following conjecture.

$$\text{Given a fraction } \frac{a}{b} \text{ and integer } m, \frac{a}{b} < \frac{a+m}{b+m}.$$

Summary Questions:
1. What strategies, if any, did you use in choosing your set of examples?

2. Which of the following strategies or procedures did you use to compare the fractions? Explain how you used the ones you chose.

   - estimating
   - drawing (or imagining) a picture
   - finding a common denominator
   - changing the fractions to decimal form (with/without using a calculator)
   - cross-multiplying
   - other (explain)

3. Did you use the same strategy or procedure for every comparison? Why or why not?

4. Was the conjecture true for all of your examples? If so, does that prove the conjecture is true? Why or why not?

5. If the conjecture did not hold for all of your examples, what can you conclude?

6. Compare your conclusions with those of other students. How are they the same or different? How are your sets of examples alike or different?

INVESTIGATION 6.5

Comparing Fractions II

Create a set of examples to explore the following conjecture.

$$\text{Given a fractions } \frac{a}{b} \text{ and } \frac{c}{d}, \text{ if } \frac{a}{b} = \frac{c}{d} \text{ then } \frac{a}{b} = \frac{c}{d} = \frac{a+c}{b+d}.$$

Summary Questions:
1. What strategies, if any, did you use in choosing your set of examples?

2. Which of the following strategies or procedures did you use to compare the fractions? Explain how you used the ones you chose.

   - ❏ estimating
   - ❏ drawing (or imagining) a picture
   - ❏ finding a common denominator
   - ❏ changing the fractions to decimal form (with/without using a calculator)
   - ❏ cross-multiplying
   - ❏ other (explain)

3. Did you use the same strategy or procedure for every comparison? Why or why not?

4. Was the conjecture true for all of your examples? If so, does that prove the conjecture is true? Why or why not?

5. If the conjecture did not hold for all of your examples, what can you conclude?

6. Consider the following conjecture:

$$\text{Given a fractions } \frac{a}{b}, \frac{c}{d}, \text{ and } \frac{e}{f} \text{ if } \frac{a}{b} = \frac{c}{d} = \frac{e}{f} \text{ then } \frac{a}{b} = \frac{c}{d} = \frac{e}{f} = \frac{a+c+e}{b+d+f}.$$

   By performing the process you applied for the original conjecture, do you believe this conjecture is true or false? Explain.

7. Compare your conclusions with those of other students. How are they the same or different? How are your sets of examples alike or different?

Chapter 6: Rational Number Operations And Properties

MANIPULATIVE ACTIVITY 6.1

Which Fraction is Greater?

For this activity you will need to use PopCubes®. If PopCubes® are not available, then visit http://wps.aw.com/aw_odaffer_mathematic_2 to download printable unit blocks.

On a homework problem, a student must insert either a <, >, or = symbol between the following fractions.

$$\frac{2}{3} \quad \frac{4}{5}$$

A student comes to you and says, "$\frac{2}{3} < \frac{4}{5}$ because 2 is less than 4 and 3 is less than 5." Use a manipulative to help this student realize that the correct response was arrived at through incorrect reasoning. Share your demonstration with a partner and discuss the following questions.

Summary Questions:
1. How did you use the manipulative to demonstrate that the student incorrectly reasoned through the problem? Did you both use the manipulative in the same way? If not, how did the demonstrations differ?

2. Besides PopCubes® or unit blocks, are there any other ways to demonstrate that the student's reasoning is incorrect?

3. Would the demonstration you performed with PopCubes® or unit blocks make the student believe that his/her reasoning wouldn't work for every pair of fractions? Explain.

MANIPULATIVE ACTIVITY 6.2

Cover a Unit

For this activity you will need a six-sided die marked $\frac{1}{2}, \frac{1}{4}, \frac{1}{4}, \frac{1}{8}, \frac{1}{8}$, and $\frac{1}{8}$. You will also need a paper-strip fraction kit consisting of 1 (one strip), $\frac{1}{2}$ (two strips), $\frac{1}{4}$ (four strips) and $\frac{1}{8}$ (eight strips) strips. Each fraction should be represented by a different color. You may visit http://wps.aw.com/aw_odaffer_mathematic_2 to download the die and strips.

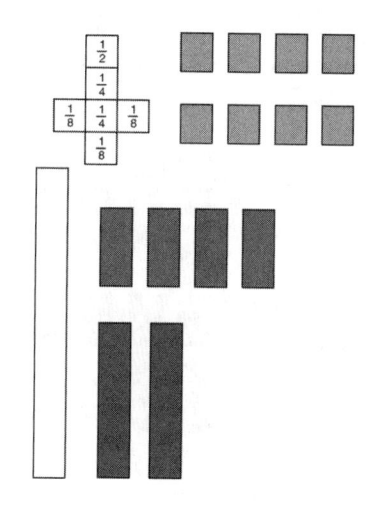

- With a partner use a 1-strip piece as a gameboard.

- Players take turns rolling the die, reading the fraction, and placing a strip representing that fraction onto the gameboard.

- Write an equation to represent each roll the game.

- The first player to cover the whole 1-strip without going over wins.

- Play the game until you are able to cover up the gameboard (without going over) at least four times.

Part A Summary Questions:
1. What is an addition equation that represents how you covered up the 1-strip piece (without going over) on each game?

2. How do the addition equations compare?

3. What observations did you make about some sums of fractions as you were playing the game?

126   Chapter 6: Rational Number Operations And Properties

Play the "Uncover a Unit" game by selecting pieces to cover the unit strip. Roll the die to determine which piece will come off. You may need to "trade" pieces in order to take off the rolled amounts. If you roll more than what is represented, then the game starts over. The winner is the person that takes off all of the strips to uncover the unit. Play this game until the unit is uncovered twice.

Part B Summary Questions:
1. What is a subtraction equation that represents how you uncovered the 1-strip piece on each successful game?

2. How do the subtraction equations compare?

Repeat the cover a unit steps with a die marked $\frac{1}{2}, \frac{1}{3}, \frac{1}{4}, \frac{1}{6}, \frac{1}{12}$, and $\frac{1}{12}$ along with the appropriate fraction strips. A download for the die and fraction strips is available on the website.

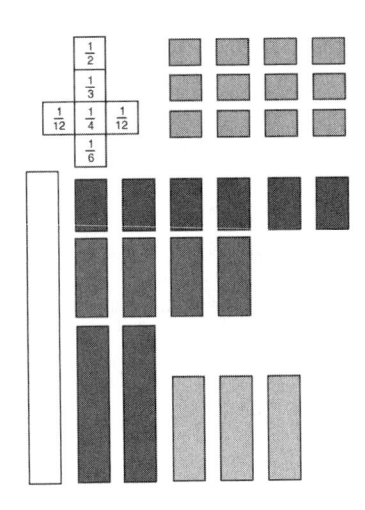

Part C Summary Questions:
1. What is an addition equation that represents how you covered up the 1-strip piece (without going over) on each game?

2. How do the addition equations compare?

3. What observations did you make about some sums of fractions as you were playing the game?

4. Was it easier or harder to cover the unit in this game verses the original game? Explain.

MANIPULATIVE ACTIVITY 6.3

Modeling Fractions

For this activity you will need PopCubes®. If PopCubes® are not available, chips can be used. You can visit http://wps.aw.com/aw_odaffer_mathematic_2 to download chips.

Working with a partner, use PopCubes® to answer the following questions.

A. If 8 cubes linked together represent 1, what represents $\frac{1}{4}$?

B. If 12 cubes linked together represent 1, what represents $\frac{1}{6}$? $\frac{2}{6} = \frac{1}{3}$? $\frac{3}{6} = \frac{1}{2}$? $\frac{4}{6} = \frac{2}{3}$? $\frac{5}{6}$?

C. If 3 cubes linked together represents $\frac{1}{3}$, what represents 1?

   If 5 cubes linked together represents $\frac{1}{2}$, what represents 1?

   If 2 cubes linked together represents $\frac{1}{4}$, what represents 1?

   If 3 cubes linked together represents $\frac{1}{5}$, what represents 1?

D. If 4 cubes linked together represents $\frac{2}{3}$, what represents $\frac{1}{3}$?

   If 8 cubes linked together represents $\frac{2}{5}$, what represents $\frac{1}{5}$?

   If 6 cubes linked together represents $\frac{3}{4}$, what represents $\frac{1}{4}$?

   If 12 cubes linked together represents $\frac{4}{9}$, what represents $\frac{1}{9}$?

E. If 6 cubes linked together represents $\frac{3}{4}$, what represents 1?

   If 8 cubes linked together represents $\frac{2}{3}$, what represents 1?

   If 9 cubes linked together represents $\frac{3}{4}$, what represents 1?

F. How many cubes could form a unit that could be used to model both $\frac{2}{3}$ and $\frac{1}{2}$?

   How many cubes could form a unit that could be used to model both $\frac{3}{5}$ and $\frac{1}{2}$?

   How many cubes could form a unit that could be used to model both $\frac{1}{3}$ and $\frac{1}{4}$?

Summary Questions:

1. How must a model of a unit be related to the fraction(s) being modeled?

2. How are the models you created for Parts A through F alike? How are they different?

3. Besides PopCubes® or counters, what other ways could Parts A through F be performed to demonstrate the answer?

128   Chapter 6: Rational Number Operations And Properties

MANIPULATIVE ACTIVITY 6.4

Mixed Up by Mixed

In Section 6.4 of your text, the quotient of two natural numbers is investigated through area models. The quotient of two fractions as well as the quotient of a mixed number and a fraction is also discussed. To extend this process we will investigate the quotient of two mixed numbers through area models. If you wish to visit http://wps.aw.com/aw_odaffer_mathematic_2, you can download and print a sheet to assist you with the Summary Questions.

Suppose we wish to investigate the quotient $3\frac{1}{4} \div 1\frac{1}{2}$. Each of these mixed numbers can be turned into improper fractions and then by using the Multiply by the Reciprocal Method we can arrive at our answer and then convert back to a mixed number if necessary.

Perform this process on the quotient to arrive at the answer of $2\frac{1}{6}$.

Now let's examine this quotient using area models. For this problem we need to start with a representation of $3\frac{1}{4}$.

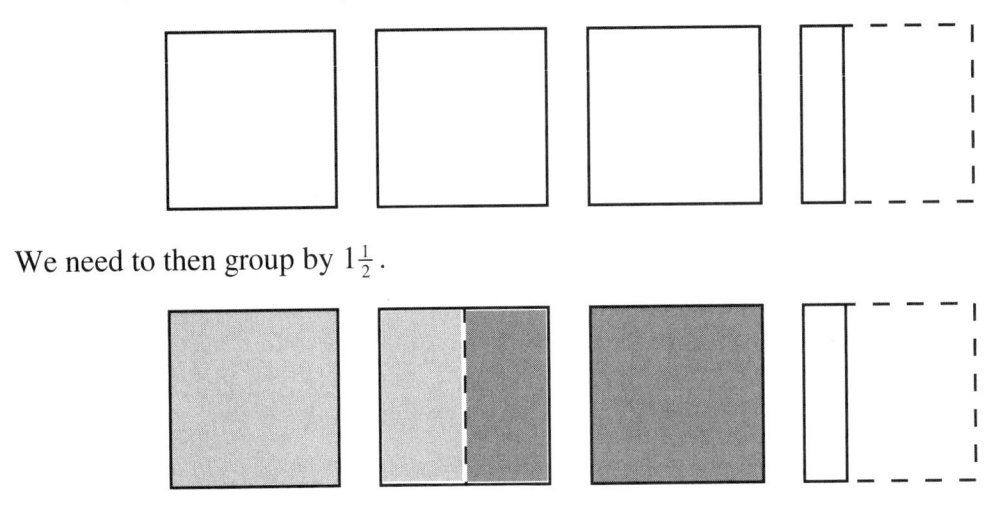

We need to then group by $1\frac{1}{2}$.

We can make two groupings of $1\frac{1}{2}$. The remaining part, although it appears to represent an area of $\frac{1}{4}$, it is interpreted as $\frac{1}{6}$.

Using additional divisions we have the following.

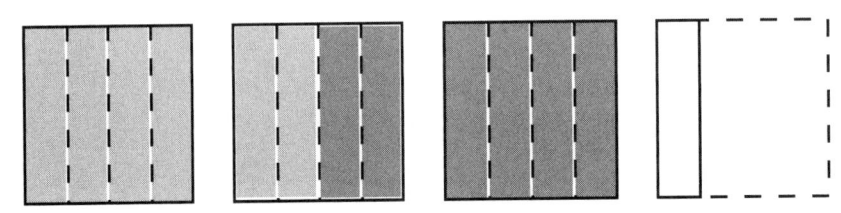

Summary Questions:
1. Why is the remaining part interpreted as $\frac{1}{6}$?

2. How must additional divisions be made to demonstrate $5\frac{1}{2} \div 2\frac{1}{2}$? Demonstrate with a drawing.

3. How must additional divisions be made to demonstrate $7\frac{1}{2} \div 1\frac{7}{8}$? Demonstrate with a drawing.

4. How must additional divisions be made to demonstrate $4\frac{3}{4} \div 1\frac{7}{8}$? Demonstrate with a drawing.

5. How must additional divisions be made to demonstrate $4\frac{2}{3} \div 1\frac{1}{2}$? Demonstrate with a drawing.

TECHNOLOGY ACTIVITY 6.1

The In-Between Game

Find a partner and a graphing calculator, such as a TI-83, to play the game described as follows.

- Player A sets up the game by entering into the graphing calculator a number between 0 and 1. Player B then enters a different number between 0 and 1. The screen below shows that Player A entered 0.45 and Player B entered 0.07.

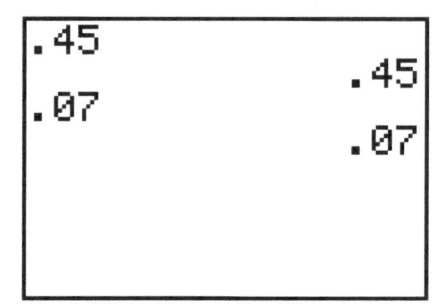

```
.45
                    .45
.07
                    .07
```

- Play now commences with each player entering a value that lies between the previous two entries. The screen below shows that Player A entered the value 0.31 and Player B entered the value 0.265. It's now Player A's turn. That player must enter a value between 0.31 and 0.265, the last two values entered into the calculator.

```
             .45
.07
             .07
.31
             .31
.265
             .265
```

- The winner if the game is the last player to display a correct value on the calculator screen. This occurs when one player proves that an incorrect entry has been made or when the calculator can no longer display new entries.

Summary Questions:
1. What strategies did you develop to help win the game?

2. What is the connection between this game and the *denseness property* of the rational numbers?

3. What occurs when an entry is made and the calculator is unable to display the new entries? What notation does the calculator display?

TECHNOLOGY ACTIVITY 6.2

Sums and Differences of Rational Numbers

For this activity, use a calculator with the capability to display fractions, such as a TI-83.

Choose from the digits below for this activity.

$$1\ 2\ 3\ 4\ 5\ 6\ 7\ 8 \text{ and } 9$$

A. Place one digit in each box to create a sum as close to $\frac{9}{10}$ as possible. Use each digit no more than once.

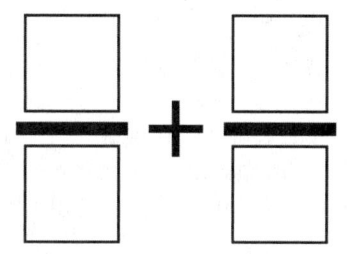

$$\frac{\Box}{\Box} + \frac{\Box}{\Box}$$

B. Place one digit in each box to create a difference as close to $\frac{3}{8}$ as possible. Use each digit no more than once.

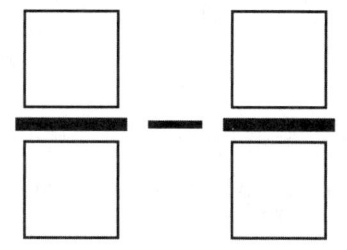

$$\frac{\Box}{\Box} - \frac{\Box}{\Box}$$

Summary Questions:
1. What strategies did you use to solve each problem?
2. How did you use rational-number computation and estimation skills?
3. What assurance do you have that you actually solved the problem?

TECHNOLOGY ACTIVITY 6.3

Simplifying Continued Fractions

Here are four fractions that together begin a pattern of *continued fractions*.

$$\frac{1}{1+1},\ \frac{1}{1+\dfrac{1}{1+1}},\ \frac{1}{1+\dfrac{1}{1+\dfrac{1}{1+1}}},\ \frac{1}{1+\dfrac{1}{1+\dfrac{1}{1+\dfrac{1}{1+1}}}}$$

Use a calculator with the capability to display fractions such as a TI-83 to simplify each of the four fractions shown above. You may find it helpful to enter each expression by starting with the "deepest" denominator in the expression and then working backwards.

Another way to generate such a sequence of fractions is to enter the second addend in the first denominator into your calculator as shown below. Then using the previous answer feature of the calculator type what is shown below, including the fraction feature.

```
1
                                    1
1/(1+Ans)▶Frac
```

Press enter once. Press it three more times to generate the remaining terms.

Summary Questions:
1. Why does the procedure using the previous answer feature of the calculator for generating this continued fraction work?

2. What patterns do you notice in the four simplified fractions?

3. What do you predict will be the simplified form of the next three terms in the sequence of continued fractions shown above? Press enter on your calculator three more times.

4. What patterns results from the following continued fractions?

$$\frac{1}{2+1}, \quad \frac{1}{2+\dfrac{1}{2+1}}, \quad \frac{1}{2+\dfrac{1}{2+\dfrac{1}{2+1}}}, \quad \frac{1}{2+\dfrac{1}{2+\dfrac{1}{2+\dfrac{1}{2+1}}}}$$

5. Create a different sequence of continued fraction and explore its pattern. Will the same general pattern as you discovered appear with any sequence of continued fractions? Explain.

TECHNOLOGY ACTIVITY 6.4

The Rebounding Ball: How Far Does It Go?

This activity can be performed with spreadsheet software such as Excel® in order to draw conclusions. This activity can also be done using any standard calculator if this software is not available.

A hard rubber ball is dropped from a window 40 feet above a cement walkway. On each bounce off the walkway, it rebounds one-half its height on the previous bounce. The ball is caught at the top of it's bounce when it first rebounds to a height less than 1 foot.

Using Excel®, we will calculate the heights reached on each bounce. Enter 40 into Cell A1 and "=A1/2" (without the quotes for all entries) in Cell B1. Then, in Cell B2 place "=B1/2". After pressing enter, the cell will change to 10.

	A	B
1	40	20
2		=B1/2
3		
4		
5		
6		
7		

On Cell B2 use the Copy and Paste features for cells below B2. Paste the contents of Cell B2 in the cells below one at a time until the cell value is less than 1. For this example, you will paste the contents of Cell B2 until you reach Cell B6. Click on Cell B7 and then on the summation (Σ) feature. The following should be displayed.

	A	B
1	40	20
2		10
3		5
4		2.5
5		1.25
6		0.625
7		39.375

Summary Questions:
1. What does the entry in Cell B7 represent?

2. How can you use the given values to determine the total distance traveled by the ball? What is this total distance?

3. If you change the entry in Cell A1 to 50, 60, 70, and 75. What do you notice about the entry in Cell B7?

4. Change the entry in Cell A1 to 100. Copy and Paste the contents of Cell B2 in B7. Use the summation feature in Cell B8 like before. What number is given in Cell B8? Interpret the results.

5. Change the entry in Cell A1 to 128. Copy and paste the contents of Cell B2 in the appropriate cells until you get a value of **less than** 1. Do the same for 250, 256, 300, 400, 500, and 512. What is a generalization regarding the number of bounces the ball will require to obtain a height of less than one for any initial height?

136 Chapter 6: Rational Number Operations And Properties

TECHNOLOGY ACTIVITY 6.5

Pi, Pi, and More Pi

As stated on page 291 of your text, π is a real number which is not rational. It can be called irrational. Since rational numbers can be expressed as the ratio of two integers, irrational numbers cannot. With irrational numbers we can get decimal approximations to any desired accuracy. The most common approximation is,

$$\pi \approx 3.14.$$

A more accurate approximation is,

$$\pi \approx 3.141592653589793238462643383279502884197169399375\,1.$$

As with decimals approximations, rational approximations are often useful.

An easy way to generate rational approximations is to determine what decimal accuracy you desire. If you choose accuracy to two decimal places, for example, then you could use the rational number $\frac{314}{100} = \frac{157}{50}$. The common rational approximation for pi is $\frac{22}{7}$ however.

Summary Questions:

1. To how many decimal places is the rational approximation to pi, $\frac{22}{7}$, accurate?

2. Why do you think $\frac{22}{7}$ is the most common rational approximation for pi?

3. If your calculator has constant π feature, how many decimal places accuracy does it have? Compare it to the approximation given above. Is the last decimal place the same? If not, explain why.

4. To how many decimal places is the rational approximation to pi, $\frac{355}{113}$, accurate?

5. To how many decimal places is the rational approximation to pi, $\frac{5419351}{1725033}$, accurate?

   You may need to perform the calculations "by hand", using the calculator to perform the individual multiplication and subtraction steps.

TECHNOLOGY ACTIVITY 6.6

Using Converter

Go to the Converter feature on the Interactiviate disk (entitled Conversions). In this activity you use this feature to draw conclusions. This activity could also be performed using the fraction feature on most calculators. The Converter feature on the Interactivate disk however has better capabilities when converting from decimal to fraction.

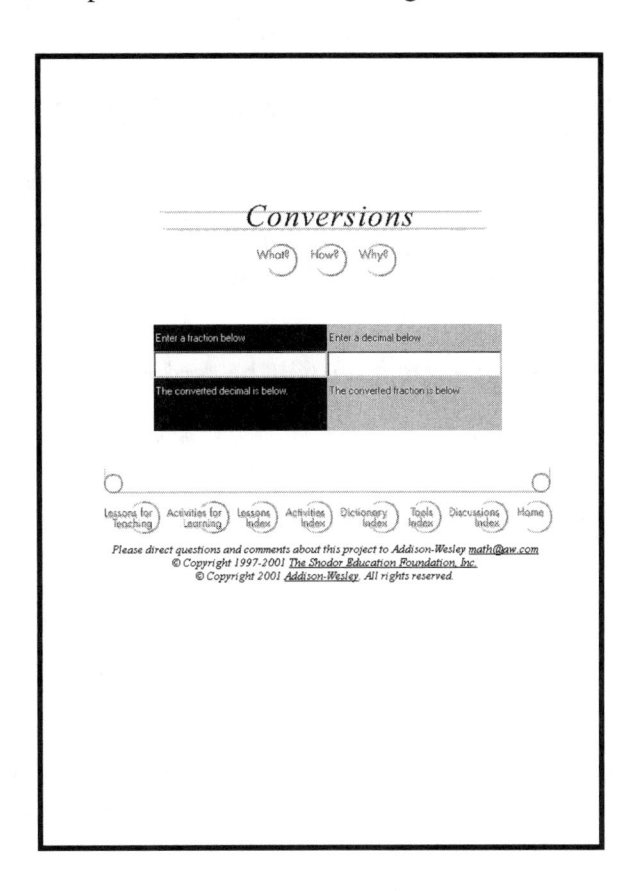

Consider the following sequence of numbers 0.1, 0.01, 0.001, 0.0001, etc. This is a geometric sequence.

Part A Summary Questions:
1. What are the next five terms in the sequence?

2. Describe the pattern in generating terms. What is the general term?

3. As the sequence progresses, what value are the terms approaching?

Using the Converter feature type in the fraction 1/0.1 and hit enter. The conversion 10.0 should be displayed. Do this for the nine remaining terms of the geometric sequence. That is type in the fraction 1/"the term". Record your results.

138 Chapter 6: Rational Number Operations And Properties

Part B Summary Questions:
1. What is happening to the terms as you progress through the sequence?

2. What is the smallest number in our sequence you can place in the denominator and have a numerical result?

3. What happens after that?

4. What does this tell you about division by zero?

In Chapter 6 (pages 288-289), it is discussed that if the denominator of a fraction can be expressed as a power of 10, then the fraction can be expressed as a terminating decimal. It is understood that the numerator should not contain a fraction itself. Ideally these fractions do not contain fractions within the numerator or denominator. To determine if a fraction in the form $\frac{a}{b}$, where a and b are natural numbers and relatively prime (see page 220 in your text), one needs only to examine the denominator in order to determine whether or not it's decimal representation will be terminating. If you find the prime factorization of b and it only contains 2's and/or 5's then, the fraction can be expressed as a terminating decimal.

Go to the Converter feature on the Interactiviate disk and enter in at least ten different fractions to test out this statement. Choose some fractions that have denominators that represent numbers that can be expressed as the product of 2's and/or 5's and some that cannot. You may choose to make all of the numerators equal to 1 to simplify your task. Record the fractions you chose and the results.

Part C Summary Questions:
1. What do the results demonstrate? Include what happened for the fractions that have denominators that represent numbers that could be expressed as the product of 2's and/or 5's and those that could not.

2. Using the other part of the Converter feature enter five arbitrary decimal numbers to be converted each to a fraction. If you get the message "Decimal too complex" then choose another decimal with less accuracy. Record your results. What do your results tell you about the conversion from decimal to fraction?

TECHNOLOGY ACTIVITY 6.7

And the Winner is……

Go to The Tortoise and Hare Race feature on the Interactiviate disk. In this activity you will be able to complete 15 stages of the fabled race between the tortoise and the hare.

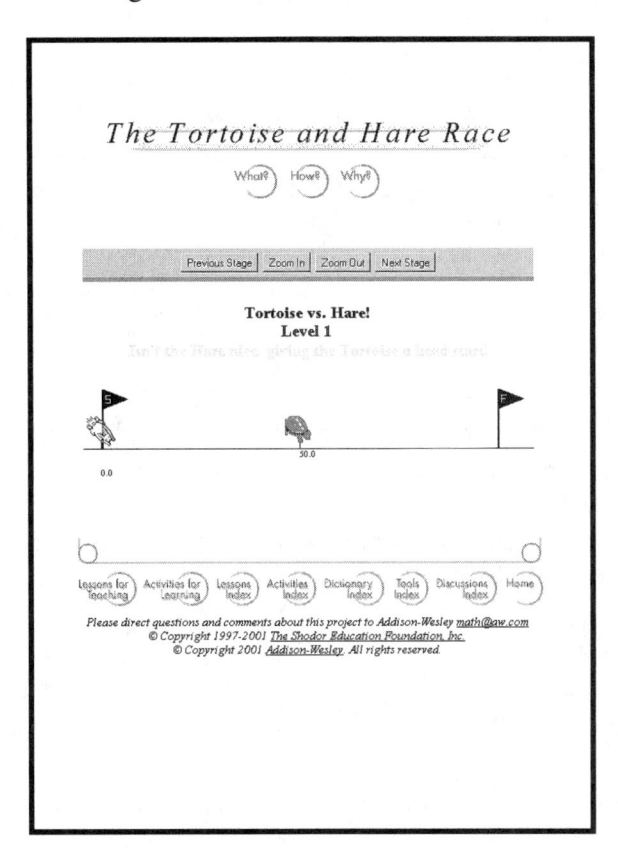

In the story, the tortoise and hare agree to a 100-mile race. The tortoise gets to have a head start of 50 miles (half the total distance). When the tortoise reaches this halfway mark, the hare then starts his race to the end. At this point stage 1 has completed. The next stage is completed when the tortoise completes $\frac{1}{2}$ of the remaining distance required to cross the finish line and the hare does the same. Each subsequent stage is completed in the same manner.

Using The Tortoise and Hare Race feature compete the table on the next page.

- Write the decimal value given at each stage, which corresponds to each animal's location between 0 and 100.
- Determine and write the corresponding fraction problem and simplify. Leave the answer as either an improper fraction or a mixed number.
- Use the simplified fraction solution to determine the distance between the tortoise and the hare. Use a calculator or the Converter feature on your Interactivate disk to check your fraction equation match the decimal location.

140   Chapter 6: Rational Number Operations And Properties

Stage	Decimal location		Fraction Problem	
	Hare	Tortoise	Hare	Tortoise
1	0.0	50.0	0	$0 + \frac{1}{2}(100) = 0 + 50 = 50$
2	50.0	75.0	$0 + \frac{1}{2}(100) = 0 + 50 = 50$	$50 + \frac{1}{2}(50) = 50 + 25 = 75$
3				
4				
5				
6				
7				
8				
9				
10				
11				
12				
13				
14				
15				

Summary Questions:
1. Who is ahead by how much after each step? Use the simplified fraction location for each of the animals to determine your answer.

Stage	Hare	Tortoise	Difference	Stage	Hare	Tortoise	Difference
1	0	50	Tortoise by $50 - 0 = 50$ miles	9			
2	50	75	Tortoise by $75 - 25 = 25$ miles	10			
3				11			
4				12			
5				13			
6				14			
7				15			
8							

2. Will the tortoise or the hare ever win? Explain.

3. By considering the location of the tortoise at each stage, what do you believe would be the following sum?

$$100\left(\frac{1}{2} + \frac{1}{4} + \frac{1}{8} + \frac{1}{16}...\right)$$

The "..." (ellipses) indicate that this goes on forever.

CHAPTER 7: PROPORTIONAL REASONING

INVESTIGATION 7.1

A "Griddy" Problem

Consider the following 10×10 grid. Let the total area represent 1 square unit.

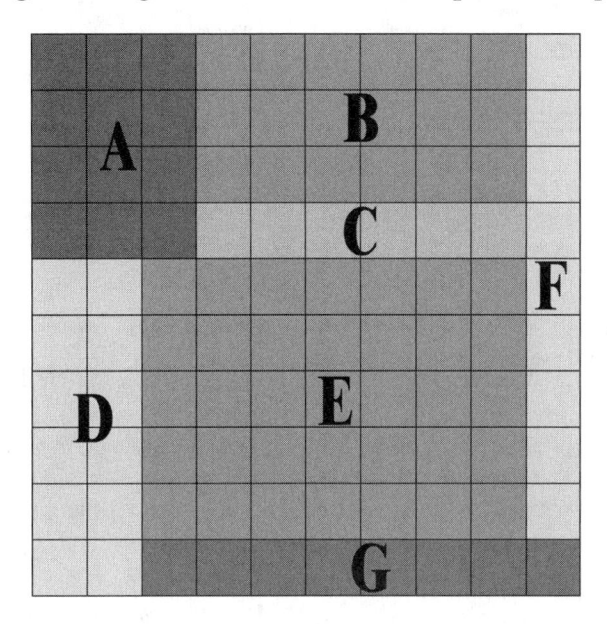

Express each of the seven rectangles as a percent of the whole and fill in the rest of the requested information in the following table.

	Percent	Ratio of shaded squares in the rectangle to the whole	Fraction expressed as a decimal	Product of two decimal factors
A				0.4 · 0.3
B				
C				
D				
E				
F				
G				
SUM				

142   Chapter 7: Proportional Reasoning

Now consider the shaded rectangles with the following subdivisions.

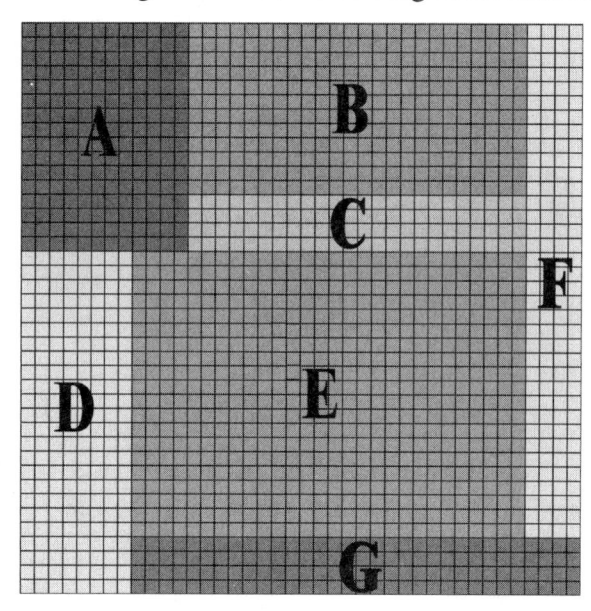

Determine how many squares are represented in the entire figure and fill in the following table.

	Number of shaded squares	Ratio of shaded squares in the rectangle to the whole
A		
B		
C		
D		
E		
F		
G		
SUM		

Summary Questions:
1. If each of the squares in the second diagram were divided into nine squares then how many squares would each of the seven rectangles contain? Would that change the ratio of the shaded squares in each rectangle to the whole?

2. Can you express the area represented by A (in the second diagram) as $1.6 \cdot 1.2$? Why or why not?

INVESTIGATION 7.2

Pieces of Eight

You may have heard the term "two bits" which describes one quarter. This term comes from Spanish coins being broken into eight pie-slice-shaped pieces called *pieces of eight* or *bits* in order to make change. The whole coins are called eight reales and served as a model for the original U.S. silver dollar. The bits usually came as one, two, or four reales. Another term that you may have heard of is "picayune". This is the name that was given to a half real or a half bit.

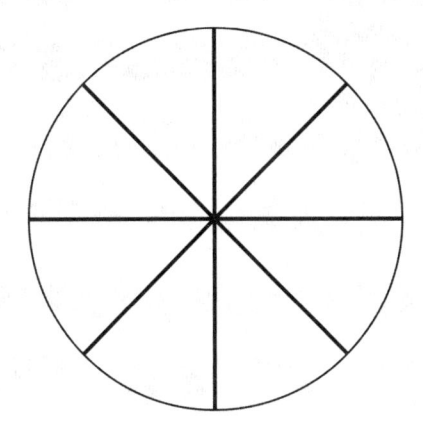

Part A Summary Questions:
1. If a Spanish coin was considered equivalent to a dollar, how many cents would the one, two, and four reales be worth? How much would a picayune be worth?

2. Why do you think there are not generally three, five, six, or seven reales as bits?

3. The practice of shaving off parts of a coin by unscrupulous people can be seen in collections. The full weight of a two reales coin is considered to be 6.77 grams. If a two reales coin weighed only 5.92 grams, then what percent has been clipped off?

When the New York Stock Exchange opened in 1792 the price per stock was quoted in New York shillings. These were valued at eight to the Spanish dollar. Changes in stock prices were then reported in eighths. It stayed this way for over 200 years. According to the Common Cents Stock Pricing Act of 1997, all U.S. stocks were required to convert their stock prices from fraction to decimals by the year 2000 (after Y2K issues were resolved). There are many financial considerations for both of these systems such as half pennies with the fractional system (when a stock increases from 100 to $100\frac{1}{8}$ for example) and narrow spreads (the difference between the asking price and the selling price) with the decimal system.

Part B Summary Question:
If an increase of 2% in many stocks is considered significant, why would a one dollar stock have to change by more than 12% to have an impact with the old system of fractions? What percent change would an increase of one eighth have on a $100 stock?

144 Chapter 7: Proportional Reasoning

INVESTIGATION 7.3

Flying Ratios

In order to make a U.S. flag in correct proportions, the ratio of the width of a flag to its length should be 10 to 19. The length of the union is 40% of the entire length.

On June 14, 1777, the Congress declared "Resolved: that the flag of the United States be thirteen stripes, alternate red and white; that the union be thirteen stars, white in a blue field, representing a new constellation." In 1795 the flag had fifteen stars and stripes for the addition of Kentucky and Vermont. However when five more states joined in 1818, Congress changed back to 13 stripes in order to represent the original 13 states. Twenty stars were placed on the Union and when an additional state joined, a new star would be added.

Part A Summary Questions:
1. If the length of the US flag is 190 inches, then what is the length of the union?

2. What is the width to length ratio of each of the six long stripes?

3. What is the width to length ratio of each of the seven short long stripes?

4. What is the width to length ratio of the union?

5. What percentage of the flag is stripes?

6. Is the width of the union more or less than half the width of the flag? Why do you believe it isn't exactly half?

There are three common ratios that appear in flags of the world. The United Kingdom, Australia, Bahamas, Canada, and Ireland all have the width to length ratio of 1:2.

United Kingdom

The German flag has a 3:5 ratio.

Germany

The flags of France, Italy, and Spain have a 2:3 ratio.

France

Part B Summary Question:
Ratios within a flag oftentimes have purpose and meaning. The proportions of the vertical stripes on the French navel flag are given to be 30:33:37. This is to enable good visual effect of the flag when flying. What do these three numbers represent in terms of the dimensions of this flag?

INVESTIGATION 7.4

Half-Baked Ratios

Often times one deals with ratios when adjusting recipes. Consider the following ingredients for a Custard Egg Tart and the two situations that follow.

$1\frac{1}{8}$ cups water
$1\frac{1}{4}$ cups all-purpose flour
$\frac{1}{2}$ cup sugar
1 tablespoon sugar
6 eggs
$\frac{1}{2}$ cup butter
2 teaspoons vanilla
2 tablespoon shortening
1 teaspoon vinegar

Situation 1: Suppose this recipe makes enough to feed 6 people and you need to make enough to feed 12 people. How would you adjust the recipe so that all ingredients are in the correct proportion?

Situation 2: Suppose you discovered that you only had three eggs. How would you adjust the recipe so that all ingredients are in the correct proportion?

Part A Summary Question:
How are these two situations alike and how are they different?

On food coloring boxes you often see ratios used to in order to create a color other than red, blue, green, or yellow. Consider the following ratios for colors and the two situations that follow.

Wild Green	Green:Yellow	3:2
Redberry Blue	Red:Blue	2:7

Situation 1: You were trying to make Wild Green and you accidentally put in 10 drops of green and 15 drops of yellow. What would you do in order to achieve the correct color?

Situation 2: You were trying to make Redberry Blue and you put in 4 drops of red and accidentally put an extra drop of blue. What would you do in order to achieve the correct color?

Part B Summary Question:
How are these two situations alike and how are they different?

INVESTIGATION 7.5

Three Short Problems III

You purchased an item on a 30% off sale. The cashier reduced the price by 20%. After you corrected the cashier they took off an additional 10%. The cashier did not give you the actual sale price.

Part A Summary Question:
How much discount off the original sale price did you receive? Explain what happened when the cashier discounted the additional 10% after the 20%.

Oftentimes we read or hear statements involving percents. When we hear 50% off sale, we know that means the original price is cut in half.

Part B Summary Questions:
1. What is meant by a percent decrease of less than 1%?

2. What is meant by a percent increase of 100% or more?

On pages 374-375 of your text, percent diagrams for *finding the percent of a number*, *finding a number when a percent of it is known*, and *finding the percent that one number is of another* were given. For each diagram below, create a problem situation using the given values and unknown. Solve each of these problems.

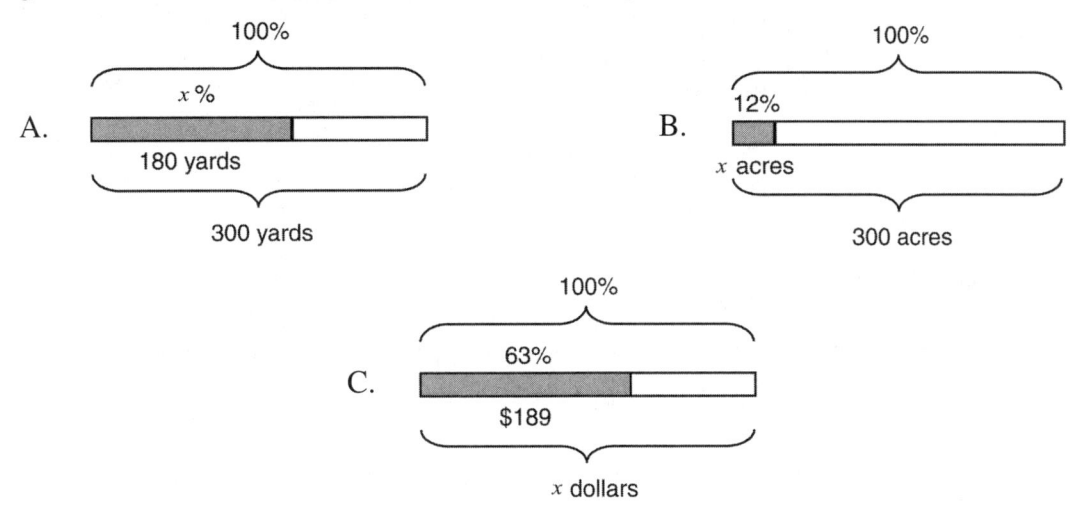

A. [Diagram: 100% total = 300 yards; shaded portion = x% = 180 yards]

B. [Diagram: 100% total = 300 acres; shaded portion = 12% = x acres]

C. [Diagram: 100% total = x dollars; shaded portion = 63% = $189]

Part C Summary Questions:
1. How are these percent diagrams alike and how are they different?

2. Are the diagrams drawn accurately (to scale)? Explain.

148 Chapter 7: Proportional Reasoning

INVESTIGATION 7.6

Summing Terms with a Common Ratio

Sequences that have a common ratio between consecutive terms are considered *geometric sequences* (See pages 19-20 in your text.). The nth term of such a sequence is ar^{n-1} where a is the first term and r is the common ratio. Such a sequence looks like

$$a, ar, ar^2, ..., ar^{n-2}, ar^{n-1}.$$

As with arithmetic sequences, we are often interested in the sum of terms. To find $S = a + ar + ar^2 + ... + ar^{n-2} + ar^{n-1}$, where S is the sum, we need to multiply both sides by the common ratio r and apply the distributive property to simplify.

$$S \cdot r = \left(a + ar + ar^2 + ... + ar^{n-2} + ar^{n-1}\right) \cdot r$$

$$Sr = ar + ar^2 + ar^3 + ... + ar^{n-1} + ar^n$$

Subtract the new equation from the old equation to obtain

$$\begin{aligned} S &= a + ar + ar^2 + ... + ar^{n-2} + ar^{n-1} \\ -Sr &= -\left(ar + ar^2 + ar^3 + ... + ar^{n-1} + ar^n\right) \\ \hline S - Sr &= a - ar^n \\ S(1-r) &= a\left(1 - r^n\right) \end{aligned}$$

Thus $S = a \cdot \dfrac{1 - r^n}{1 - r}$.

Part A Summary Questions:

1. Consider the geometric sequence $6, 4, \dfrac{8}{3}, \dfrac{16}{9}, \dfrac{32}{27}, \dfrac{64}{81}, \dfrac{128}{243}, \dfrac{256}{729}, \dfrac{512}{2187}, \dfrac{1024}{6561}$.
   What are the terms expressed in the form ar^{n-1}?

2. By first finding a least common denominator of all of the terms, add the terms together by hand. Use a calculator and the formula $S = a \cdot \dfrac{r^n - 1}{r - 1}$ to find the sum of the terms. What is the sum? What are some advantages and disadvantages of each method of summation?

Unlike arithmetic sequences such as 2, 5, 8, 11, 14, 17, 20,... it is possible to find the sum of an infinite number of terms of a geometric sequence if the common ratio r is between

0 and 1. To find such a sum, we proceed in the same manner as before to find
$S = a + ar + ar^2 + ... + ar^{n-2} + ar^{n-1} + ...$.

$$S \cdot r = \left(a + ar + ar^2 + ... + ar^{n-2} + ar^{n-1} + ...\right) \cdot r$$

$$Sr = ar + ar^2 + ar^3 + ... + ar^{n-1} + ar^n + ...$$

Subtract the new equation from the old equation to obtain

$$\begin{aligned} S \quad &= a + ar + ar^2 + ... + ar^{n-2} + ar^{n-1} + ... \\ -Sr &= -\left(ar + ar^2 + ar^3 + ... + ar^{n-1} + ar^n + ...\right) \\ \hline S - Sr &= a \\ S(1-r) &= a \end{aligned}$$

Thus $S = a \cdot \dfrac{1}{1-r}$.

Part B Summary Questions:

1. Consider the first summation formula $S = a \cdot \dfrac{1-r^n}{1-r}$. If $0 < r < 1$, what happens to r^n as n increases? What if $r > 1$?

2. Why is it not possible to find the sum of an infinite number of terms of an arithmetic sequence? Consider two cases, where the common difference is positive and the common difference is negative.

3. What is the sum of $6, 4, \dfrac{8}{3}, \dfrac{16}{9}, \dfrac{32}{27}, \dfrac{64}{81}, \dfrac{128}{243}, \dfrac{256}{729}, \dfrac{512}{2187}, \dfrac{1024}{6561} ...$?

4. What percentage does the sum of the first 10 terms represent of the sum of the whole sequence (the infinite sequence)?

MANIPULATIVE ACTIVITY 7.1

Representing Proportional Relationships

Using the following as a ruler, measure each of the labeled sides of the triangle as accurately as possible. Record each value in the table provided. You can visit http://wps.aw.com/aw_odaffer_mathematic_2 to download the ruler, triangles, table, and blank scatterplot.

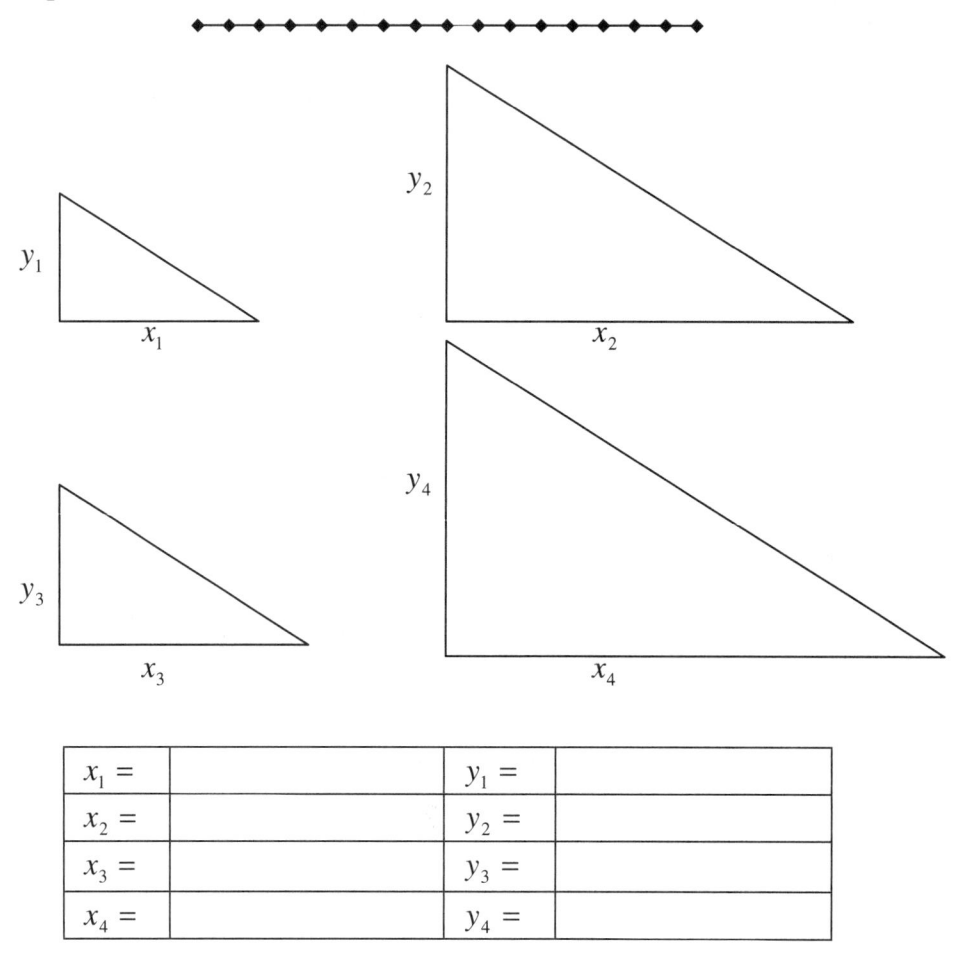

$x_1 =$		$y_1 =$	
$x_2 =$		$y_2 =$	
$x_3 =$		$y_3 =$	
$x_4 =$		$y_4 =$	

Do a scatterplot, which shows the relation between the x- and the y-values for each triangle. There should be a total of four dots.

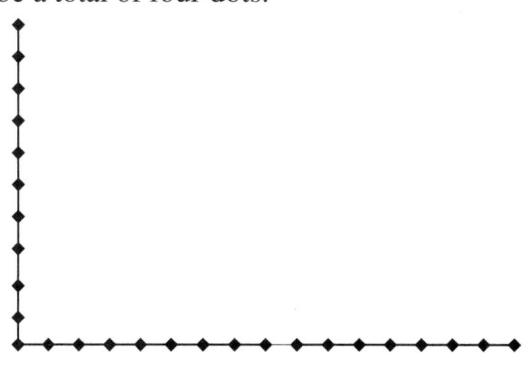

For each of the four pairs of numbers find $\frac{y}{x}$. Express each as a decimal (rounded to the nearest hundredth) and as a rational number.

Summary Questions:
1. What can you conclude about the labeled sides of each of the four triangles?

2. Using your scatterplot, what would the y-value of a triangle be if the x-value was 10? Explain how you used the scatterplot. How could you use the $\frac{y}{x}$ ratio(s) found before to verify this result?

3. Would the following triangles have the same characteristics as the four original triangles? Explain your response using both scatterplot information and $\frac{y}{x}$ ratios.

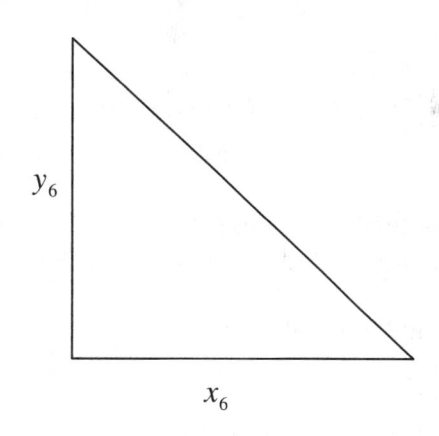

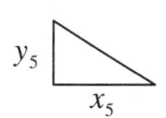

152   Chapter 7: Proportional Reasoning

MANIPULATIVE ACTIVITY 7.2

Popping the Question(s)

Use PopCubes® to solve the following problem. Determine which colors would represent men and which would represent women. If PopCubes® are not available, then you can download red and blue chips at http://wps.aw.com/aw_odaffer_mathematic_2.

In a small town $\frac{1}{6}$ of the adult women are married to $\frac{1}{4}$ of the adult men. What percentage of the adult population is not married?

Part A Summary Questions:
1. What strategy (strategies) did you use to solve this problem?

2. If the number of adults in the population were asked for, would the answer be unique? Explain.

Use PopCubes® to solve the following. If PopCubes® are not available, then you can download red, blue, and green chips at http://wps.aw.com/aw_odaffer_mathematic_2.

I have PopCubes® divided up into three piles. The largest pile has four times as many cubes as the medium-sized pile and the medium-sized pile has three times as many cubes as the smallest pile. What is the ratio of the number of cubes in the large pile to the number of cubes in the small pile?

Part B Summary Questions:
1. What strategy (strategies) did you use to solve this problem?

2. What percentage of the total does each pile represent?

3. If the number of PopCubes® were asked for, would the answer be unique? Explain.

MANIPULATIVE ACTIVITY 7.3

Going in Circles

Draw four circles of various sizes and make sure to mark the center on each. If you wish, you may visit http://wps.aw.com/aw_odaffer_mathematic_2 to download a sheet with circles printed along with a ruler. Label your four circles A-D from smallest to largest.

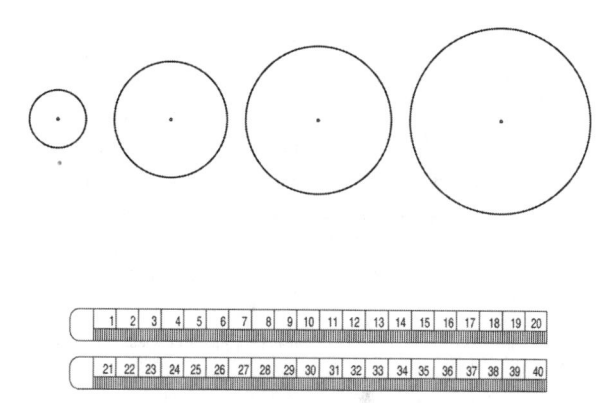

For each of the four circles, find the length around (circumference) and the distance passing through the center (diameter). You may measure in inches, centimeters, or with the downloaded ruler. To measure the circumference, you can cut out the downloaded ruler and wrap it around each circle. If you use a standard ruler, you can cut out your circles, mark a beginning/ending point and "roll" it onto your ruler. Record your results in the following table.

	Circumference (x)	Diameter (y)	$x \cdot y$	$\dfrac{x}{y}$
Circle A				
Circle B				
Circle C				
Circle D				

Summary Questions:
1. What can be said about the product $x \cdot y$ for these various circles?

2. What can be said about the ratio $\dfrac{x}{y}$ for these various circles?

3. If a circle has a diameter of 20 units, what would you predict the circumference to be? Create such a circle to test you results.

154   Chapter 7: Proportional Reasoning

MANIPULATIVE ACTIVITY 7.4

A Body of (in) Great Proportions

For this activity, you will need a measuring tape or a yard/meter stick. If one is not available, you can visit http://wps.aw.com/aw_odaffer_mathematic_2 to download a ruler to be cut and pasted together. For ease of measurements, the download is in the metric system.

Working in groups, find the following body measurements:

- Height without shoes (**HS**)

- Distance from floor to belly button while standing (**BS**)

- Distance from floor to belly button while kneeling (**BK**)

- Height while kneeling (**HK**)

- Vertical length of face (**LF**)

- Vertical length of chin (**LC**)

- Horizontal distance across shoulders (**DS**)

- Horizontal distance of arm span from fingertip to fingertip (**DA**)

Fill in a table like the one on the next page.

NAME					
HS					
BS					
BK					
HK					
LF					
LC					
DS					
DA					

Summary Questions:
1. What seems to be the ratio of DA to HS?

2. What seems to be the ratio of HK to HS?

3. What seems to be the ratio of DS to HS?

4. What seems to be the ratio of BS to HS?

5. What seems to be the ratio of BK to BS?

6. What seems to be the ratio of LC to LF?

Describe the procedure you implemented to arrive at your answers.

156 Chapter 7: Proportional Reasoning

MANIPULATIVE ACTIVITY 7.5

Expanding and Shrinking Rectangles

For this activity you will need graph paper. If graph paper is not available, it can be downloaded at http://wps.aw.com/aw_odaffer_mathematic_2. You may choose to print about five pieces.

- On graph paper create a 12×12 square in one of the corners.
- Distort the square so that its sides measure twice the sides of the original square.
- Distort the original square so that the sides measure half the sides of the original square.
- Distort the original square so that the sides measure one-third the sides of the original square.
- Distort the original square so that opposite sides measure twice the original and the other two sides measure three times the original.
- Distort the original square so that opposite sides measure three times the original and the other two sides measure one-third the original.

Keep tract of the results of the distortions compared to the original square in the table below.

Dimensions	Area (number of squares in the interior)
12×12	

Summary Questions:
1. When you distort a square by the same amount on each side, how does that affect the area? Describe the distortion in terms of ratios.

2. When you distort a square by different amounts on pairs of sides, how does that affect the area? Describe the distortion in terms of ratios.

3. Using the corner of the graph paper, create a triangle with a height of 12 units and a base of 6 units. Perform the distortions in similar manner to that of the square. There are only single sides to distort, not pairs. Connecting the endpoints of the two distorted sides should create the longest side of the triangle. Approximate the area of the interior as much as possible. Do the responses for Questions 1 and 2 hold the same for the triangle? Explain.

TECHNOLOGY ACTIVITY 7.1

Summing Terms with a Common Ratio II

This activity can be performed with spreadsheet software such as Excel® in order to draw conclusions. This activity can also be done using any standard calculator if this software is not available.

To begin this activity, we will be using a starting value of 120. In Cell A1 type "120" without the quotation marks. In Cells B1 through H1 type "1/2", "1/3", "1/4", "1/5", "1/6", "1/10", and "1/12" as shown below. For these cells, which are included for labeling purposes, you will need to include the quotation marks. Without the quotation marks, you could get a date entered (such as January 2nd for 1/2) or a decimal conversion. In Cell B2 type "=A1/2" and in Cell B3 type "=B2/3" (both without quotation marks). The results are shown below.

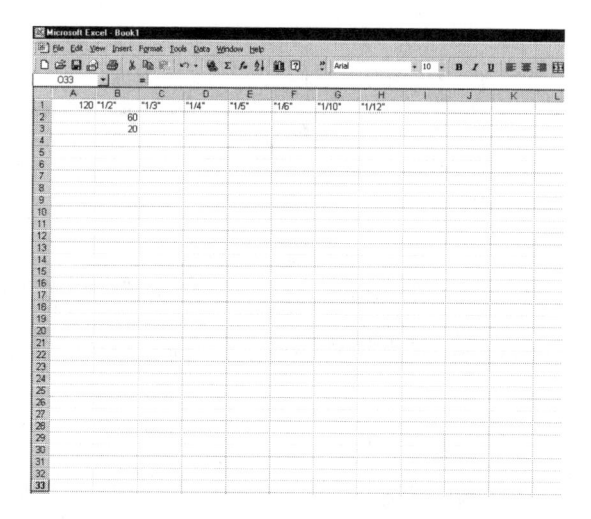

Copy the Cell B3 and paste it in Cells B4 through B30. In Cell B31 use the summation ($\sum$) feature to obtain the screen below.

158   Chapter 7: Proportional Reasoning

Repeat this process for Columns C through H. Entries in Row 2 use the initial value divided by the appropriate corresponding value (or multiplied by the labeled ratio). Entries in Row 3 will be the entries in Row 2 divided by the appropriate corresponding value (or multiplied by the labeled ratio). Sum each of the columns. The copy/paste feature can be used to copy the contents of Cell B31 and paste it to Cells C31 through H31.

Using the calculated values, fill in the following table.

n	$\dfrac{1}{n}$	Sum	Sum expressed as a fraction with a numerator of 120
2	$\dfrac{1}{2}$	120	$\dfrac{120}{1}$
3	$\dfrac{1}{3}$		
4	$\dfrac{1}{4}$		
5	$\dfrac{1}{5}$		
6	$\dfrac{1}{6}$		
⋮	-	-	-
10	$\dfrac{1}{10}$		
11	-	-	-
12	$\dfrac{1}{12}$		

Summary Questions:
1. What is the relationship between the starting value, ratio between consecutive terms, and the sum?

2. If you change the starting value from 120 to other values (such as 1000 or 1600), how does that affect the relationship you found in Question 1?

3. Have you found a relationship for summing a finite number of terms or an infinite number of terms? Explain.

TECHNOLOGY ACTIVITY 7.2

Representing Proportional and Inverse Relationships

For this activity, you can use a graphing calculator or a spreadsheet program that has a scatterplot grapher. For each part sketch or print your results.

- Create a scatterplot of a proportional relationship between two quantities x and y. This is a visual or graphical representation.

- Create a table of values showing x and y. Show at least six pairs of values in your table, including the pair with $x = 0$. This is a *tabular* or *numerical* representation.

- Represent a proportional relationship with symbols in the form $y = kx$. Determine the appropriate value of k for your proportional relationship. This is a *symbolic* or *algebraic* representation.

Part A Summary Questions:
1. What are some characteristics of proportional relationships apparent in the representations you created above?

2. How would you describe the relationship between x and y when the k value is negative? Examine the similarities and differences in the three representations.

Proportional variation is also called direct variation, that is the ratio or quotient of the two variables remains constant. Inverse variation has the relationship that the product of the two variables remains constant. Choose a non-zero constant and create a symbolic, tabular, and graphical representation of the inverse variation relationship between x and y.

Part B Summary Questions:
1. What are some characteristics of inverse relationships apparent in the representations you created?

2. How would you describe the relationship between x and y when the k value is negative? Examine the similarities and differences in the three representations.

3. Why does the constant value k need to be non-zero?

4. Can you obtain a pair in which either x or y is zero? Explain.

160 Chapter 7: Proportional Reasoning

TECHNOLOGY ACTIVITY 7.3

Sierpinski's Triangle

Go to the Sierpinski's Triangle feature on the Interactiviate disk. In this activity you use this feature to draw conclusions.

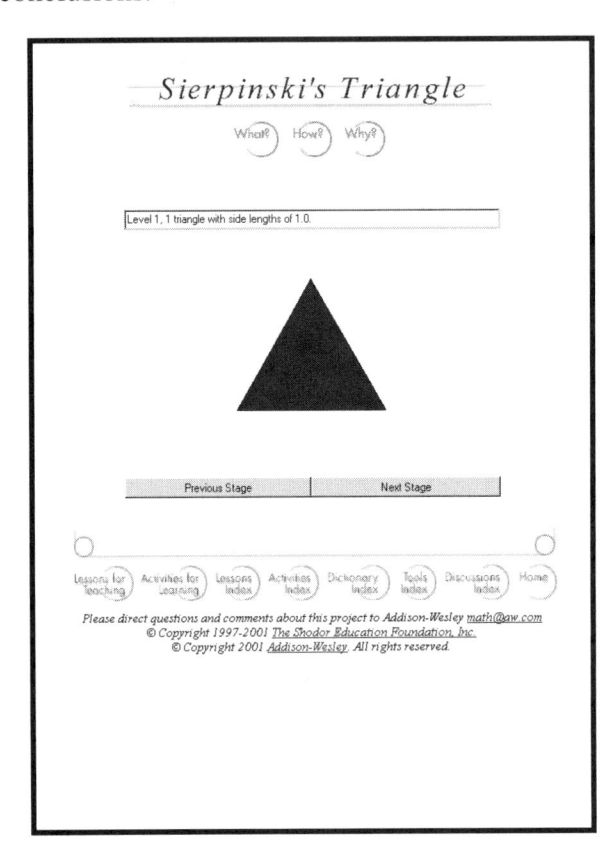

Go through the seven stages of the Sierpinski's Triangle feature and record your results in the table below.

Level (l)	1	2	3	4	5	6	7
A. Number of triangles (equal sized shaded and unshaded) (t)	1						
B. Number of shaded triangles (s)	1						
C. Side lengths m	1.0						
D. Area of one of the shaded triangles $a = \dfrac{1}{t}$	1						
E. Percent Shaded $a \cdot s \cdot 100\%$							

Part A Summary Questions:
1. What is the procedure that the Sierpinski's Triangle feature on the Interactiviate disk follows in order to yield each level? Describe what happens as you progress through the levels.

2. For A through E, do consecutive stages vary proportionally? For those that do, find the k value. (See page 353 in your text.)

3. For A through E, what is a formula that yields entries at the lth level?

4. For A through E, what happens as the level approaches infinity?

Sierpinski's Triangle can be created through the process in which triangles are removed according to the method used on the Sierpinski's Triangle feature on the Interactiviate disk. In such a process, the lengths of the sides of the triangles removed in consecutive levels vary proportionally. If m_l represents the length of the triangle removed at stage l and m_{l+1} represents the length at the next stage, then $m_{l+1} = \frac{1}{2} m_l$.

Another method to create Sierpinski's Triangle involves placing points in a triangle. To do this draw two triangles and label the three vertices "1", "2", and "3". One triangle should have all three sides the same length and the other should have all three sides of different lengths. For a download of two such triangles visit http://wps.aw.com/aw_odaffer_mathematic_2. If you are working in a group, have half of your classmates work on one sheet and the other half work on the other sheet. It is recommended that you obtain a ruler that has centimeters and millimeters marked to make calculations and markings easier.

You are going to be generating the numbers "1", "2", and "3" randomly. This can be done by the roll of a six-sided die where "1 and 4" correspond to "1", "2 and 5" correspond to "2", and "3 and 6" correspond to "3". If a die is not available, you can use your graphing calculator to generate the numbers "1", "2", and "3" randomly. The following shows how. If you press the MATH button you will see the first screen on a TI-83.

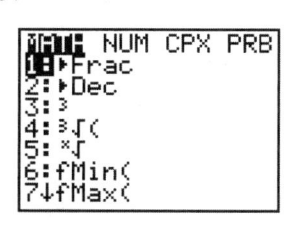

Toggle over to NUM. Then toggle down to 5:INT(or press 5.

Press MATH again and toggle over to PRB. Then press enter to choose 1:rand.

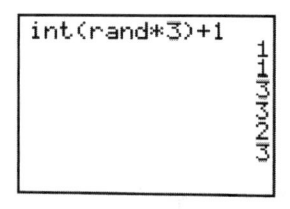

162   Chapter 7: Proportional Reasoning

Type in the rest of the expression as shown is the last screen. If you continue to hit enter, the calculator will display the digits 1 through 3

To start the process, pick an arbitrary point not on the boundary of the triangle. Generate either a "1", "2", or "3". Use the ruler to plot the point that is halfway between your first point and the numbered vertex generated. Use this new point as the starting place for the next iteration. Continue the process (at least 100 times) of generating a number ("1", "2", or "3") and finding the midpoint between a vertex and the last point plotted.

Part B Summary Question:
What would happen if you choose an initial point that is on the boundary of the triangle?

TECHNOLOGY ACTIVITY 7.4

Playing with Pies

Go to the Pie Chart feature on the Interactiviate disk.

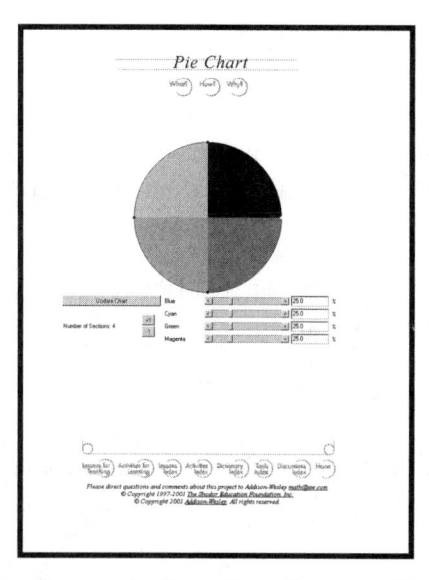

This feature will allow you to slice a pie from 1 to 9 parts. For each of the 9 possibilities, adjust the percents using the sliding bar until all colors represent the same percentage. Record the results for each stage in the table below.

	Blue	Cyan	Green	Magenta	Orange	Pink	Red	White	Yellow	Sum
1	100.0%									100.0%
2	50.0%	50.0%								100.0%
3										
4										
5										
6										
7										
8										
9										

Summary Questions:
1. Were you able to get all of the levels the same amount? If not, which could you not?

2. What was your technique in adjusting the colors to achieve optimum results?

3. Which of the nine levels had a sum of exactly 100%?

4. What determines if sum is exactly 100%, more than 100%, or less than 100%?

Chapter 7: Proportional Reasoning

TECHNOLOGY ACTIVITY 7.5

A Topic of Interest

On page 381 of your text, the formula for calculating the amount of compound interest is given to be $a = p\left(1 + \dfrac{i}{n}\right)^{nt}$ where a is the total amount of principle plus interest, p is the principal, i is the annual rate of interest, n is the number of times the interest is compounded per year, and t is the number of years. Using this formula, you can determine how much money you will have in an account when you make regular deposits.

Suppose you made an annual investment of $100 at the beginning of every year. Every year the money compounds at a rate of 5%. How much money will you have at the beginning of the 10th year (after you make the 10th deposit)? Using a calculator or spreadsheet, complete in the table below.

Year	Deposit	Total in account before interest added	Interest earned at end of the year (round to the nearest penny)	Total in account at the end of the year
1	$100	$100.00	$5.00	$105.00
2	$100	$205.00	$10.25	$215.25
3	$100			
4	$100			
5	$100			
6	$100			
7	$100			
8	$100			
9	$100			
10	$100		-	-
	$1000			

Part A Summary Questions:

1. If each $100 is earning 5% per year then why is total in account at the end of the 2nd year $215.25 and not $210?

2. In this scenario, how many times did the first payment go through the compounding process? Second payment? Third payment? Tenth payment?

3. Calculate

$$100 + 100(1+0.05) + 100(1+0.05)^2 + 100(1+0.05)^3 + 100(1+0.05)^4 +$$
$$100(1+0.05)^5 + 100(1+0.05)^6 + 100(1+0.05)^7 + 100(1+0.05)^8 + 100(1+0.05)^9.$$

Do you get the same results as before after the 10th deposit? Explain what each term of this expression represents.

In Investigation 7.5, the formula for the sum of the terms of a geometric sequence was derived. This formula is $S = a \cdot \dfrac{1-r^n}{1-r}$ where S is the sum, a is the first term, r is the common ratio, and n is the number of terms. If you consider the expression

$$100 + 100(1+0.05) + 100(1+0.05)^2 + 100(1+0.05)^3 + 100(1+0.05)^4 +$$
$$100(1+0.05)^5 + 100(1+0.05)^6 + 100(1+0.05)^7 + 100(1+0.05)^8 + 100(1+0.05)^9$$

100 is the first term, $(1+0.05)$ is the common ratio, and 10 is the number of terms. Verify that is expression will yield the same sum as found before.

In general, if you deposit d dollars into an account with an annual interest rate of i compounded n times a year then you will have in your account

$$a = d \cdot \dfrac{1-\left(1+\dfrac{i}{n}\right)^{nt}}{1-\left(1+\dfrac{i}{n}\right)} = d \cdot \dfrac{1-\left(1+\dfrac{i}{n}\right)^{nt}}{1-1-\dfrac{i}{n}} = d \cdot \dfrac{1-\left(1+\dfrac{i}{n}\right)^{nt}}{-\dfrac{i}{n}} = d \cdot \dfrac{\left(1+\dfrac{i}{n}\right)^{nt}-1}{\dfrac{i}{n}}$$

after t years. The number of times you deposit in a year is the same as how many compounding periods are in a year.

This formula can be used to determine monthly payments on such things as furniture, cars, and houses. With a typical loan, you have an amount borrowed (p), an annual interest rate (i), and the number of years (t) you wish to pay off this loan. What you need to do is determine the value of d that satisfies the following:

$$p\left(1+\dfrac{i}{n}\right)^{nt} = d \cdot \dfrac{\left(1+\dfrac{i}{n}\right)^{nt}-1}{\dfrac{i}{n}},$$

where n is generally 12 to reflect monthly payments.

Part B Summary Questions:
1. Given a $20,000 loan on a car, what would the monthly payments be on a two-year loan if the interest rate is 7%? Calculate $p\left(1+\dfrac{i}{n}\right)^{nt}$ first and $\dfrac{\left(1+\dfrac{i}{n}\right)^{nt}-1}{\dfrac{i}{n}}$ second.

Divide the two quantities to find d.

166   Chapter 7: Proportional Reasoning

2. How much of your payment is going to pay off the loan (from Question 1) each month? How much interest did you pay on this loan? You can use a spreadsheet or a calculator to fill in the following table.

Payment number	Amount of payment	Amount of interest	Amount towards principal	Amount after principal payment
1				
2				
3				
4				
5				
6				
7				
8				
9				
10				
11				
12				
13				
14				
15				
16				
17				
18				
19				
20				
21				
22				
23				
24				
Sum				

3. Typically the monthly payment on these types of loans is rounded up to the next penny. Why is this the case?

CHAPTER 8: ANALYZING DATA

INVESTIGATION 8.1

Population Data

Consider the following Census 2000 data. The eight most populated states along with data relating to age, income, and housing is given. A housing unit may be a house, an apartment, a mobile home, a group of rooms, or a single room that is occupied (or, if vacant, is intended for occupancy) as separate living quarters according to the Census.

Ranked in terms of total population	State	Total resident population (1,000)	Average annual pay (in dollars)	Number of housing units	Population 85 years and older
1	California	33,872	37,564	12,214,549	425,657
2	Texas	20,852	32,895	8,157,575	237,940
3	New York	18,976	42,133	7,679,307	311,488
4	Florida	15,982	28,911	7,302,947	331,287
5	Illinois	12,419	36,279	4,885,615	192,031
6	Pennsylvania	12,281	32,694	5,249,750	237,567
7	Ohio	11,353	31,396	4,783,051	176,796
8	Michigan	9,938	35,734	4,234,279	142,460

- Make a dot plot of the *Average annual pay* for the eight states.
- Make a dot plot of the *Number of housing units* for the eight states.
- Make a dot plot of the *Population 85 years and older* for the eight states.

Summary Questions:

1. For each of the dot plots, what patterns are evident? What kind of scaling did you use and why?

2. For each of the dot plots, are there any clusters? Are there any outliers?

3. For each state determine the percent the *Population 85 years and older* with respect to the entire population. If you made a dot plot of those percents, would you get the same ranking and type of variability compared to that of the *Population of 85 years and older*? Explain.

4. For each state determine the number of housing units per thousand residents. How does the ranking compare to the other categories?

INVESTIGATION 8.2

...And the Older Get Older

Consider the following Census 2000 data for the fifty states.

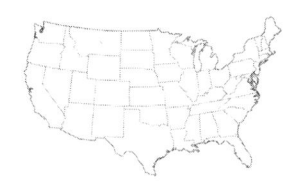

State	Percent of population 65 years and older	Percent of population 85 years and older	State	Percent of population 65 years and older	Percent of population 85 years and older
Alabama	13.0	1.5	Montana	13.4	1.7
Alaska	5.7	0.4	Nebraska	13.6	2.0
Arizona	13.0	1.3	Nevada	11.0	0.9
Arkansas	14.0	1.1	New Hampshire	12.0	1.5
California	10.6	1.3	New Jersey	13.2	1.6
Colorado	9.7	1.1	New Mexico	11.7	1.3
Connecticut	13.8	1.9	New York	12.9	1.6
Delaware	13.0	1.3	North Carolina	12.0	2.3
Florida	17.6	2.1	North Dakota	14.7	1.3
Georgia	9.6	1.1	Ohio	13.3	1.6
Hawaii	13.3	1.4	Oklahoma	13.2	1.7
Idaho	11.3	1.4	Oregon	12.8	1.7
Illinois	12.1	1.5	Pennsylvania	15.6	1.9
Indiana	12.4	1.5	Rhode Island	14.5	2.0
Iowa	14.9	2.2	South Carolina	12.1	1.3
Kansas	13.3	1.9	South Dakota	14.3	2.1
Kentucky	12.5	1.4	Tennessee	12.4	1.4
Louisiana	11.6	1.3	Texas	9.9	1.1
Maine	14.4	1.8	Utah	8.5	1.0
Maryland	11.3	1.3	Vermont	12.7	1.6
Massachusetts	13.5	1.8	Virginia	11.2	1.2
Michigan	12.3	1.4	Washington	11.2	1.4
Minnesota	12.1	1.7	West Virginia	15.3	1.8
Mississippi	12.1	1.5	Wisconsin	13.1	1.8
Missouri	13.5	1.8	Wyoming	11.7	1.4

- Make a combined stem-and-leaf plot for the given data.

- Make a histogram for each of the data sets.

- Make a scatterplot for *Percent of population 65 years and older* verses *Percent of population 85 years and older*.

- Calculate the mean and standard deviation for each data set. You may choose to use a calculator with statistical capabilities such as a TI-83.

Summary Question:
What comparisons can be made between these two data sets? Write a report which includes the information you have gathered.

INVESTIGATION 8.3

Speed Skating Times

During the Winter Olympics Speed Skating has become a popular event. The gold-medal times, in seconds, for men's and women's 500-meter speed skating are given below.

Men Time	Country	Year	Women Time	Country
44.1	USA	1924		
43.4	FIN/NOR	1928		
43.4	USA	1932		
43.4	NOR	1936		
43.1	NOR	1948		
43.5	USA	1952		
40.2	URS	1956		
40.2	URS	1960	45.9	GER
40.1	USA	1964	45.0	URS
40.3	FRG	1968	46.1	URS
39.44	FRG	1972	43.33	USA
39.17	URS	1976	42.76	USA
38.03	USA	1980	41.78	GDR
38.19	URS	1984	41.02	GDR
36.45	GDR	1988	39.10	USA
37.14	GER	1992	40.33	USA
36.33	RUS	1994	39.25	USA
35.68	JPN	1998	38.30	CAN
34.62	USA	2002	37.38	CAN

In 1998 and 2002, the gold-medal was determined by combining the times of two runs. In order to be able to compare table value, we added the times of the two runs and divided them by two (rounding to the nearest hundredth of a second).

In 1998 the men's winner, Hiroyasu Shimizu of Japan, had a 1st run of 35.76 and a 2nd run of 35.59 for a combined total of 71.35. The women's winner, Catriona LeMay-Doan of Canada, had a 1st run of 38.59 and a 2nd run of 38.21 for a combined total of 76.60.

In 2002 the men's winner, Casey FitzRandolph of the United States of America, had a 1st run of 34.42 and a 2nd run of 34.81 for a combined total of 69.23. The women's winner, Catriona LeMay-Doan of Canada, had a 1st run of 37.30 and a 2nd run of 37.45 for a combined total of 74.75.

- Create a combined Stem-and Leaf Plot for the Men's and Women's 500-meter Speed Skating times. (See page 396 of your text.)

- For each year that men and women have both been competing, determine the ratio of the men's time to the women's time.

Summary Questions:
1. A sportswriter studied the data and suggested that women's times will eventually be less than the men's times. Do you agree or disagree with this statement? Use your combined stem-and-leaf plot, analysis of ratio of times, or any other numerical/ graphical summaries to justify your response.

2. Can you draw any conclusions regarding the men's/women's nationality of the gold-medal winners? Discuss any differences in conclusions that can be drawn depending on your grouping nationalities. Keep in mind that URS and RUS represent the Soviet Union and Russia. The abbreviations FRG, GDR and GER are for West Germany (Federal Republic of), East Germany (German Democratic Republic) and Germany, respectively. Up to World War II, Germany was one country. After the war they were split in two, joining again at the end of 1989. However, for the Olympics, the split took place only in 1968, so up to 1964, athletes from both countries took part in a common team, denoted by GER (Germany). From 1968 to 1988, the two countries took part as separated teams, joining again in 1992. It should be noted that in 1952, the German team consisted entirely of West-German athletes, but there were no champions in speed skating from Germany that year.

INVESTIGATION 8.4

Three Short Problems IV

Consider the following graph of time verses the water level in the bathtub.

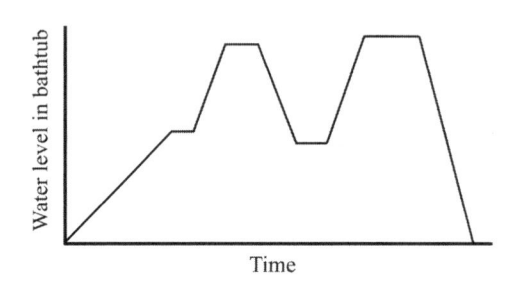

Part A Summary Question:
What story could you tell about the person taking the bath?

Consider the following statement:

> "Patients using toothpaste brand A improved 100 percent more than patients using toothpaste brand B."

Part B Summary Question:
What questions would you ask when evaluating the way data were collected that led to this statement?

Consider the following data and graphs.

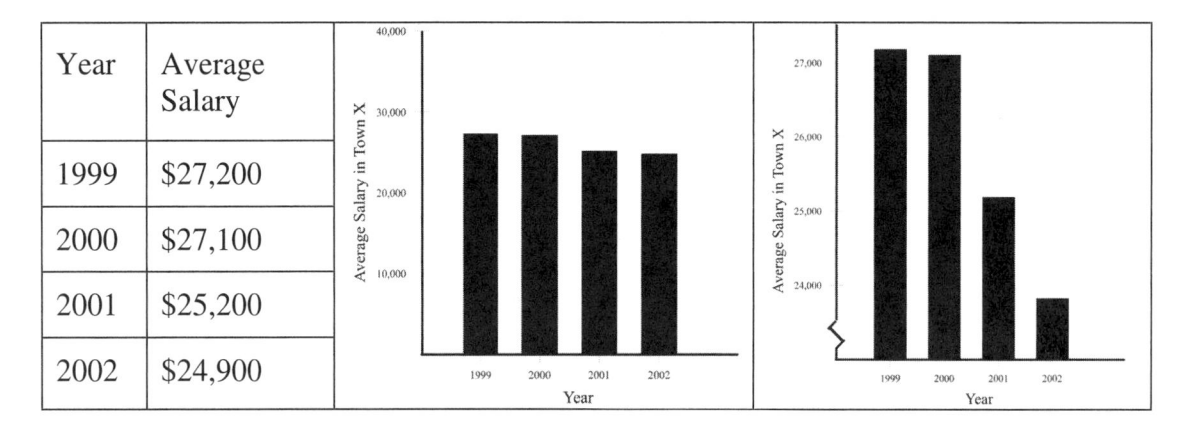

Year	Average Salary
1999	$27,200
2000	$27,100
2001	$25,200
2002	$24,900

Part C Summary Questions:
1. Why do these graphs look so different?

2. Which do you believe accurately displays the data and why?

3. If a political competitor used the second graph to show *massive decline* in salaries over the past few years, how would you show the decline exists, but it is not that massive?

INVESTIGATION 8.5

How Honorable is Honorable?

Working with classmates, consider following three situations presented below.

A. A (very) small town advertising agency boasts the following.

Come live and work in our small town.
The average yearly salary for our residents is $100,000!*

* Calculations: $\bar{x} = \dfrac{1{,}000{,}000 + 10 \cdot 10{,}000}{11} = \dfrac{1{,}100{,}000}{11} = 100{,}000$

B. Dr. Richard Hartert accurately predicted the sex of the upcoming baby for three out of four of his last patients. He reported that he was correct 75% of the time.

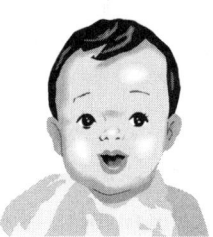

C. Jaime Bailey took a survey of the members of her stock club. Each of the members indicated that they owned stock outside of the stock that they held collectively as members of the club. Jaime concluded that almost all of the women of her age probably own stock.

Summary Questions:

1. Is the information presented reputable, or are the conclusions drawn valid?

2. Can the generalizations made really be supported with the information available in each of the situations?

3. Discuss these questions and reach an agreement among your group and then join another group to discuss your conclusions verses theirs. Did your groups agree?

Chapter 8: Analyzing Data

MANIPULATIVE ACTIVITY 8.1

Take a Survey

For this activity you will need to create survey forms for classmates to fill out.

A. Create a survey form that asks your classmates for responses to a number (approximately five) of statements and a small amount of demographics information, such as age and gender. The statements should be about attitudes towards a given topic.

B. Have them respond to each statement with one of the following responses:

    Strongly Disagree   Disagree   Neutral   Agree   Strongly Agree

C. Collect survey forms from at least ten of your classmates. If there are not enough students in your class, then ask students from other classes or relatives to help you in the data collection.

D. Score the responses to each statement giving a
- Strongly Disagree a score of -2.
- Disagree a score of -1.
- Neutral a score of 0.
- Agree a score of 1.
- Strongly Agree a score of 2.

E. Find the mean and the variance of the responses for each statement.

F. Develop a report on the findings from your survey.

Example: A statement on a survey about attitudes toward gender equality might be:

Girls do as well as boys in mathematics.

    Strongly Disagree   Disagree   Neutral   Agree   Strongly Agree

Had the statement been *Boys do better than girls in mathematics*, the statement would have been considered to have a *negative direction*. Hence, a Strongly Agree would have a score of -2, an Agree a score of -1, a Neutral a score of 0, a Disagree a score of 1, and a Strongly Disagree a score of 2.

Summary Questions:
1. In doing this activity, what did you discover about writing statements for a survey?

2. What role can variance play in looking at a set of responses to two statements if the two statements have the same mean response?

MANIPULATIVE ACTIVITY 8.2

Trendy Lines

For this activity, you will need a measuring tape. If one is not available, you can visit http://wps.aw.com/aw_odaffer_mathematic_2 to download a ruler to be cut and pasted together.

A. Working in groups, find the following body measurements.

- Height without shoes (**HS**)
- Distance from floor to belly button while standing (**BS**)
- Distance from floor to belly button while kneeling (**BK**)
- Height while kneeling (**HK**)
- Vertical length of face (**LF**)
- Horizontal distance of arm span from fingertip to fingertip (**DA**)

NAME					
HS					
BS					
BK					
HK					
LF					
DA					

B. Create a scatterplot for at least 3 relations, including the relation between **HS** and **DA**.

C. Analyze the scatterplot for these relationships, including identification of a trend line.

Summary Questions:
1. Did anyone have exactly the same height and armspan? If so, they are a "square".

2. What other "body measures" might be examined or have you examined?

3. How can you account for the patterns of relationships observed?

Chapter 8: Analyzing Data

MANIPULATIVE ACTIVITY 8.3

How Many Reds?

For this activity, you will need a set of 50 PopCubes®. Five of the cubes should be red (or any color that you designate) and the others not. If PopCubes® are not available, you may visit http://wps.aw.com/aw_odaffer_mathematic_2 to download a set of chips.

Place the cubes in a bag and take out one cube noting its color. Replace this cube and take out two cubes, again noting color. Continue this process until you have taken out twenty-five cubes, replacing cubes after each round. Fill in a table like the one below.

Number of cubes	Number of red	Number of non-red
1		
2		
3		
4		
5		
6		
7		
8		
9		
10		
11		
12		
13		
14		
15		
16		
17		
18		
19		
20		
21		
22		
23		
24		
25		

Create a scatterplot for the *Number of red cubes* verses the *Number of cubes*.

Summary Questions:
1. Does there appear to be a trend line in your scatterplot? Explain.

2. How could this type of sampling be done in the wild to estimate populations such as bears or fish?

MANIPULATIVE ACTIVITY 8.4

Three Coin Toss

For this activity you will need one quarter, one dime, and one nickel.

- Toss the set of three coins forty times, recording the appearance of heads or tails.

Toss	Quarter	Dime	Nickel	Toss	Quarter	Dime	Nickel
1.				21.			
2.				22.			
3.				23.			
4.				24.			
5.				25.			
6.				26.			
7.				27.			
8.				28.			
9.				29.			
10.				30.			
11.				31.			
12.				32.			
13.				33.			
14.				34.			
15.				35.			
16.				36.			
17.				37.			
18.				38.			
19.				39.			
20.				40.			

- Make a histograph and a circle graph showing how many times the different possible number of heads (0 - 3) appeared.
- Make a histograph and a circle graph for each the quarter, dime and nickel showing how many times heads (0 - 1) appeared.

Summary Questions:
1. Which of the types of graphs is the best type for displaying the number of heads observed in each toss? Why?

2. Suppose that you were to toss the coin 100 times. How many times would you expect to get three heads? Two heads? One head? No heads?

3. How did you reason to your answers in Question 2? Were the graphs you made helpful?

4. Are there any similarities or differences between the graphs made separately for the quarter, dime, and nickel? If so, what are they?

MANIPULATIVE ACTIVITY 8.5

A Dicey Game

For this activity, you will need a standard die. If one is not available, you can visit http://wps.aw.com/aw_odaffer_mathematic_2 for a download to be cut and taped.

In this variation of a famous game, you are going to roll the die and keep track of the values shown in a table like the one shown below. For each round, you use tally marks to represent the occurrence of a side showing. For the first experiment, you are going to roll the die until a "1" appears. Perform this activity fifteen times.

	1	2	3	4	5	6	7	8	9	10	11	12	13	14	15
2															
3															
4															
5															
6															
Total Number of Rolls															
Total Sum															

Perform this experiment again by rolling the die until a "2", "3", "4", "5", or "6" appears. A download is available at http://wps.aw.com/aw_odaffer_mathematic_2 for the six tables.

For each of the six tables, determine the mean, median, mode, and standard deviation of both the *Total Number of Rolls* and the *Total Sum*.

Summary Questions:
1. What are some similarities and differences between the calculations you made for the six tables?

2. Does there appear to be a relationship between the number that stops the game (1 - 6) and the total number of rolls? Justify with a scatterplot or some other graphical evidence.

3. Does there appear to be a relationship between the number that stops the game (1 - 6) and the total sum? Justify with a scatterplot or some other graphical evidence.

TECHNOLOGY ACTIVITY 8.1

Sled Dog Race Times

The table below shows the top 25 finishers in the 2002 Iditarod Dog Sled Race. The information under "Days Hrs Min Sec" indicates the time it took each team to complete the race. You will need a calculator with statistical capabilities such as a TI-83 or a spreadsheet for the activity.

Place	Musher	Dogs	Days	Hrs	Min	Sec	Avg mph
1.	Martin Buser	10	8	22	46	2	5.13
2.	Ramy Brooks	7	9	0	49	18	5.08
3.	John Baker	7	9	5	46	30	4.96
4.	Jon Little	9	9	7	22	44	4.93
5.	Vern Halter	9	9	7	47	48	4.92
6.	Jeff King	10	9	10	42	19	4.86
7.	Ramey Smyth	7	9	12	2	29	4.83
8.	Charlie Boulding	8	9	13	36	32	4.79
9.	Robert Sorlie	8	9	13	44	52	4.79
10.	Kjetil Backen	10	9	13	47	42	4.79
11.	Mitch Seavey	6	9	14	25	10	4.78
12.	Harald Tunheim	9	9	15	10	3	4.76
13.	Sonny Lindner	11	9	19	8	29	4.68
14.	Ray Redington, Jr.	7	9	21	26	18	4.64
15.	Tim Osmar	10	9	21	48	19	4.63
16.	Dee Dee Jonrowe	6	9	22	7	20	4.62
17.	Jerry Riley	5	9	22	11	31	4.62
18.	Ken Anderson	6	9	22	29	49	4.62
19.	Rick Swenson	8	9	23	41	11	4.59
20.	Lynda Plettner	13	10	2	34	24	4.54
21.	Al Hardman	12	10	4	20	30	4.51
22.	John Barron	9	10	6	25	40	4.47
23.	Hans Gatt	10	10	8	54	4	4.42
24.	Bruce Lee	8	10	11	20	17	4.38
25.	Jim Lanier	9	10	12	43	0	4.36

Determine the length of the race in miles.

Summary Questions:
1. How did you determine the length of the race? Explain you reasoning.

2. Does there appear to be any relationship between the number of dogs on a race team and the time required to complete the race? Provide evidence and explain your response.

TECHNOLOGY ACTIVITY 8.2

First Digit Analysis

For this activity you will need to use the Histograph feature on your Interactivate disk or a calculator with statistical capabilities such as a TI-83.

Consider the following Census 2000 data for the fifty states.

State	2000 Total resident population (1,000)	Gross state product in chained dollars for 1998	State	2000 total resident population (1,000)	Gross state product in chained dollars for 1998
Alabama	4,447	129	Montana	902	21
Alaska	627	32	Nebraska	1,711	58
Arizona	5,131	107	Nevada	1,998	51
Arkansas	2,673	61	New Hampshire	1,236	38
California	33,872	1,094	New Jersey	8,414	308
Colorado	4,301	132	New Mexico	1,819	39
Connecticut	3,406	158	New York	18,976	688
Delaware	784	31	North Carolina	8,049	228
Florida	15,982	405	North Dakota	642	16
Georgia	8,186	222	Ohio	11,353	334
Hawaii	1,212	60	Oklahoma	3,451	85
Idaho	1,294	24	Oregon	3,421	98
Illinois	12,419	416	Pennsylvania	12,281	353
Indiana	6,080	159	Rhode Island	1,048	29
Iowa	2,926	80	South Carolina	4,012	104
Kansas	2,688	76	South Dakota	755	19
Kentucky	4,042	106	Tennessee	5,689	138
Louisiana	4,469	138	Texas	20,852	640
Maine	1,275	31	Utah	2,233	49
Maryland	5,296	187	Vermont	609	17
Massachusetts	6,349	246	Virginia	7,079	233
Michigan	9,938	288	Washington	5,894	171
Minnesota	4,919	155	West Virginia	1,808	41
Mississippi	2,845	61	Wisconsin	5,364	155
Missouri	5,595	158	Wyoming	494	18

For each category tally the first digit (1 - 9) for all fifty states. Organize each of these data sets into a histogram.

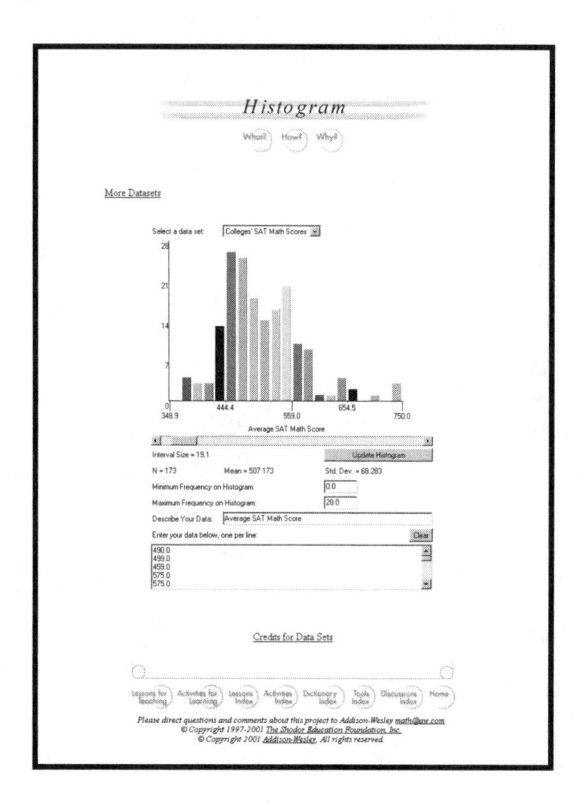

Summary Question:
What comparisons can be made between these two data sets?

TECHNOLOGY ACTIVITY 8.3

Hot is Hot and Cold is Cold

For this activity you will need to use a calculator with statistical capabilities such as a TI-83 or a spreadsheet program such as Excel®.

Consider the following data for the fifty states. The lowest and highest recorded temperatures are given. The data set from *The World Almanac and Book of Facts*, 2002. New York, NY: World Almanac Books, 2002, p.176.

State	Lowest $°F$	Highest $°F$	State	Lowest $°F$	Highest $°F$
Alabama	-27	112	Montana	-70	117
Alaska	-80	100	Nebraska	-47	118
Arizona	-40	128	Nevada	-50	125
Arkansas	-29	120	New Hampshire	-46	106
California	-45	134	New Jersey	-34	110
Colorado	-61	118	New Mexico	-50	122
Connecticut	-32	106	New York	-52	108
Delaware	-17	110	North Carolina	-34	110
Florida	-2	109	North Dakota	-60	121
Georgia	-17	112	Ohio	-39	113
Hawaii	12	100	Oklahoma	-27	120
Idaho	-60	118	Oregon	-54	119
Illinois	-36	117	Pennsylvania	-42	111
Indiana	-36	116	Rhode Island	-25	104
Iowa	-47	118	South Carolina	-19	111
Kansas	-40	121	South Dakota	-58	120
Kentucky	-37	114	Tennessee	-32	113
Louisiana	-16	114	Texas	-23	120
Maine	-48	105	Utah	-69	117
Maryland	-40	109	Vermont	-50	105
Massachusetts	-35	107	Virginia	-30	110
Michigan	-51	112	Washington	-48	118
Minnesota	-60	114	West Virginia	-37	112
Mississippi	-19	115	Wisconsin	-54	114
Missouri	-40	118	Wyoming	-66	114

- Make a histograph for each of the two data sets.
- Make a box-and-whisker plot for each data set.
- Find the mean and standard deviation for each of the data sets.
- Make a scatterplot of the high temperatures verses the low temperatures.

Summary Questions:
1. Are there any outliers in either of the data sets? Is there a possible geographical or geological explanation? Explain

2. Which seems to have more variability, the high temperatures or the low temperatures? Is there a possible geographical or geological explanation? Explain

3. Does there appear to be a correlation between the high temperatures and the low temperatures? Explain.

184 Chapter 8: Analyzing Data

TECHNOLOGY ACTIVITY 8.4

Top Tunes

For this activity you will need to use the Box Plot and Simple Plot features on your Interactivate disk or a calculator with statistical capabilities such as a TI-83.

The table shows the top 15 song titles and recording artists for the week of April 6, 2002 as reported on the Billboard Hot 100 ® web page.

This week	Last week	Two weeks ago	Weeks on chart	Title/Artist
1	1	1	15	Ain't It Funny, Jennifer Lopez Featuring Ja Rule
2	5	8	8	What's Luv?, Fat Joe Featuring Ashanti
3	2	3	23	In The End, Linkin Park
4	9	11	8	Foolish, Ashanti
5	6	14	9	Girlfriend, 'N Sync Featuring Nelly
6	3	4	31	How You Remind Me, Nickelback
7	7	6	16	Blurry, Puddle Of Mudd
8	12	12	9	U Don't Have To Call, Usher
9	4	2	21	Always On Time, Ja Rule Featuring Ashanti
10	11	10	9	Oops (Oh My), Tweet
11	10	7	11	Can't Get You Out Of My Head, Kylie Minogue
12	8	5	22	Wherever You Will Go, The Calling
13	13	9	11	What About Us?, Brandy
14	15	18	11	I Love You, Faith Evans
15	22	29	5	Don't Let Me Get Me, Pink

❑ Go to the Interactivate disk feature Box Plot. Create a box-and-whisker plot to represent the number of weeks on the Top 100 for the 15 entries in the table by first clearing the data that is currently displayed. The 15 entries must be entered as ordered pairs. The first entry can be inputted as "15,1" (without the quotation marks). Create a box-and-whisker plot by clicking on the "Update Boxplot" button.

❑ Report the 5-number summary for this data set.

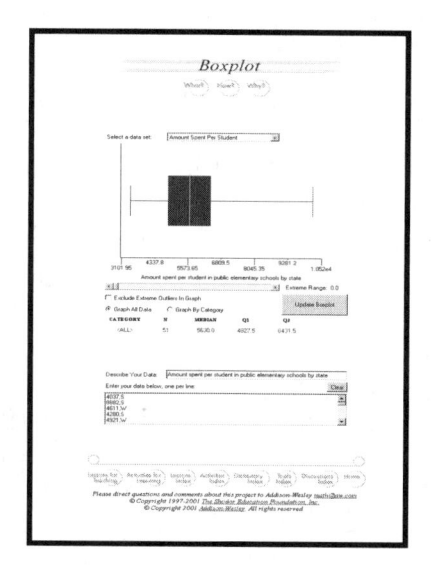

- Determine the average rating change from last week to this week for the songs on the list.

- Create some measure to represent the stability of The Billboard Hot 100® ratings for these 15 songs. Describe your measure and use it to report the most and least stable songs on the list.

Summary Questions:

1. How many new entries are on the list? How can you tell?

2. Does there appear to be a relationship between a song's current rating and the total number of weeks it has appeared on the Top 100 list? Use the Simple Plot feature on your Interactive disk to provide a scatterplot as evidence and give an explanation for your response.

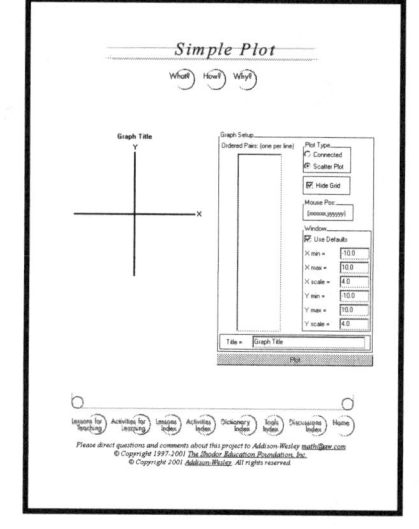

Chapter 8: Analyzing Data

TECHNOLOGY ACTIVITY 8.5

Harrison Ford's Films

Harrison Ford, the actor, was born on July 13, 1942 in Chicago, Illinois. In a period of more than 30 years he has appeared in more than 30 films. The name, year, and running time for films that Harrison Ford has appeared in are given in the following table.

Name of Film	Year	Running Time in minutes
What Lies Beneath	2000	126
Random Hearts	1999	133
Six Days, Seven Nights	1998	101
The Devil's Own	1997	110
Air Force One	1997	124
Les Cent et une Nuits de Simon Cinema (aka A Hundred and One Nights of Simon Cinema)	1995	125
Sabina	1995	127
Clear and Present Danger	1994	142
Jimmy Hollywood	1994	110
The Fugitive	1993	127
Patriot Games	1992	113
Regarding Henry	1991	107
Presumed Innocent	1990	127
Indiana Jones and the Last Crusade	1989	127
Working Girl	1988	113
Frantic	1988	120
The Mosquito Coast	1986	117
Witness	1985	112
Indiana Jones and the Temple of Doom	1984	118
Return of the Jedi	1983	133
Blade Runner	1982	114
Raiders of the Lost Ark	1981	115
The Empire Strikes Back	1980	124
Apocalypse Now	1979	139
Hanover Street	1979	109
More American Graffiti	1979	111
The Frisco Kid (aka No Knife)	1979	122
Force 10 from Navarone	1978	118
Heroes	1977	113

The Possessed	1977	75
Star Wars (aka Star Wars: Episode IV-A New Hope)	1977	121
James Michener's Dynasty (aka Dynasty)	1976	100
The Conversation	1974	113
American Graffiti	1973	110
Zabriskie Point	1970	112
Getting Straight	1970	126
Journey to Shiloh	1968	101
Luv	1967	95
The Intruders	1967	100
A Time for Killing	1967	83
Dead Heat on a Merry-Go-Round	1966	108

Go to the Interactivate disk features Histogram and Boxplot. Create both a histograph and a box-and-whisker plot of the film years and running times.

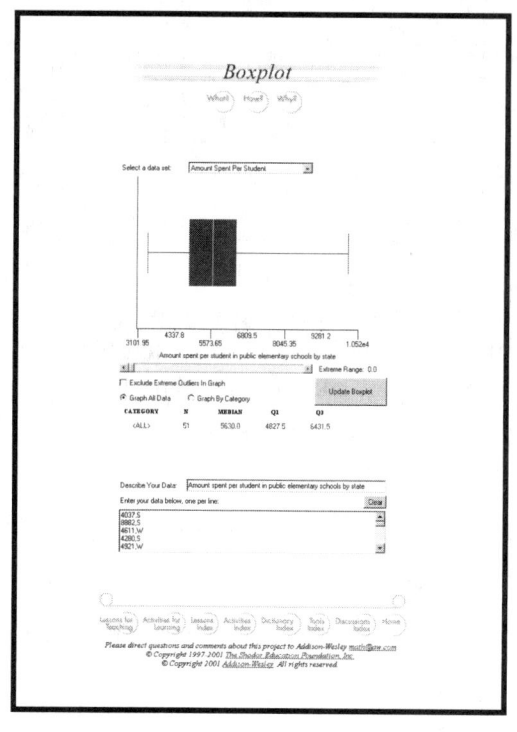

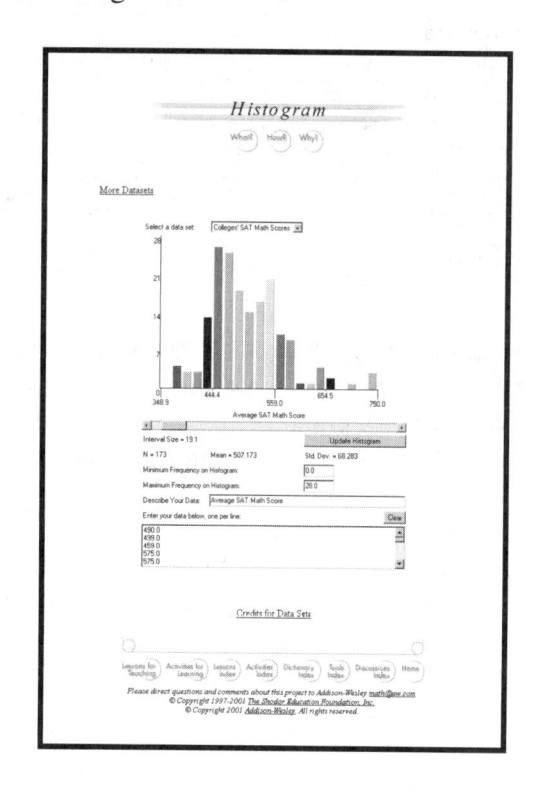

Summary Questions:

1. How can you use the graphical displays to describe variation in the years Harrison Ford appeared in films?

2. How can you use the graphical displays to describe the running time for the films Harrison Ford appeared in?

188   Chapter 8: Analyzing Data

TECHNOLOGY ACTIVITY 8.6

TV Junkies

For this activity you will need to use a calculator with statistical capabilities such as a TI-83 or a spreadsheet program such as Excel®.

Consider the data on television watching in hours:minutes per week in the following table. The data sets from *The World Almanac and Book of Facts*, 2002. New York, NY: World Almanac Books, 2002, p.280.

Group	Ages	Total per week	Early Morning Mon.-Fri. 7am-10am	Daytime Mon.-Fri. 10am-4pm	Primetime Mon.-Sat. 8pm-11pm & Sun. 7-11pm	Late Night Mon.-Fri. 11:30pm-1am	Sat. 7am-1pm	Sun. 1pm-7pm
Women	18+	33:16	2:07	4:55	9:34	2:13	0:47	1:33
	18-24	21:50	0:59	3:47	7:17	1:43	0:32	1:04
	25-54	31:35	2:05	4:08	9:12	2:15	0:48	1:30
	55+	41:10	2:38	6:49	11:50	2:21	0:51	1:49
Working Women		28:34	1:35	2:58	8:58	2:07	0:45	1:29
Men	18+	30:14	1:29	3:14	9:13	2:15	0:44	1:55
	18-24	21:10	0:50	2:44	5:18	1:51	0:31	1:18
	25-54	29:04	1:21	2:40	9:02	2:21	0:44	1:55
	55+	37:28	2:09	4:46	11:28	2:13	0:49	2:12
Teens	12-17	19:40	0:41	1:41	5:56	1:14	0:43	1:13
Children	2-11	20:30	0:50	3:05	4:50	0:42	1:10	1:05
All People		29:04	1:44	3:45	8:24	1:55	0:49	1:34

Working with other classmates, select some 2-variable subsets of the data on television watching in the table and prepare a report. Decide on a comparison involving 2-variable data (such as time watched by male age groups) and then have each member of your group make a graph of the data. Compare the graphs you each made. Then, as a group, prepare a short report on the patterns you observed among your different graphs.

Summary Questions:
1. What patterns did you notice in your data set? Did there appear to be a positive or negative correlation in the data you examined?

2. Would your patterns hold up for a similar type of 2-variable group by changing one of your underlying variables?

3. Which data set did you find most interesting of those presented by your classmates? Why?

CHAPTER 9: PROBABILITY

INVESTIGATION 9.1

A Gate to Somewhere or Nowhere

Consider the following diagram in which you start at Position A and need to pass through gates (indicated by dots) in order to make it out. Initially you will need to make a choice as to heading towards Gate B or C. Assume that you flip a coin, so the probability of heading towards either gate is $\frac{1}{2}$. You may only travel in the direction indicated on each path. For each gate there is a probability of $\frac{1}{2}$ that it is open. If a gate is not open, you can choose an alternate path if one is available. If an alternate path is not available, the game is over and you do not successfully complete your journey.

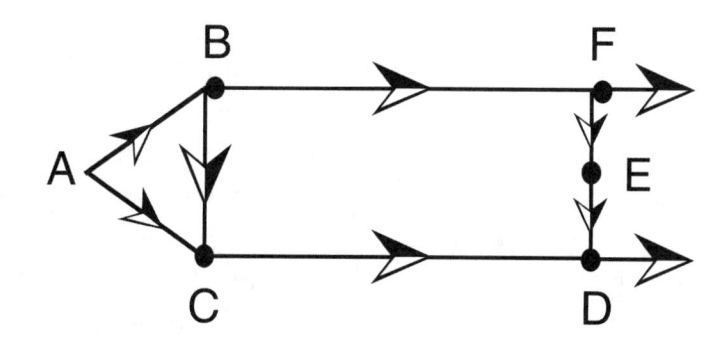

Study the diagram above and make a tree diagram of all possible journeys (including the incomplete ones). Determine the probability that you will complete your journey.

Using a coin to simulate the status of the gate (heads for open and tails for closed), start at Position A and determine whether or not you complete your journey. Do this simulation twenty times while keeping track of the journeys taken (including the incomplete ones).

Summary Questions:
1. Do your experimental results agree with your tree diagram and the associated probabilities? Compare your results with your classmates.

2. If you wanted to increase your probability of completing your journey, instead of flipping a coin which gate should you always head towards initially? Explain using conditional probability.

3. Assume that Gate E is always open. What is the probability that you will complete your journey?

4. Assume that you may travel any direction on any path. What is the probability that you will complete your journey?

Chapter 9: Probability

INVESTIGATION 9.2

Three Short Problems V

Suppose you were channel surfing one evening and listened to the weather forecast on four different stations. You heard the following statements made:

Station 1: *There is a 50% chance of rain tomorrow.*
Station 2: *The odds in favor of rain are 1 to 1.*
Station 3: *The odds against rain are 1 to 1.*
Station 4: *The probability of rain is $\frac{1}{2}$.*

Part A Summary Question:
What are the differences and similarities between the forecasts?

Three friends were walking down the street and noticed a couple with a boy and a girl. Paul Rowe noted that the probability of having a boy and a girl is $\frac{1}{2}$ because it is balanced in the sense that they have one of each and each sex occurs half the time. Katerina Kucera argued that the probability would be $\frac{1}{3}$ because there are three possibilities, two boys, two girls, or a boy and a girl. Scott Hochwald was adamant that Paul was correct about his assertion that the probability of having a boy and a girl is $\frac{1}{2}$. He went on however to contend that there are four possible arrangements of having two children, Boy Boy, Boy Girl, Girl Boy, and Girl Girl. Two of the four, or $\frac{1}{2}$, involve having a boy and a girl.

Part B Summary Questions:
1. Whose argument is correct?

2. What probabilities would each of these friends state if they saw a couple walking down the street with two boys and two girls? With three boys and three girls?

When you toss a fair coin, the probability of either heads or tails is $\frac{1}{2}$. Each toss is independent of another. So if you have tossed 9 heads in a row, the probability of tossing heads again is still $\frac{1}{2}$.

Part C Summary Questions:
1. What is the probability of tossing 10 heads in a row? How does this differ from the event described above?

2. What is the probability of never getting a tails? Explain.

INVESTIGATION 9.3

How Fortunate We Are

Consider a lottery game that consists of 53 numbers from which you choose 6. If you choose 3 of the 6 winning numbers, you are eligible for a cash prize.

- Using a calculator, determine the number of ways of choosing 6 correct numbers.

- What is the probability of choosing 6 out of the 6 winning numbers? The jackpot is split among the winners.

- The probability of choosing 5 out of the 6 winning numbers in this game is given by $\frac{_{47}C_1 \cdot _6C_5}{_{53}C_6}$. Simplify the numerator and denominator of this expression. Rewrite this expression with a numerator of 1. Round the denominator to the nearest whole number.

Summary Questions:

1. Why is the probability of choosing 5 out of the 6 winning numbers in this game given by $\frac{_{47}C_1 \cdot _6C_5}{_{53}C_6}$ instead of $\frac{1}{_{53}C_5}$?

2. What would the probability of choosing 4 out of the 6 winning numbers in this game? Choosing 3 out of 6?

3. Why do we use combinations instead of permutations in the calculations?

4. Would the probability of winning this lotto be higher, lower, or the same if the game was changed to choosing 47 numbers out of the 53? Explain.

5. The following appears on the website for a state lottery in which a player chooses 6 out of 53 numbers. Considering your calculations and the information in your text regarding odds (pages 481-482), do you have any concerns about the information in the table? Explain.

Prize Level	Odds of Winning	Average Payout
6-of-6	1:22,957,480	Jackpot
5-of-6	1:81,410	$5,000
4-of-6	1:1,416	$70
3-of-6	1:71	$5

6. Assuming that the average jackpot is $10,000,000, what is the expected value of a $1 lottery ticket for the game described in this activity?

Chapter 9: Probability

INVESTIGATION 9.4

Conditional Probability and Venn Diagrams

Examples of conditional probability given both a sample space and geometric figures are on pages 468-469 of your text. Using the notation for set intersection, the probability of A given that B has occurred is

$$P(A \mid B) = \frac{P(A \cap B)}{P(B)}.$$

Assuming that the Sets A and B are not empty, consider four possible Venn diagram arrangements. Assign probabilities in each arrangement to the enclosed regions. Note that since we are only considering the enclosed regions, the sum of the probabilities will be 1 for each arrangement. Compute $P(A \mid B)$ using the formula given above.

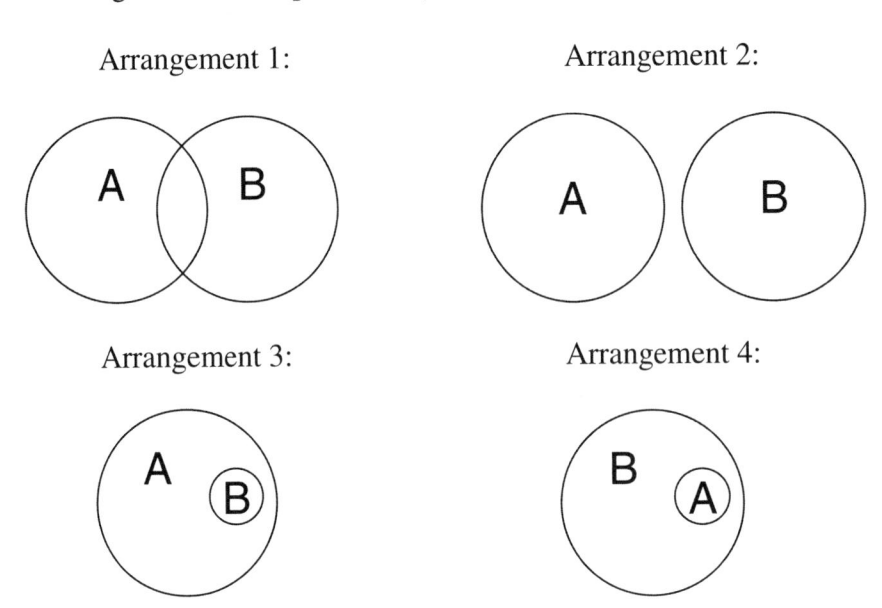

Arrangement 1:

Arrangement 2:

Arrangement 3:

Arrangement 4:

Summary Questions:

1. What is an explanation of the formula, $P(A \mid B) = \dfrac{P(A \cap B)}{P(B)}$, for each of the three arrangements?

2. Since conditional probability must yield a value between 0 and 1, inclusive, which of the above arrangements will yield the extreme cases?

3. We made the assumption that the Sets A and B are not empty. Why was this done? Is it necessary that they both be non-empty? Explain.

INVESTIGATION 9.5

Other Dicey Games

A common die is a six-sided solid in which all sides look alike, except for the numbering. A die, or cube, is a kind of regular polyhedron (*poly* meaning many and *hedron* meaning face). The term regular indicates that all the sides are the same size and shape. In turn each of these shapes have sides all the same measure.

Suppose you threw two die with the standard labeling of sides 1 through 6 and recorded their sum. Fill out the table below and determine the probability of throwing each possible sum. You may choose to visit http://wps.aw.com/aw_odaffer_mathematic_2 to download this table along with tables for the rest of this activity.

	1	2	3	4	5	6
1						
2						
3						
4						
5						
6						

Besides the cube there are four other regular polyhedra. These are known collectively as Platonic solids, named after the Greek philosopher Plato.

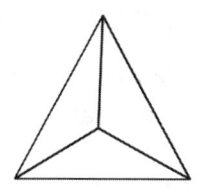

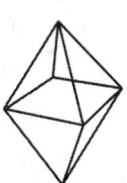

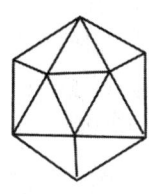

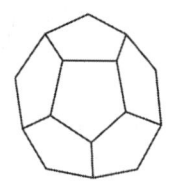

Tetrahedron   Octahedron   Icosahedron   Dodecahedron

The Greeks believed that water, fire, air, and earth were four basic elements and associated the icosahedron (20 faces), tetrahedron (four faces), octahedron (8 faces), and cube (respectively) with them. The universe was associated with the dodecahedron (12 faces). There may have been a connection between the twelve faces and the twelve signs of the zodiac.

For each of the above solids, imagine having two of each of the solids as dice with standard labeling. Like the cube, determine all possible sums of the two die and the probability of throwing each sum.

Summary Questions:
1. What are similarities and differences among the tables you created for throwing the possible sums for these Platonic Solids?

2. What are similarities and differences among the probabilities of throwing the possible sums for these Platonic Solids?

INVESTIGATION 9.6

Benford's Law

Benford's Law is also known as the First Digit Law. This law maintains that 1 appears as the first non-zero digit approximately 30% of the time in tables of physical constants or statistical data. The probability of the rest of the digits occurring as the first digit decreases as you increase to 9. The astronomer Simon Newcomb first noticed this phenomenon in 1881 when he was looking in a well-used book of logarithms. Pages that had logarithmic values which started with 1 or 2 were much more tattered than others. The physicist Frank Benford found the same type of occurrence in data in 1963. He tried out his theory in over 20,000 data sets such as baseball statistics and found that this theory worked. The theory wasn't proven until 1996 by a math professor at Georgia Tech named Ted Hill.

The actual probability of the first digit being n is

$$P(n) = \log_{10}\left(1 + \frac{1}{n}\right) \text{ where } n = 1, 2, 3, \ldots, 9.$$

For example if $n = 1$, $P(1) = \log_{10}\left(1 + \frac{1}{1}\right) = \log_{10} 2 \approx 0.3010$.

Using a calculator, determine the approximate value of $P(2), P(3), P(4), \ldots, P(9)$. On most calculators, $\log_{10}$ is indicated by log. Keep track of the values in a table like the one below. Write down all the decimal places that your calculator displays.

n	$P(n) = \log_{10}\left(1 + \frac{1}{n}\right)$
1	
2	
3	
4	
5	
6	
7	
8	
9	

Construct a histograph with the above information.

Summary Questions:
1. What is the sum of all the probabilities?

2. Why could Benford's Law be applied to data sets that occur such as information gathered from IRS tax returns, but not the lottery?

Investigate a data set such as closing stock prices on any given day that trading has occurred. Stock prices can be influenced from a host of other numbers and appear as a large random set of numbers. Determine the probability of 1 through 9 appearing as the first digit in your data set. Refer also to Technology Activity 8.2. Working in a group, write a report to share with the class describing how you gathered your data and if the probabilities you calculated agreed with Benford's Law.

Chapter 9: Probability

MANIPULATIVE ACTIVITY 9.1

Taking Your Chances

For this activity you will need four coins. Quarters are preferred. With a marker you will need to clearly label each side. If you chose, you can visit http://wps.aw.com/aw_odaffer_mathematic_2 to download labels that can but cut out and taped over your coins as well as tables to help keep track of your results. The coins should be labeled as follows.

- Coin 1: One side should be marked A and the other side B.
- Coin 2: One side should be marked C and the other side A.
- Coin 3: One side should be marked B and the other side C.
- Coin 4: One side should be marked A and the other side A.

Find a partner and identify which player is Player I and which player is Player II. Players will take turns tossing coins at once. Record in a table the outcome of each toss, giving Player I one point if there are matching letters. Otherwise, give Player II one point. Perform the following steps with Coins 1, 2, and 3.

A. Toss the coins ten times

B. Determine the winner of the game.

C. Repeat the game two more times.

Toss	Coin 1	Coin 2	Coin 3	Outcome Player I (match)	Player II (no match)
1					
2					
3					
4					
5					
6					
7					
8					
9					
10					

Summary Questions:

1. Based on your experiment as recorded in the table, does it make a difference which player you are? If so, is it better to be Player I or Player II?

2. What are P(match) and P(no match) for a given flip? How did you determine the probabilities?

Repeat the steps and record the outcomes with Coins 1, 2, and 4. Then repeat the steps and record the outcomes with Coins 1, 2, 3, and 4. Respond to both Summary Questions for each experiment. Compare the three experiments and note any similarities and differences.

MANIPULATIVE ACTIVITY 9.2

It All Depends

For this activity you will need two sets of ten paper cards numbered 1 through 10. You can visit http://wps.aw.com/aw_odaffer_mathematic_2 to download both a blue set and a red set. The following deals with information one can obtain by drawing pairs of card from the twenty colored and labeled cards, one at a time. Some of the draws are made with replacement, others without replacement.

A. Find the following probabilities using a logical analysis of the situation where the draws are made without replacement.

    a. $P(red|red)$ b. $P(10|red)$ c. $P(6|5)$ d. $P(red|blue)$

B. Find the following probabilities using a logical analysis of the situation where the draws are made with replacement after each draw.

    a. $P(red|red)$ b. $P(10|red)$ c. $P(6|5)$ d. $P(red|blue)$

C. Consider the probabilities in Parts A and B. Would it ever be the case that the probability without replacement would be the same as the probability with replacement for this setting?

D. Consider the probabilities in Parts A and B. How would changing the conditions allow for the probability with replacement to be the same as the probability without replacement for a similar card setting?

E. Work with a partner and draw 50 pairs of cards without replacement using the given information for your first draw. Keep track of how many of the 50 attempts are successful (you pull the desired second card) and how many attempts are failures (you do not pull the desired second card) for each of the following.

    a. $P(red|red)$ b. $P(10|red)$ c. $P(6|5)$ d. $P(red|blue)$

Calculate the results that you observed for the above four conditional probabilities. How close did your results match the probabilities that you determined in Part A?

F. Work with a partner and draw 50 pairs of cards with replacement after each draw using the given information for your first draw. Keep track of how many of the 50 attempts are successful (you pull the desired second card) and how many attempts are failures (you do not pull the desired second card) for each of the following.

    a. $P(red|red)$ b. $P(10|red)$ c. $P(6|5)$ d. $P(red|blue)$

Calculate the results that you observed for the above four conditional probabilities. How close did your results match the probabilities that you determined in Part B?

Summary Question:
Why are conditional probabilities important probabilities? Explain your answer using a common situation where conditional probabilities may apply to your everyday life.

198   Chapter 9: Probability

MANIPULATIVE ACTIVITY 9.3

Take a Walk

For this activity you will need a coin and a 3×3 grid like the one below to trace over.

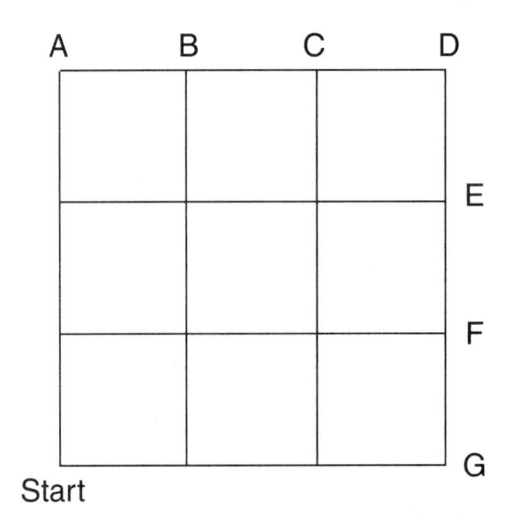

```
    A     B     C     D
    +-----+-----+-----+
    |     |     |     |
    |     |     |     |
    +-----+-----+-----+ E
    |     |     |     |
    |     |     |     |
    +-----+-----+-----+ F
    |     |     |     |
    |     |     |     |
    +-----+-----+-----+ G
   Start
```

Working with another classmates, the game begins in the lower left hand corner. Have one student flip the coin and another trace the path. If the coin lands heads, move one unit up. If the coin lands on tails, move to the right one unit. When you reach the top or the right side the game is over. Repeat the game ten times, keeping track of the paths and the termination place.

Summary Questions:
1. What point can you not reach and why?

2. What is the maximum number of flips necessary to play a single game?

3. Did you reach the same point(s) while tracing different paths?

4. Based on your observations, what is the probability of reaching each of the Points A through G?

5. Determine the number of ways to reach Points A through G. What is the theoretical probability of reaching Points A through G?

6. How are probabilities of the game ending at each of the points along the top and right borders related to combinatorics?

Manipulative Activity 9.3   **199**

Consider the following diagram.

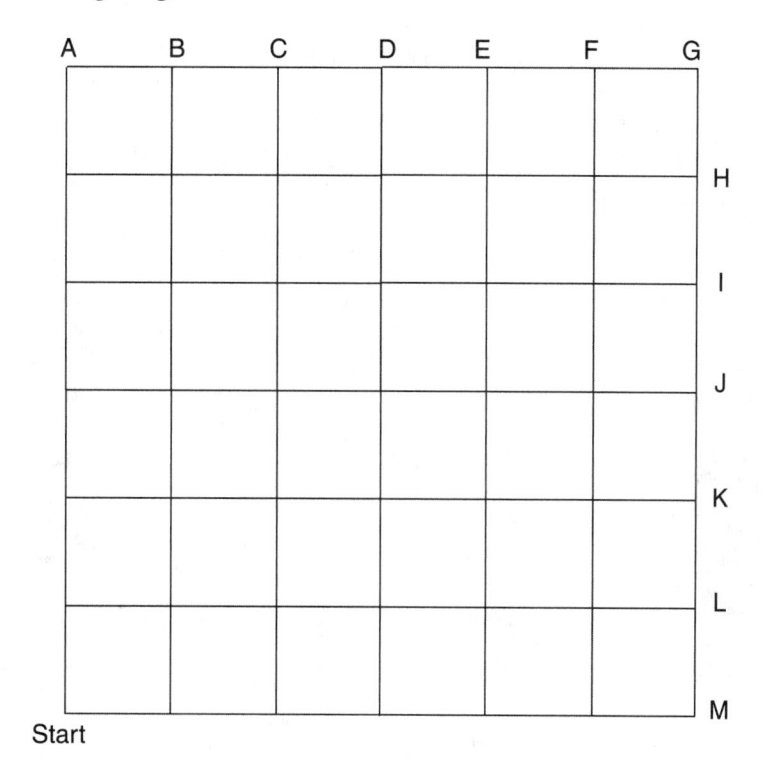

```
      A    B    C    D    E    F    G
     ┌────┬────┬────┬────┬────┬────┐
     │    │    │    │    │    │    │
     ├────┼────┼────┼────┼────┼────┤ H
     │    │    │    │    │    │    │
     ├────┼────┼────┼────┼────┼────┤ I
     │    │    │    │    │    │    │
     ├────┼────┼────┼────┼────┼────┤ J
     │    │    │    │    │    │    │
     ├────┼────┼────┼────┼────┼────┤ K
     │    │    │    │    │    │    │
     ├────┼────┼────┼────┼────┼────┤ L
     │    │    │    │    │    │    │
     └────┴────┴────┴────┴────┴────┘ M
    Start
```

Apply what you learned in the first grid to determine the theoretical probability of reaching Points A through M. Compare your group's results with classmates.

Chapter 9: Probability

MANIPULATIVE ACTIVITY 9.4

Making the Lineup

For this activity you will need pictures of five boys, five girls, five men, and five women. A download is available at http://wps.aw.com/aw_odaffer_mathematic_2 to be cut out. There is no distinction within any single category. For example, all figures of men are alike.

Using the cutouts, determine the number of ways you can arrange

- one boy, one girl, one man, and one woman.
- one boy, one girl, and two women.
- one boy, one girl, one man, and two women.
- one boy, two girls, one man, and three women.

Part A Summary Question:
What are similarities and differences among the four different types of arrangements?

Now consider the cutouts in two categories, adults and children. Using the cutouts, determine the number of ways you can arrange

- five adults and three children in a line so that no two children are standing next to each other.
- five adults and three children in a circle so that no two children are standing next to each other.

Part B Summary Question:
What are similarities and differences between the two different types of arrangements?

MANIPULATIVE ACTIVITY 9.5

One-Son Policy

For this activity, you will need two different colors of PopCubes®, pink and blue or any other color combination will suffice.

The country of China, concerned with overpopulation, has debated the merits and the outcomes of government population control. An option that has been considered is a "one-son" policy. That is, couples may continue to have children until the family has one son and then they may have no more children.

To simulate this, place five pink cubes and five blue cubes in a bag and mix them up. Have one student draw a cube out of the bag. If the cube is blue, a boy has been born. The couple may no more children and your game is over. If the cube is pink, a girl has been born. The couple will try again and your game continues. Return the pink cube to the bag, mix them up and draw again. Keep returning pink cubes to the bag until a blue is drawn. One student should be keeping track of the number of girls born before a boy. Run this experiment 10 times.

Part A Summary Questions:
1. What do you believe, based on your observations, will be the expected number of children per Chinese family?

2. Why do we return the pink cube to the bag?

3. What would the tree diagram which describes possible outcomes look like? Assign probabilities to each of the branches.

Run this experiment again without returning the pink cube. The game is still over when a blue cube is drawn.

Part B Summary Questions:
1. Based on your observations, how many pink cubes would you expect before a blue cube?

2. What would the tree diagram which describes possible outcomes look like? Assign probabilities to each of the branches.

3. What are similarities and differences between the two experiments (with replacing pink cubes and without)?

TECHNOLOGY ACTIVITY 9.1

Funny Funnel

Imagine a "number sorting" funnel that, when you drop in a number, sorts the integers by the following set of rules:

- If an integer is odd, it is funneled into a left branch inside the funnel. An odd integers is then dropped from this left branch into one of two bins:
    - prime numbers or
    - composite numbers.
- If an integer is even, it its funneled into a right branch inside the funnel. An even integers is then dropped from this right branch into one of two bins:
    - integers divisible by 4 or
    - integers not divisible by 4.

Draw a picture of this funnel machine and funnel 40 randomly chosen integers n, such that $70 < n \leq 90$. One option to generate these 40 random numbers is to make use of a calculator such as the TI-83.

Press the MATH button, toggle over to PRB and choose option 5 which is randInt(.

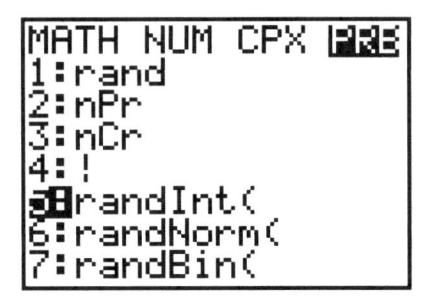

```
MATH NUM CPX PRB
1:rand
2:nPr
3:nCr
4:!
5:randInt(
6:randNorm(
7:randBin(
```

Press enter and then type "71,90)" (without quotation marks). Notice the inequality does not include 70, so the first integer included is 71.

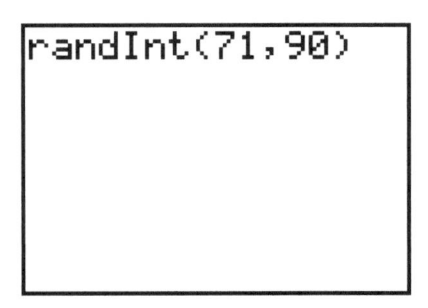

```
randInt(71,90)
```

Press enter and keep pressing enter to generate the required number of random integers.

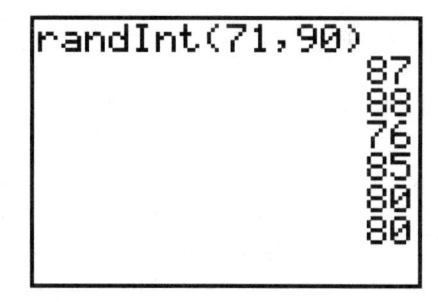

```
randInt(71,90)
              87
              88
              76
              85
              80
              80
```

Summary Questions:
1. What is the probability that the number you select is a prime number? What is the probability that the number you select drops in the "prime number" bin? Explain your reasoning.

2. What is the probability that the number you select is a composite number? What is the probability that the number you select drops in the "composite number" bin? Explain your reasoning.

3. What is the probability that the number you select is divisible by 4? What is the probability that the number you select drops in the "integers divisible by 4" bin? Explain your reasoning.

4. What is the probability that the number you select is not divisible by 4? What is the probability that the number you select drops in the "integers not divisible by 4" bin? Explain your reasoning.

5. Suppose you randomly choose n such that $0 < n \leq 20$. How does that change the probabilities in Questions 1 - 4? Explain your reasoning.

6. Should the four probabilities for the number falling into each of the four bins add up to 1? Why or why not? Did the probabilities you found in Question 5 add up to 1? Explain.

TECHNOLOGY ACTIVITY 9.2

It's Perfectly Normal

For this project you will need a program such as Excel® which is capable of calculations and creating statistical graphs.

Consider tossing a coin. There are two possible outcomes, either no heads or one head. If you toss the coin twice, there are three possible outcomes. You could toss no heads, one head, or two heads. There are two ways you can toss two heads however. If you toss a coin four times, there are five possible outcomes summarized in the table below. The probability of each event is also indicated.

Number of Heads	Results of Flips	Number of Ways	Probability
0	TTTT	1	$\frac{1}{16} = 0.0625$
1	TTTH TTHT THTT HTTT	4	$\frac{4}{16} = 0.25$
2	TTHH THTH THHT HTTH HTHT HHTT	6	$\frac{6}{16} = 0.375$
3	THHH HTHH HHTH HHHT	4	$\frac{4}{16} = 0.25$
4	HHHH	1	$\frac{1}{16} = 0.0625$

Using a program such as Excel® make a histograph like the one below showing the possible number of heads on the horizontal axis and the probability of the events on the vertical axis.

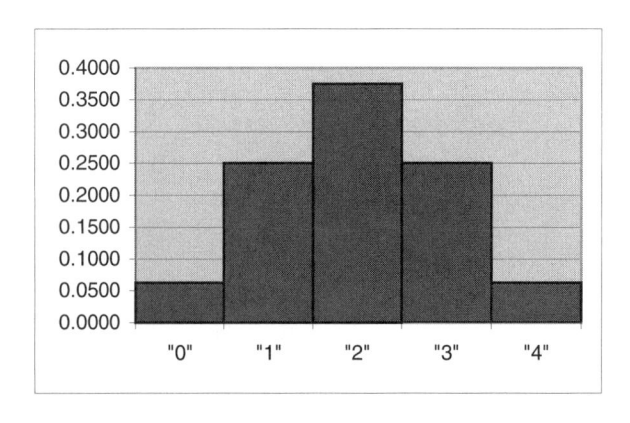

Technology Activity 9.2 **205**

To do this, enter the following information into your spreadsheet.

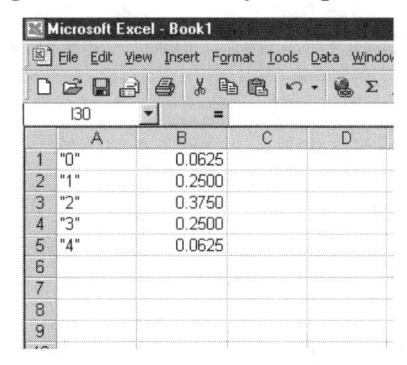

	A	B
1	"0"	0.0625
2	"1"	0.2500
3	"2"	0.3750
4	"3"	0.2500
5	"4"	0.0625

Highlight the ten cells and then hit Chart Wizard.

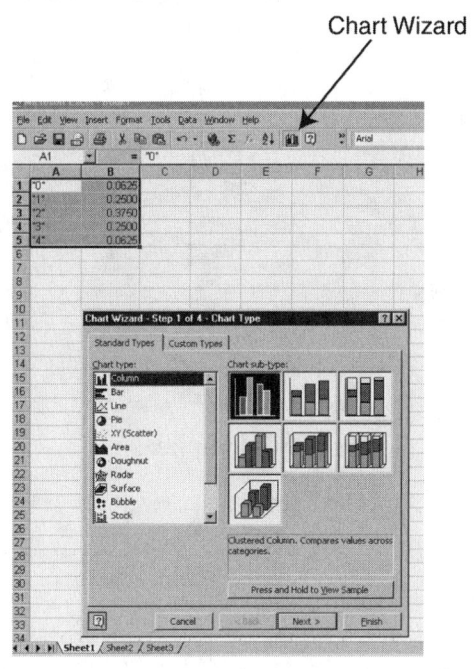

Hit the Next > button and the following should appear.

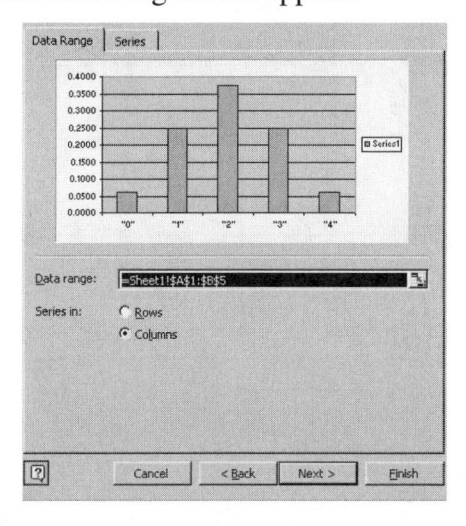

206 Chapter 9: Probability

Hit the Next > button and the following should appear.

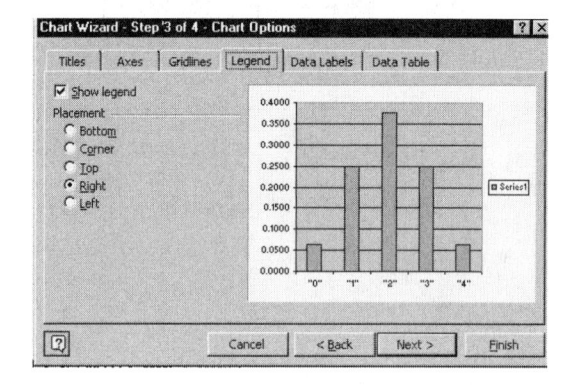

Deselect the Show legend feature to allow more room for the graph.

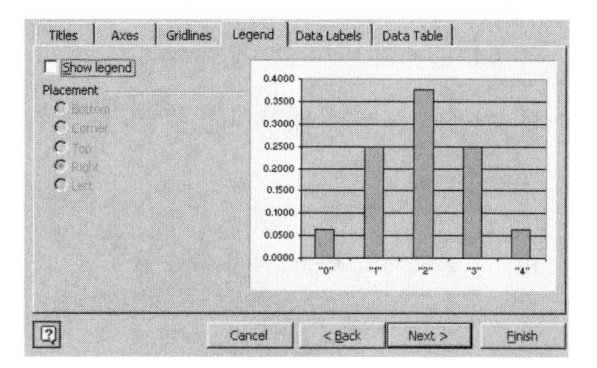

Hit the Next > button and the following should appear.

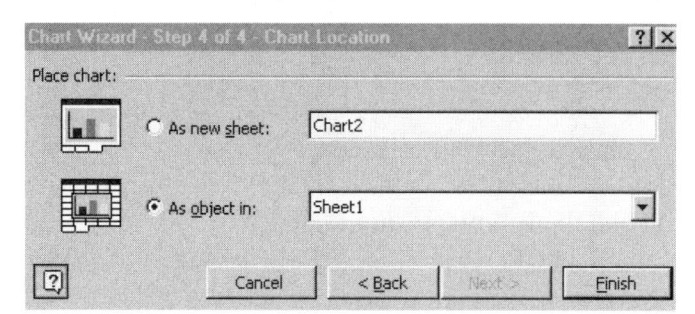

Hit the Finish button and the following should appear.

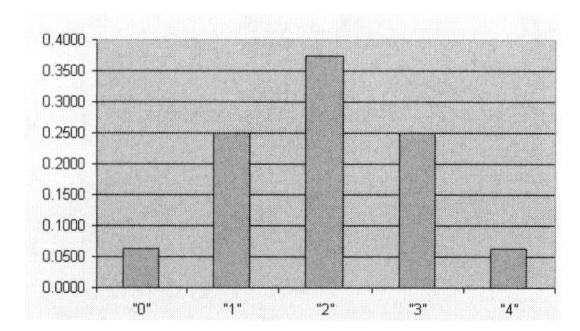

Click on any of the vertical bars and the following should appear. Adjust the Gap Width to be 0 in order to get the columns to touch.

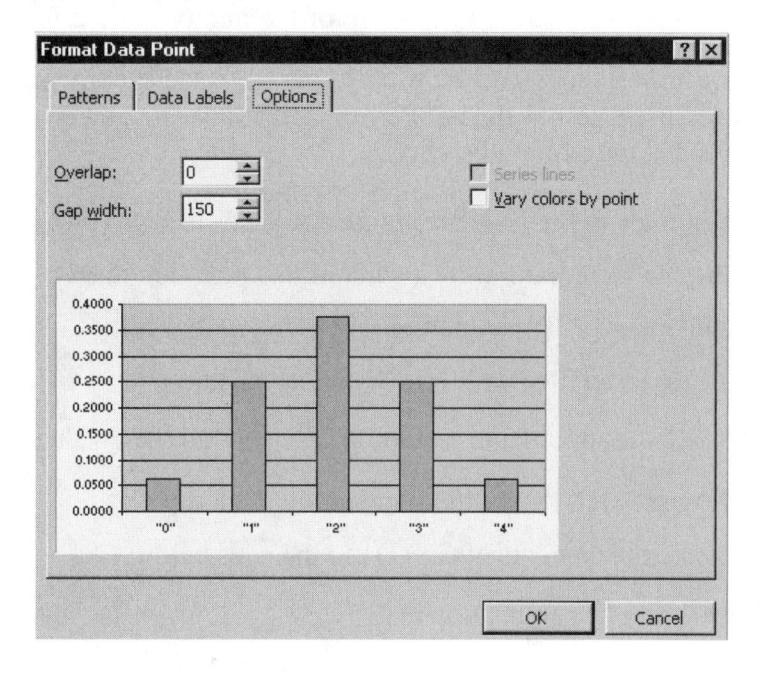

Hit the OK button and the correct histograph should appear. You may choose to copy and paste this graph into a program such as Word® in order to summarize the results of this activity.

Now in taking a closer look at the table for tossing a coin 4 times, the number of ways a certain number of heads occurs can be generated by combinations instead of brute force.

Number of Heads	Number of Ways
0	$_4C_0 = \dfrac{4!}{(4-0)!\,0!} = 1$
1	$_4C_1 = \dfrac{4!}{(4-1)!\,1!} = 4$
2	$_4C_2 = \dfrac{4!}{(4-2)!\,2!} = 6$
3	$_4C_1 = \dfrac{4!}{(4-1)!\,1!} = 4$
4	$_4C_0 = \dfrac{4!}{(4-0)!\,0!} = 1$

In general, if you toss a coin n times the number of ways r heads can occur is $_nC_r = \dfrac{n!}{(n-r)!\,r!}$. The probability of tossing a coin n times and having a head occur r

Chapter 9: Probability

times is $\dfrac{{}_nC_r}{S} = \dfrac{\dfrac{n!}{(n-r)!\,r!}}{S}$, where S is the sum of the number of the number of ways all possibilities can occur. Excel® can be used to generate these combinations. Consider the same case of tossing a coin 4 times. Perform the following and have the spreadsheet calculate the values that we explored earlier.

- In Column A, type in the possible number of heads as data (no quotation marks).
- In Cell B1, type "=combin(4,A1)", without the quotation marks.
- When you hit enter, a "1" should appear as data in that cell.
- Copy and paste the contents of Cell B1 to the cells below.
- In Cell B6, use the summation feature ($\sum$) to find the S value.
- In Cell D1, type "=B1/16", without quotation marks.
- Copy and paste the contents of Cell D1 to the cells below.
- In Cell D6, use the summation feature ($\sum$) to check that the sum of the probabilities is 1.
- In Column C, place the labels that will be on the histograph. You will need to use quotation marks.
- Highlight the ten cells that will be used as labels and data in your histograph and follow the steps outlined previously to make the histograph if desired.

	A	B	C	D
1	0	1	"0"	0.0625
2	1	4	"1"	0.25
3	2	6	"2"	0.375
4	3	4	"3"	0.25
5	4	1	"4"	0.0625
6		16		1
7				

Follow the procedures outlined to determine the histograph for the number of heads when 8 flips, 16 flips, 32 flips, and 64 flips are performed. Summarize you results in a report. Include in your report responses to the following Summary Questions.

Summary Questions:
1. What are similarities and differences between the information generated in the spreadsheet?

2. As more flips are performed what shape does the histograph approach?

TECHNOLOGY ACTIVITY 9.3

The Birthday Problem

For this activity you will need a graphing calculator or a spreadsheet program such as Excel®. Excel® is preferred over a calculator, such as a TI-83, because of the potential of an overflow error due to the level of calculations that must be performed.

Suppose you are in a room with five other people. You might think that the probability that two of you have the same birthday is small and you would be correct. The probability that at least two people in your room have the same birthday is about 3%.

To determine the probability that at least two people have the same birthday, we would have to consider the probability that two people, three people, four people, or all five people have the same birthday. However a more direct route would be to consider the *Definition of Complementary Events* (page 458). We will think of the complement of the event that at least two people have the same birthday to be the event that no two people have the same birthday. In this case the probability be seek would be

$$1 - \frac{365}{365} \cdot \frac{364}{365} \cdot \frac{363}{365} \cdot \frac{362}{365} \cdot \frac{361}{365} \approx 0.0271355737 \text{ or about } 3\%.$$

Explain what each of the factors in the term $\frac{365}{365} \cdot \frac{364}{365} \cdot \frac{363}{365} \cdot \frac{362}{365} \cdot \frac{361}{365}$ mean.

Using alternate notation, $1 - \frac{365}{365} \cdot \frac{364}{365} \cdot \frac{363}{365} \cdot \frac{362}{365} \cdot \frac{361}{365} = 1 - \frac{{}_{365}P_5}{365^5}$. In general, the probability that at least two people in a room of n people will have the same birthday is

$$1 - \frac{{}_{365}P_n}{365^n}.$$

Now to investigate what happens to the probability of a match as the number of people increases we will use a program such as Excel®. Follow the following steps to generate the desired probabilities.

- In Column A start in Cell A1 and enter 1.

- You can either continue entering in consecutive natural numbers or enter "=A1+1" (without the quotes) in Cell A2. You can then copy and paste the contents of Cell A2 to the cells below. You should have values appear down to Cell A50, indicating a room with 50 people.

- In Cell B1 type "=1−PERMUT(365,A1)/365^A1" (without the quotes).

- You can then copy and paste the contents of Cell B2 to the cells below.

The following screen shows the first few rows that should be displayed.

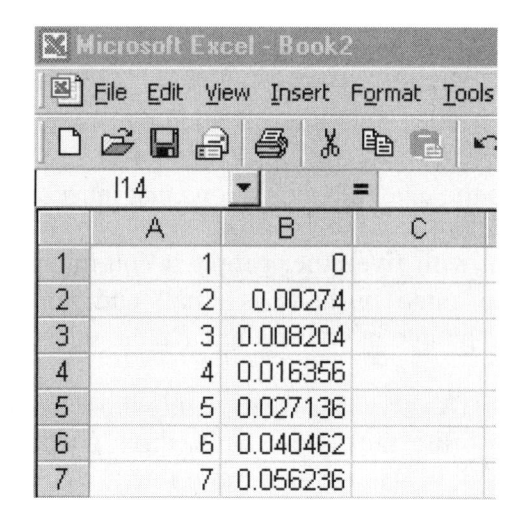

	A	B
1	1	0
2	2	0.00274
3	3	0.008204
4	4	0.016356
5	5	0.027136
6	6	0.040462
7	7	0.056236

Part A Summary Questions:
1. How many people would you need in a room in order to have the probability of a birthday match to be at least 50%? Are the results surprising? Explain.

2. If you have 50 people in a room, what is the probability of a birthday match? Are the results surprising? Explain.

3. Construct a histogram by highlighting the cells in Column B. Follow the instructions in Technology Activity 9.2. How would you describe the graph?

4. How would you adjust your calculations to determine the probability that a group of people in a room were born in the same month? On the same day of the week?

Consider the following example of the *Pigeon-Hole Principle.*

If you put 8 pigeons in 7 holes then at least one hole would have more than one pigeon.

Arguments of this type are used in solutions to many mathematical problems. Many theorems have been proven with the help of the Pigeon-Hole Principle.

Consider the following.

Is there a minimum number of people in a room that would guarantee a "birth month" match? A "birth day of the week" match?

Part B Summary Questions:
1. How could the example given of the Pigeon-Hole Principle explain your answer?

2. How does your answer in Question 1 compare to calculations made with a program such as Excel®?

TECHNOLOGY ACTIVITY 9.4

Spinning Around

Go to the Spinner feature on the Interactiviate disk. This feature will display a spinner with four possible outcomes. Adjust the Number of Sections to 3. On page 458 of your text, you were asked to determine the theoretical probabilities that the spinner shows

- Red,
- Not blue,
- Not red,
- Not green.

In order to see if the theoretical results are consistent with the observable results allow the sector labeled "Cyan" to represent the red sector depicted in your text.

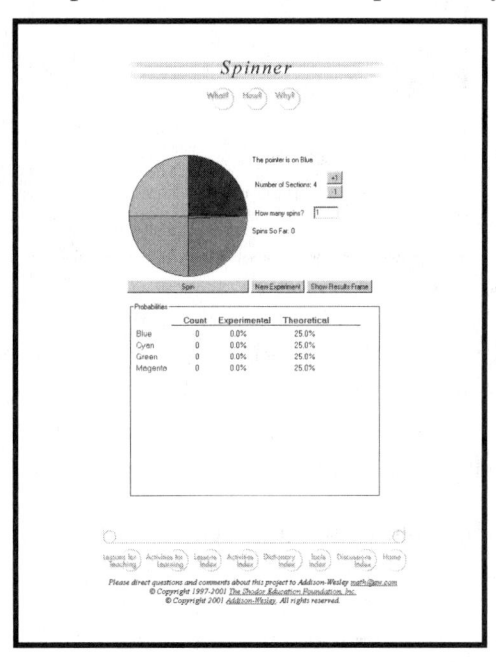

Start with performing the experiment one spin at a time. Press the spin button four times and observe the Experimental results. Press the Show Results Frame to give a graphical representation of the results. Spin the spinner four more times and again observe the Experimental results and graphical representation. Increase the "How many spins?" option and continue to observe the results, both numerical and graphical.

Summary Questions:
1. What do you notice about the long-term behavior of the probabilities associated with the spinner?

2. Do your long-term results agree with the answers that you gave to the problem posed on page 458 of your text? Explain.

TECHNOLOGY ACTIVITY 9.5

Hit the Target

A parachutist is trying to hit a square target that measures 100 meters on each side. The only obstacles in the target area are four trees; the center of each is at a vertex of the square. The trees are identical and when seen from above their braches appear to be the shape of congruent circles. We assume that the parachutist lands randomly somewhere within the square.

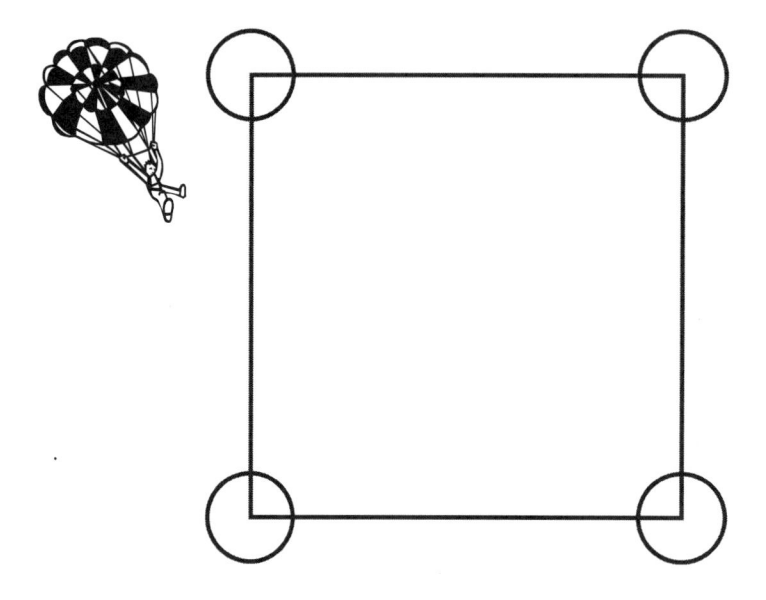

Create a dynamic illustration of the situation using The Geometer's Sketchpad® or a similar geometry exploration software (GES). Allow for the common radius of the tree-branch circles to change using the GES. Record measurements from your dynamic illustration to solve the following two problems.

A. Determine the probability that parachutist will land safely in the square and not in the trees when each tree-branch has a radius of 10 meters.

B. Determine the radius of the trees so that the probability is 0.90 that the parachutist will land safely in the square and not in the trees.

Summary Questions:
1. What strategies did you use to solve Problem A?

2. What strategies did you use to solve Problem B?

3. How would the problem situation change if there was one tree in the interior of the square instead of the four trees as described before? Consider the center of tree in various locations in the interior of the square.

Instructions for required constructions are given on the next few pages.

Some of the terms such as **Pointer, Point Tool**, and **Line Tool** are described in more detail in Appendix B of your text.

In this problem the parachutist is trying to hit a square target that measures 100 meters on each side. The Geometer's Sketchpad has three measurement options. They are cm, inches, and pixels. Go to the **Edit** menu and choose **Preferences**. The following menu will appear.

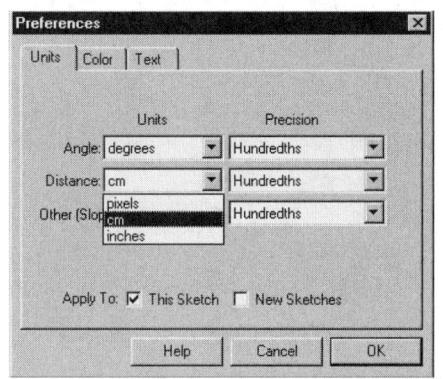

For this construction, you can either leave the units in centimeters and then scale in order to create the construction or use pixels to allow for a square that measures 100 units (pixels) on each side. We will choose to perform the constructions with the pixel measurement.

One way to construct a square is to use your **Line Tool** to select a starting place. You click with your mouse a beginning place and drag the line to an ending place. Make the line segment horizontal. You can tell that it is a horizontal line because it should be perfectly straight. Once the line has been constructed, go to the **Measure** menu and select **Length**. The labeled segment along with the length will be displayed in the upper left-hand corner of your screen. Most likely your length will need to be adjusted to measure 100 pixels. Using your **Pointer Tool** select one of the end points. You can either drag the endpoint until you get the desired measure of use the arrows on your keyboard to adjust the length. One advantage of using the keyboard is that your line segment will remain horizontal.

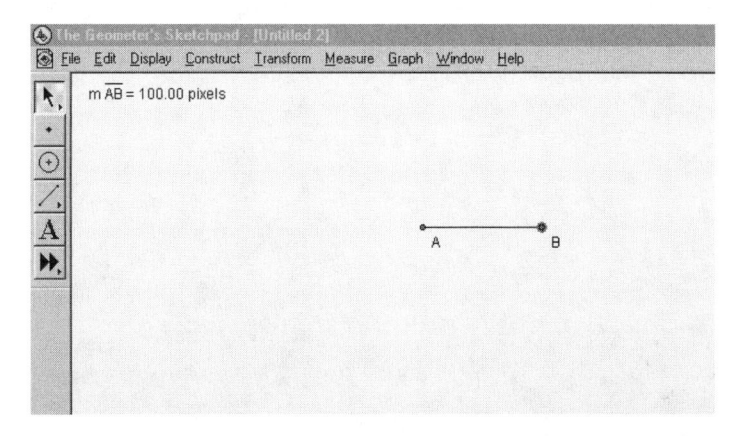

214 Chapter 9: Probability

Using your **Pointer Tool** select the line segment. It should change its appearance by becoming much "fatter" with a pink outline. Go to the **Edit** menu and select **Copy** and then go back to the **Edit** menu and select **Paste**. The copy will appear selected. Using your keyboard arrows move it left or right until it is directly under your first line segment. If after adjustment it does not appear directly under your original, select it and try again.

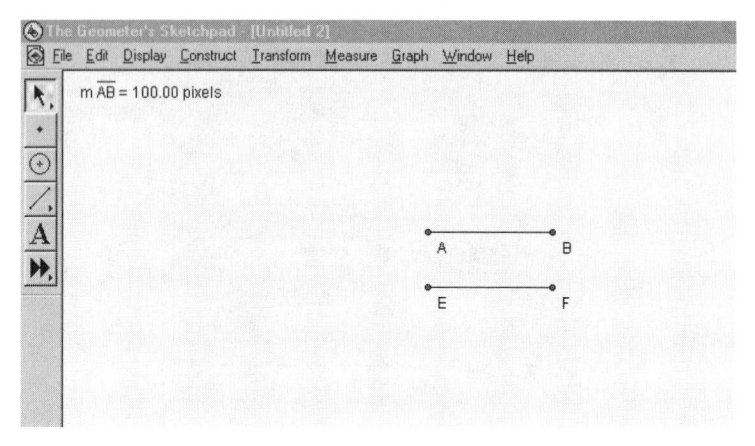

Using the **Line Tool** we need to construct the third side of what will be the square. After selecting the **Line Tool**, go to one of the four labeled endpoints. You will know you are about to select an endpoint because it will be encircled. Click on the endpoint and drag the line segment down to the endpoint either directly above or below. Click on that endpoint. Again, this other endpoint will be encircled if you are directly over it. The new side should be drawn and selected. Go to the **Measure** menu and select **Length**. Using your **Pointer Tool** select either the top or bottom side. Using your keyboard's up/down arrows adjust the position of the side until it measures 100 pixels. Construct the fourth side of the square using the **Line Tool** and the method described above.

Using your **Pointer Tool**, select some point not on the square. Click on the four vertices of your square either in a clockwise or counter-clockwise fashion. As you select a vertex, it will change size. Go to the **Construct** menu and select **Quadrilateral Interior**. Go to the **Measure** menu and select **Area**. The area will appear in the upper left-hand corner.

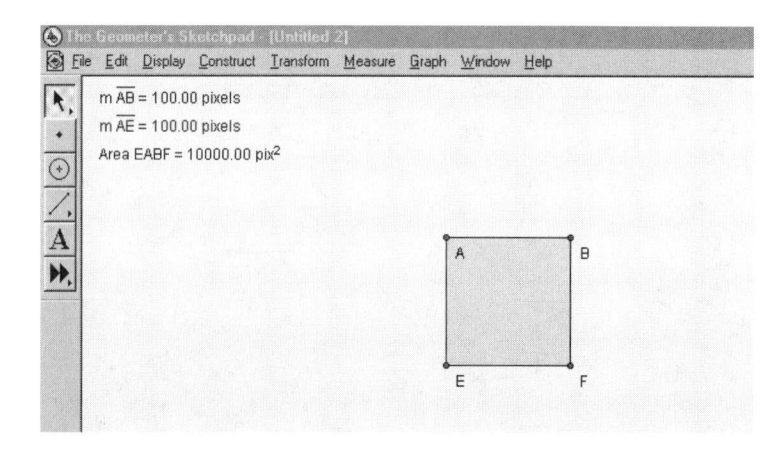

We next need to construct circles whose centers are on the corners of the square and measure the area that lies inside the square. To do this select the **Circle Tool** and click on one of the vertices of the square. Drag outside the square until you have a small circle. Click on your mouse to mark this circle. Go to the **Measure** menu and select **Radius**. In Part A of the activity, we will need a circle of radius 10 meters (here 10 pixels). Select the point on the circle and using your keyboard arrows, adjust the radius until it is 10 pixels. You may need to use the up/down as well as the left/right arrows.

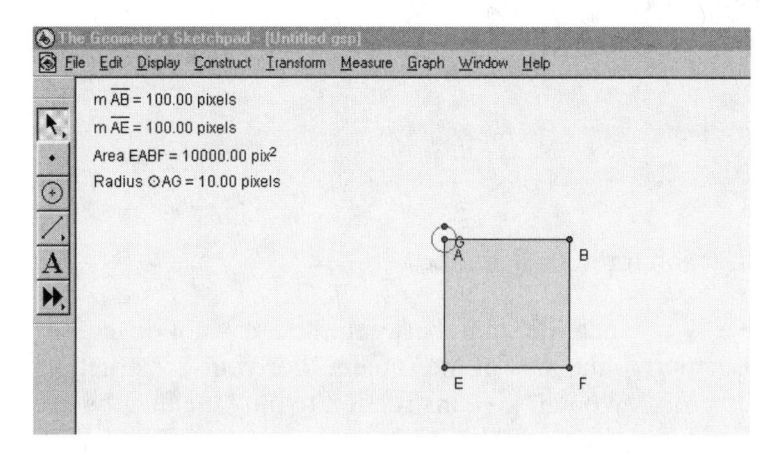

In order to ensure a common radius among the four circles, select the circle you constructed and go to the **Edit** menu and select **Copy**. Go back to the **Edit** menu and select **Paste**. The copy will appear selected. Move the circle until its center is on one of the remaining three vertices. Repeat this process until you have placed circles on all four vertices.

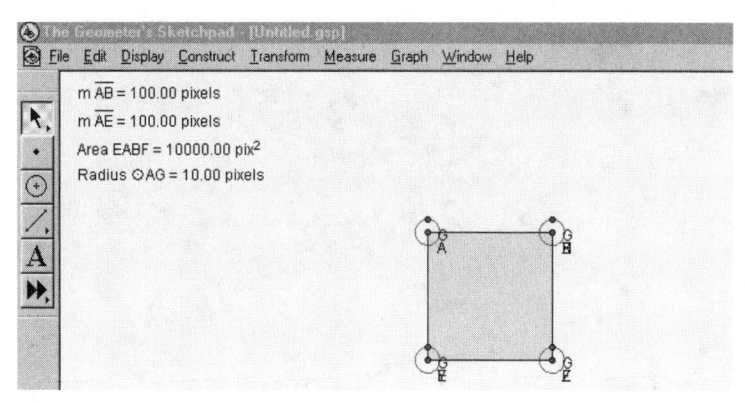

We next need to create sectors, which will represent the overlap between the circle and the square. To do this you will need two points that are on the circle and adjacent sides of the square. Using the **Point Tool**, find points of intersection by noting where both a side and the circle are highlighted. Select a point by clicking on your mouse. You should have created two new points. Using the **Pointer Tool** select a point not on your figure. Select only the circle and then the two points on the circle and square in a counter-clockwise fashion. Go to the **Construct** menu and select **Arc On Circle**. A small arc will be highlighted. Go to the Construct menu and select **Arc Interior** and then

216 Chapter 9: Probability

Arc Sector. The sector will be highlighted. Go to the **Measure** menu and select **Area**. The area of the sector will appear in the upper left-hand corner.

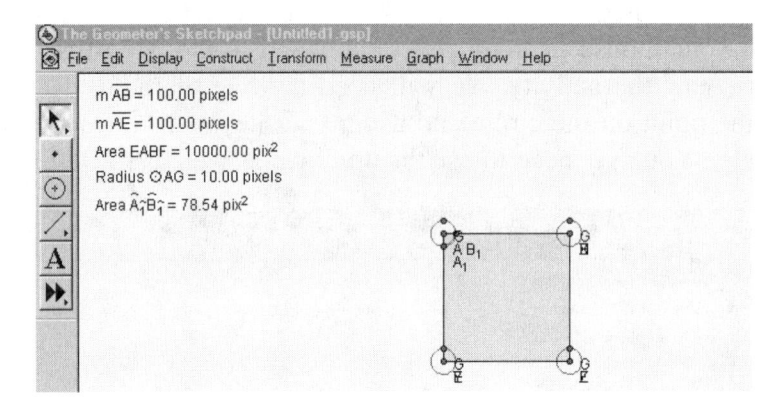

Repeat this construction for the other three vertices.

We will next have to calculate the ratio between the areas not covered by the trees in the square (the four sectors) to the area of the square. For your construction you will need to consider all four sectors. We will give instruction to only include the one sector shown in the previous screen dump.

Go to **Measure** menu and select **Calculate**. Select which measurements you wish to use in your calculations.

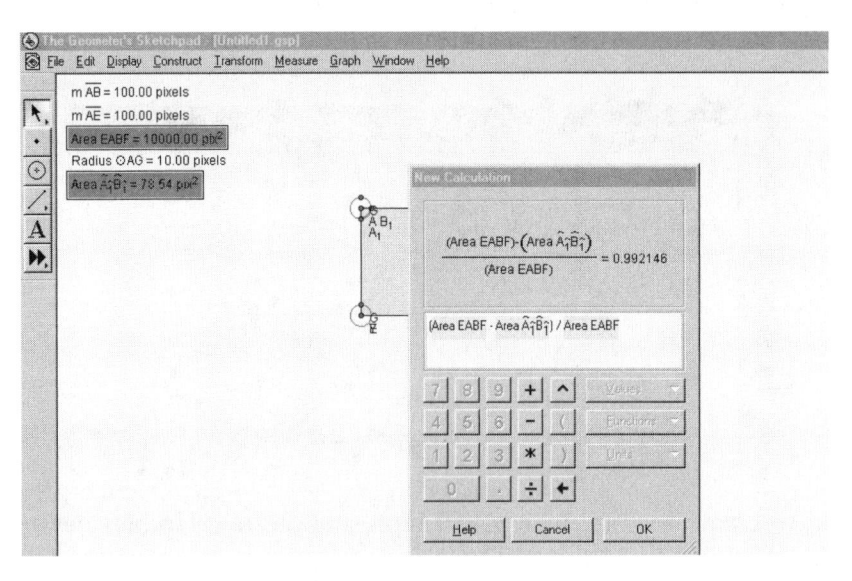

Click on the **OK** button when you are done.

In Part B of the activity, you will need to adjust your radii so that you can then determine what size radii will produce the desired ratio. To do this, use your **Pointer Tool** and select only the four points (one per circle) that are common endpoints of the radii. Drag one of these points and the others should follow by either enlarging or shrinking all circles simultaneously. Adjust the radius size until you get the ratio to be 0.90.

CHAPTER 10: INTRODUCING GEOMETRY

INVESTIGATION 10.1

What's in a Name?

On page 517, the generally accepted names for a 3-, 4- 5-, 6-, 7-, 8-, 9-, 10-, and 12-sided polygons are given. For a figure with more sides, one generally calls the figure an *n*-gon, where *n* indicates the number of sides.

Looking at these names, one notices the absence of an 11-sided figure. Although it is not commonly used, an 11-sided figure can be called a *undecagon* or preferably a *hendecagon*. It should be noted that a 9-sided figure is generally called a *nonagon*, but has an alternate name of *enneagon*. In fact any *n*-gon can be given a name according to the number of sides. For multiples of ten, we have the following.

Decagon 10-sided   Icosagon 20-sided   Triacontagon 30-sided
Tetracontagon 40-sided   Pentacontagon 50-sided   Hexacontagon 60-sided
Heptacontagon 70-sided   Octacontagon 80-sided
Enneacontagon 90-sided   Hectogon or Hecatontagon 100-sided

In general, to construct a name you need to combine a prefix and a suffix.

Sides	Prefix	Sides	Suffix
20	Icosikai…	+1	…henagon
30	Triacontakai…	+2	…digon
40	Tetracontakai…	+3	…trigon
50	Pentacontakai…	+4	…tetragon
60	Hexacontakai…	+5	…pentagon
70	Heptacontakai…	+6	…hexagon
80	Octacontakai…	+7	…heptagon
90	Enneacontakai…	+8	…octagon
		+9	…enneagon

Summary Questions:
1. What would a Tetracontakaihexagon be?

2. What would you call a 99-sided figure?

   o Make up a name for a regular *n*-sided figure where *n* is between 20 and 100. Ask a classmate to give the exact measurement of each interior angle.

   o Choose a different number, *n*, between 20 and 100 and determine the measurement of an exterior angle for this regular *n*-gon. Ask a classmate to give you the name of that *n*-gon.

218 Chapter 10: Introducing Geometry

INVESTIGATION 10.2

Polygon Angles

How are the angles in a regular polygon related? Tell as much as you can about the angles of a regular polygon and the sums of these angles.

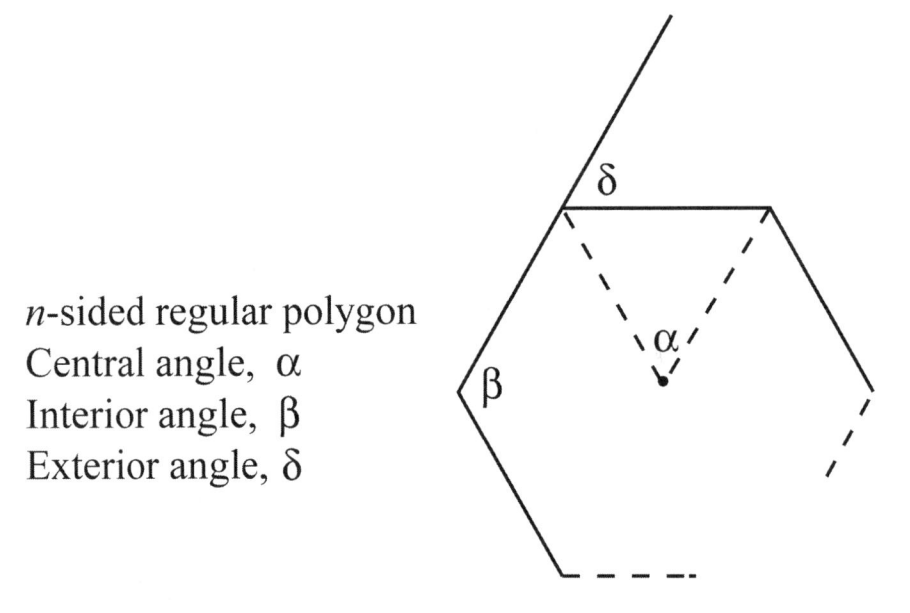

n-sided regular polygon
Central angle, α
Interior angle, β
Exterior angle, δ

Summary Questions:
1. What is the measure of the central angle of an n-sided regular polygon? Explain how you know that this is true.

2. How is the central angle, α, related to the interior angle, β? Write an equation to show this relationship, and explain how you know that this relationship is true.

3. How is the interior angle, β, related to the exterior angle, δ? Write an equation to show this relationship, and explain how you know that this relationship is true.

4. How is the exterior angle, δ, related to the central angle, α? Write an equation to show this relationship, and explain how you know that this relationship is true.

5. What is the sum of the exterior angles of the polygon? (Hint: Use what you know about the sum of the central angles of the polygon and the equation you wrote in Question 4.) Verify your answer.

6. What is the sum of the interior angles of the polygon? Verify your answer.

INVESTIGATION 10.3

Network Traversability

Which of the following networks, 1 - 17, are traversable?

Networks with all Even Vertices

1)   2) 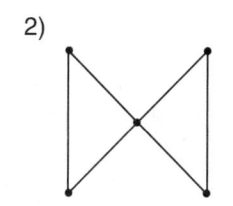   3) 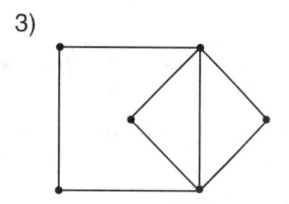   4)

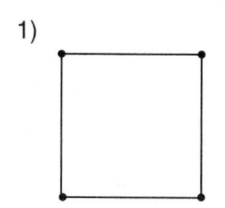

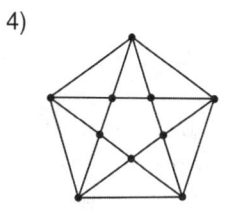

Networks with all Odd Vertices

5)   6) 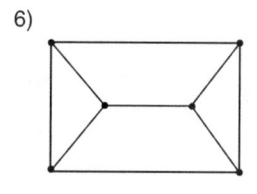   7) 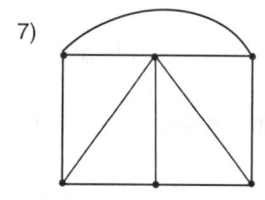   8)

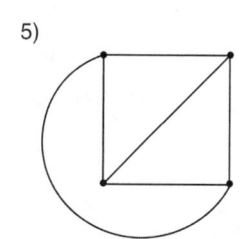

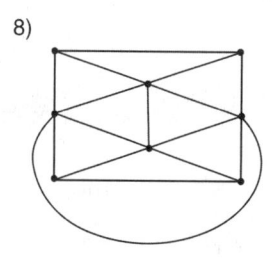

Networks with both Odd and Even Vertices

9)   10) 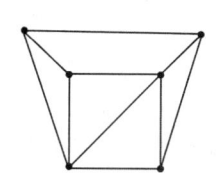   11) 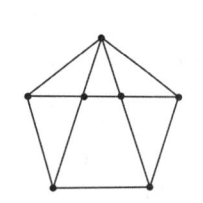   12)

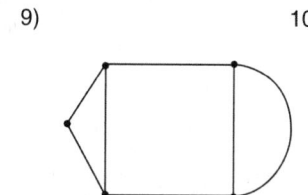

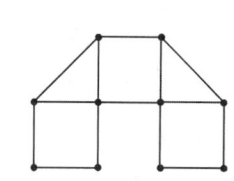

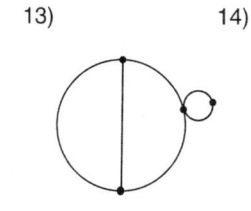

13)   14) 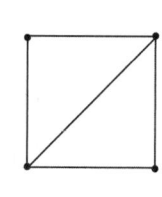   15) 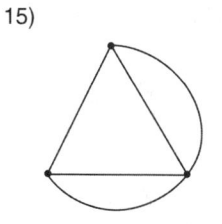   16) 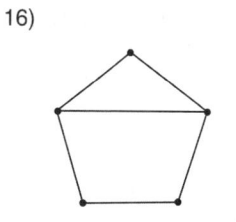   17)

Summary Questions:
1. For which of the networks can you go along each edge only once and return to the starting vertex?

2. For which of the networks can you go along each edge only once and return to a different vertex?

3. What generalizations can you state about which types of networks are traversable?

INVESTIGATION 10.4

Quadrilateral Generalizations

Working in a small group, make drawings or use a Geometry Exploration Software to inductively support, or find a counterexample to disprove, the following generalizations.

A quadrilateral is a parallelogram if and only if…

- A. both pairs of opposite sides are parallel.
- B. both pairs of opposite sides are congruent.
- C. it has a pair of congruent _____.
- D. it has a pair of opposite sides that are both congruent and parallel.
- E. both pairs of opposite angles are congruent.
- F. a pair of opposite angles are congruent.
- G. the diagonals bisect each other.
- H. a pair of opposite sides are congruent.
- I. the consecutive angles are supplementary.
- J. a pair of opposite sides are parallel.

Summary Questions:

1. Is there a generalization about a rectangle that is not true for a parallelogram? If so, state it.

2. Is there a generalization about a rhombus that is not true for a parallelogram? If so, state it.

3. Is there a generalization about a kite that is not true for a parallelogram? If so, state it.

4. Do you think any generalization true for a parallelogram and a rectangle and a rhombus would also be true for a square? Explain.

INVESTIGATION 10.5

What's Right is Right

Consider the diagrams in Figure 10.25 on page 549 of your textbook. Which of the three diagrams can be used to justify the following statement.

"Any angle inscribed in a semi-circle is a right angle."

Part A Summary Question:
How can you use the diagram to justify this statement?

Consider the following diagram.

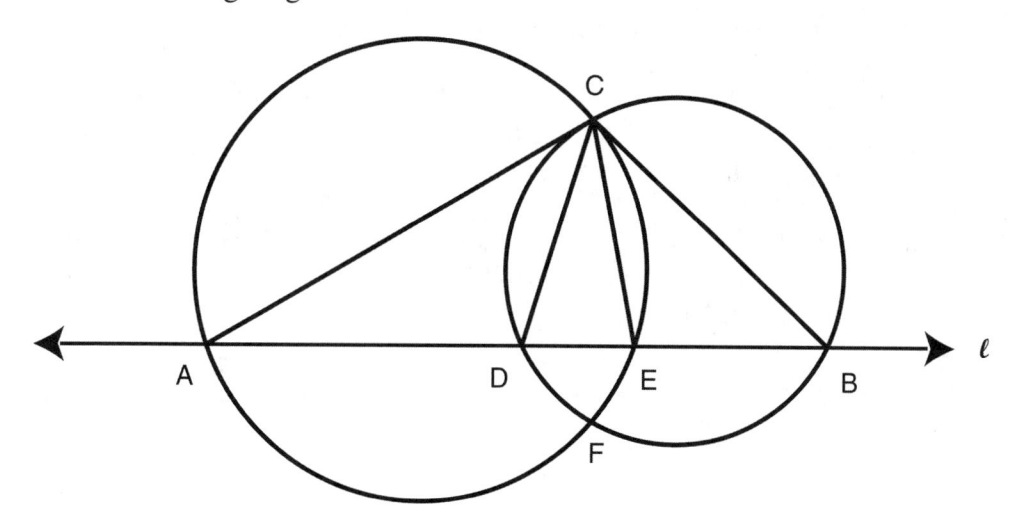

There are two circles with diameters $\overline{AC}$ and $\overline{BC}$. These two circles meet at Points C and F. Line ℓ passes through the two circles and intersects at the indicated points. Since $\overline{AC}$ is a diameter, angle $\angle AEC$ is a right angle and hence $\overline{CE}$ is perpendicular to Line ℓ. because $\overline{BC}$ is also a diameter, a similar justification to be made in order to state that $\overline{CD}$ is perpendicular to Line ℓ.

Part B Summary Questions:
1. Since $\overline{CE}$ and $\overline{CD}$ pass through Point C, then according to this argument, how many lines passing through Point C are perpendicular to Line ℓ? Is this possible? Explain.

2. Make a similar drawing as above only make the line pass through the two circles below Point F. Can the same argument be made regarding the number of lines that pass through a given point and are perpendicular to a given line? Explain.

3. Is there a third possibility as to the location of the line that passes through the two circles? If so, what is it? Can the same argument be made regarding the number of lines that pass through a given point and are perpendicular to a given line? Explain.

MANIPULATIVE ACTIVITY 10.1

Try a Different Angle!

For this activity you will need paper, scissors, and glue (or stapler). If you chose, you can visit http://wps.aw.com/aw_odaffer_mathematic_2 to download regular and irregular polygons required for the constructions.

In the text, the sum of the interior angles of a polygon was found by cutting off the corner angles of the polygon and placing them around a circle or semi-circle. (See page 543 in your textbook.) We could call this the *angle-cutoff model*. The sum of the exterior angles of a polygon was modeled by rotating a cut-out arrow through each of the exterior angles and determining the extent of the rotation. (See page 546 in your textbook.) We could call this the *arrow-rotation model*. Now let's switch these models.

A. Discuss how you would use the angle-cutoff model to determine the sum of the *exterior* angles of a polygon. Demonstrate this by using a cut-out for regular and irregular triangles, quadrilaterals, and pentagons

B. Discuss how you would use the arrow-rotation model to determine the sum of the *interior* angles of a polygon. Demonstrate this by using a cut-out for regular and irregular triangles, quadrilaterals, and pentagons.

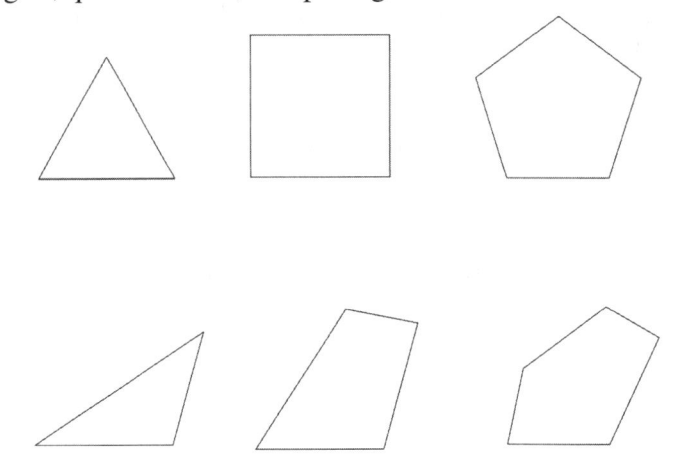

Summary Questions:
1. Which of the models, if either, do you think is best for demonstrating the sum of the interior angles of a polygon? The exterior angles of a polygon?

2. Why do the sums of the interior angles of polygons with increasing numbers of sides increase, while the sums of the exterior angles of polygons with increasing numbers of sides stay the same?

3. How could you use the models to help you explain your answer to Question 2?

MANIPULATIVE ACTIVITY 10.2

Disappearing and Appearing Units

For this activity you will need a straight edge, scissors and some grid paper. On a piece of grid paper create the four figures according to the diagram below and carefully cut them out. If you chose, you can visit http://wps.aw.com/aw_odaffer_mathematic_2 to download the grid paper.

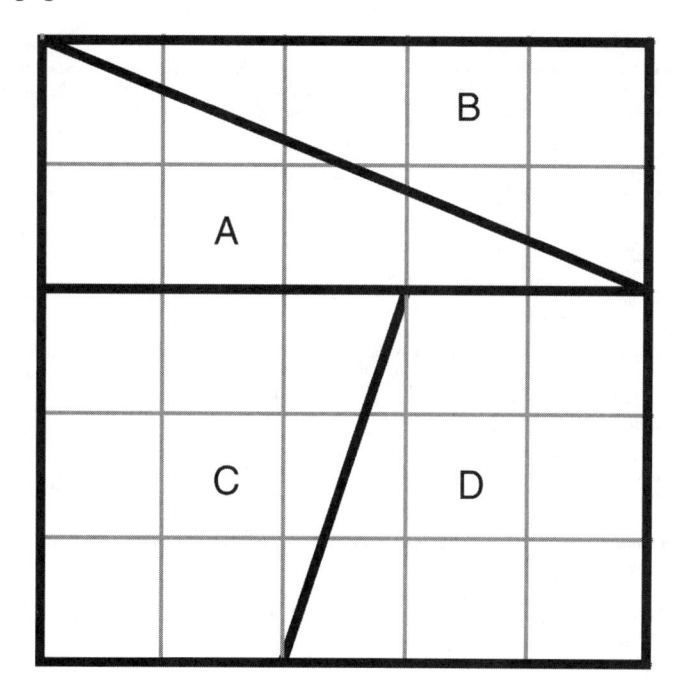

Figure A

Rearrange the cut-out figures to form a 3 unit by 8 unit rectangle like Figure B. Count up the number of squares.

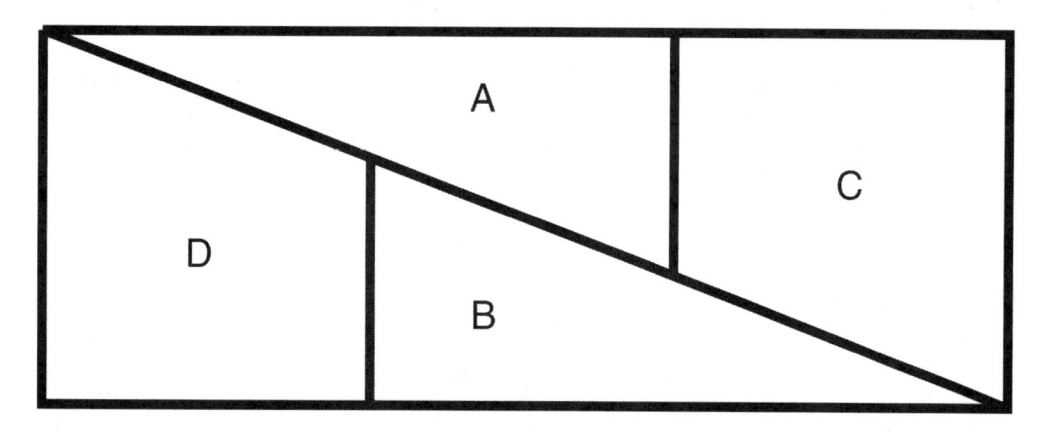

Figure B

224   Chapter 10: Introducing Geometry

Consider a similar design to Figure A.

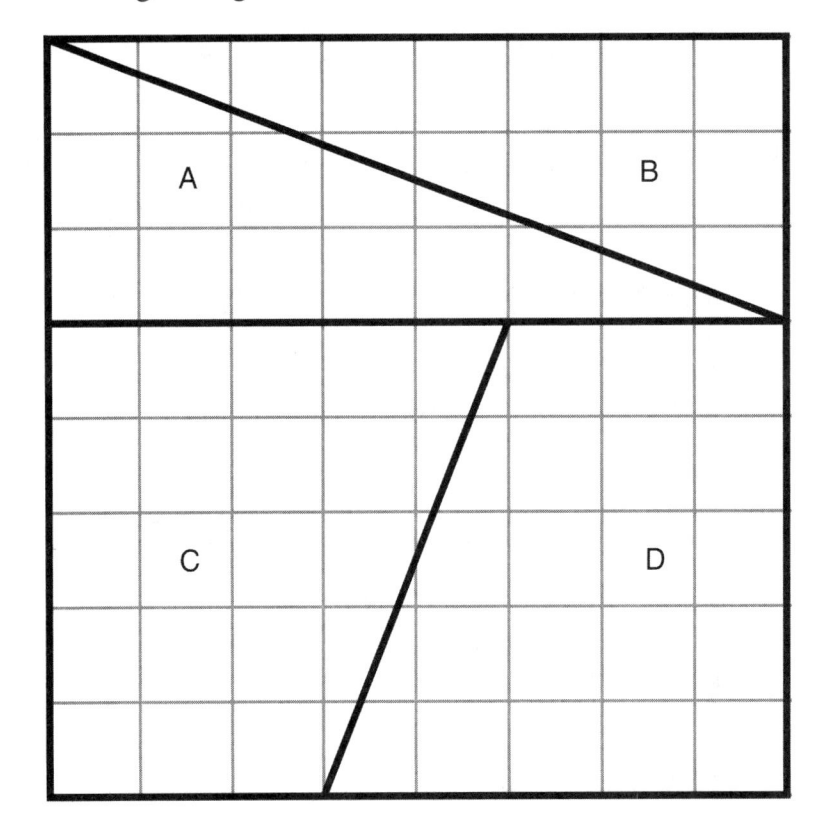

Rearrange the cut-out figures to form a rectangle like Figure B. Count up the number of squares.

Part A Summary Questions:
1. What, if any, are discrepancies between the original square figures and the rectangular figures created?

2. Is there a difference is the two constructions? Explain

The unit numbers involved in the first construction are 2, 3, 5, and 8. In the second construction they are 3, 5, 8, and 13. The numbers occur in the Fibonacci sequence. (See pages 504-505 of your textbook.) The Fibonacci sequence is defined as follows:

$$a_1 = a_2 = 1 \text{ and } a_{n+1} = a_n + a_{n-1}, \text{ where } n \geq 2.$$

One of the interesting properties of this sequence is the fact that

$$a_n^2 - a_{n-1} \cdot a_{n+1} = (-1)^{n-1}.$$

Part B Summary Question:
How can you use this formula to explain what has occurred in your two constructions?

Create a larger square figure with the appropriate divisions of triangles and trapezoids.
Hint: The grid size should be 13 units by 13 units.

Create a smaller square figure with the appropriate divisions of triangles and trapezoids.
Hint: The grid size should be 3 units by 3 units.

Part C Summary Questions:
1. According to the relation, $a_n^2 - a_{n-1} \cdot a_{n+1} = (-1)^{n-1}$, what should occur in each of the constructions?

2. Does your prediction hold for these two constructions? Explain.

MANIPULATIVE ACTIVITY 10.3

The Pythagorean Connection

For this activity you will need paper, scissors, and glue (or stapler). Make one or more of the models described below to verify the Pythagorean theorem.

Model A:
Make a version of a right triangle whose legs are the sides of square connected to the triangle. (See the model shown in Figure 10.2b on page 558 of your textbook.)
- o Note that only the triangle and the squares on the two legs need to be made, since using the model involves placing the squares from the legs to make a square on the hypotenuse.
- o Note also that the divisions of the square on the longest leg can be found by the following procedure:
  Step 1:   Use diagonals to find the center of the square.
  Step 2:   Construct a line through the center of the square and perpendicular to the hypotenuse.
  Step 3:   Construct a line through the center of the square that is perpendicular to the line you constructed in Step 2.

Ask several people to try the model. Write about their reaction to the model and their level of success.

Model B:
Make a "motion picture book" that one could thumb through to see the motions used to verify the Pythagorean theorem in the model in Figure 10.30 on page 560 of your textbook.
- o You will need to determine how many intermediate pages you want to include that show transitions between the stages shown in the text. The more pages you have, the more continuous the picture show will appear.
- o You may wish to include some explanation to introduce the motion picture show and some follow-up comments or questions for the viewer.

Ask several people to try the motion picture book model. Write about their reactions to the model and their level of understanding.

Model C:
Make a version of the model shown in Exercise 58 on page 568 of your textbook.

Use the model to demonstrate the Pythagorean theorem to several people. Write about their reactions to the model and their level of understanding.

Summary Question:
Which of the models described above that you or your classmates made do you think is the best to use to demonstrate the Pythagorean theorem? Give reasons to support your conclusion.

MANIPULATIVE ACTIVITY 10.4

Right, Obtuse, Acute, or None

For this activity you will need three die (one dice can be rolled three times). If die are not available, you can use the random number generator feature available on most graphing utilities. You will need to construct three sets of lengths of one-, two-, three-, four-, five-, and six- units. If you chose, you can visit http://wps.aw.com/aw_odaffer_mathematic_2 to download the lengths to be cut out.

```
_____
                 6 units
    _____
                 5 units
       _____
                 4 units
          _____
                 3 units
            _____
                 2 units
              _____
                 1 unit
```

Perform the following steps 20 times, keeping track of your results.

Step 1: Toss three die or generate three random numbers between 1 and 6, inclusive.

Step 2: Determine if these three numbers will form a triangle. If so, determine what kind of triangle it is (right, obtuse, or acute).

Part A Summary Questions:
1. How many of trials resulted in an acute triangle? Obtuse triangle? Right triangle? No triangle?

2. In looking at the trials that resulted in no triangle, what kind of relationship is common?

There are 56 different possible outcomes when you roll the three dice. A 2-3-1 is considered the same outcome as a 1-2-3. Systematically determine these different possibilities. For each of the possibilities, determine if an acute triangle, obtuse triangle, right triangle, or no triangle can be formed with the unit lengths.

Part B Summary Question:
On your list, there should only be one right triangle that can be formed from the unit lengths. These three sides satisfy the Pythagorean theorem. Without actually performing the constructions is there a test you can perform of the lengths to determine if a triangle is acute or obtuse? If so, what is it? Verify your conjecture with at least five constructions not already performed.

MANIPULATIVE ACTIVITY 10.5

Dominos, Triomonos, Tetrominos, and More

For this activity you will need PopCubes® to assemble figures.

The game of dominos requires pieces that connect two squares together. There is essentially only one way to connect two squares together so that two squares touch each other along complete sides only. Any other arrangement of the two squares would be a rotation of the diagram below. Of course the actual game is played with markings on each of the squares.

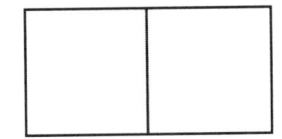

If we were to create a game of Triominos with the condition that any two squares must touch along complete sides only then we would have two distinct arrangements.

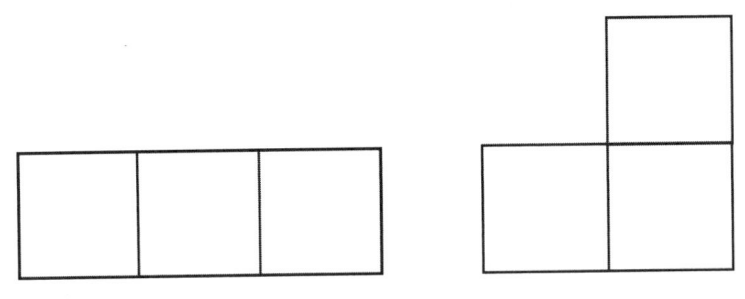

Using PopCubes® create the five shapes involved with connecting four squares together. Two shapes are considered the same if one can obtain the other by turning or flipping one to obtain the other. Justify to a partner that there are only five distinct pieces that would be involved in a game of Tetrominos. You may have seen these shapes in a popular video game with a similar name.

Summary Questions:
1. How many distinct pieces would be involved with a game of Pentominoes? What are they? Find these pieces using your PopCubes®. If you have more than one set of PopCubes® (50 per set) then you will have enough to make a complete set. Otherwise once you find a piece draw it on paper before it is altered.

2. Considering the prefixes involved with the names of polygons, what would be an appropriate name be for a game that involves six squares? How many distinct pieces would be involved? Hint: You would need five sets of PopCubes® to create a complete set of the pieces. Describe the process you went through to find the pieces. Was it systematic or random?

3. If you extend these types of games, what would the names be involved for pieces that have seven squares? Eight squares? Draw an example of a piece from each game.

TECHNOLOGY ACTIVITY 10.1

Inscribed Quadrilaterals

For this activity you will need to use The Geometer's Sketchpad® or a similar geometry exploration software (GES).

- Create a circle and plot Points A, B, C, and D on the circle.

Once you've created a circle and plotted four points on the circle, you can right-click on a point and choose **Show Label**. Because we will not want to change the size of the circle, you should not use the point on the circle made during the construction of the circle.

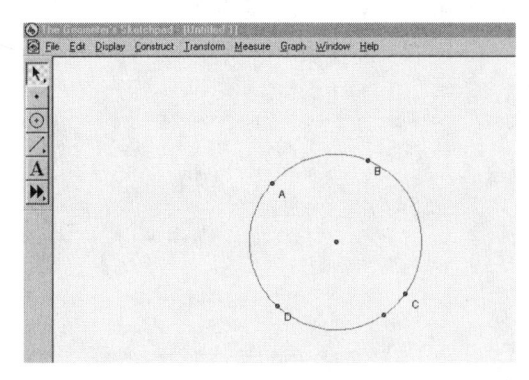

- Create Quadrilateral ABCD and measure its area. Your quadrilateral will vary in size and similarity to the one shown below.

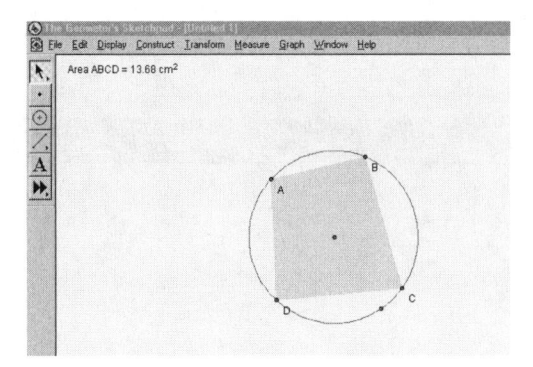

- Distort the figure by moving the vertices of the Quadrilateral ABCD along the circle. Do not change the size of the circle.

Determine the type of quadrilateral that seems to generate the largest area for ABCD. Measure side lengths and angles of Quadrilateral ABCD to help confirm your conjecture.

Summary Question:
Do you think your conjecture will hold for other polygons? Use GES to find out and then refer to geometric properties to explain what you see.

230 Chapter 10: Introducing Geometry

TECHNOLOGY ACTIVITY 10.2

Parallelograms and Squares

For this activity you will need to use The Geometer's Sketchpad® or a similar geometry exploration software (GES).

o   Create a parallelogram. One way to do this is to first draw a line. Copy and paste this line and adjust its position by using your arrows on your keyboard.

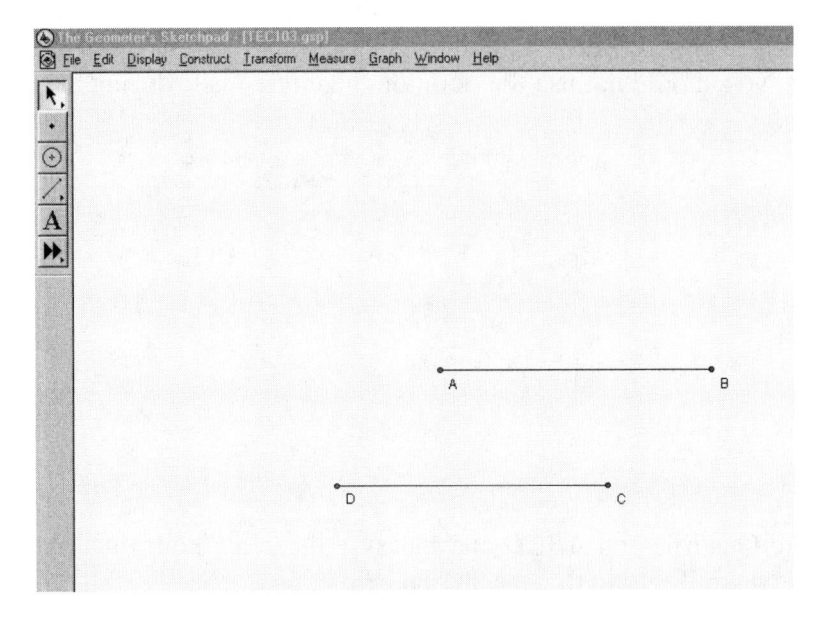

Create the other two sides by connecting the endpoints of the drawn segments as shown below.

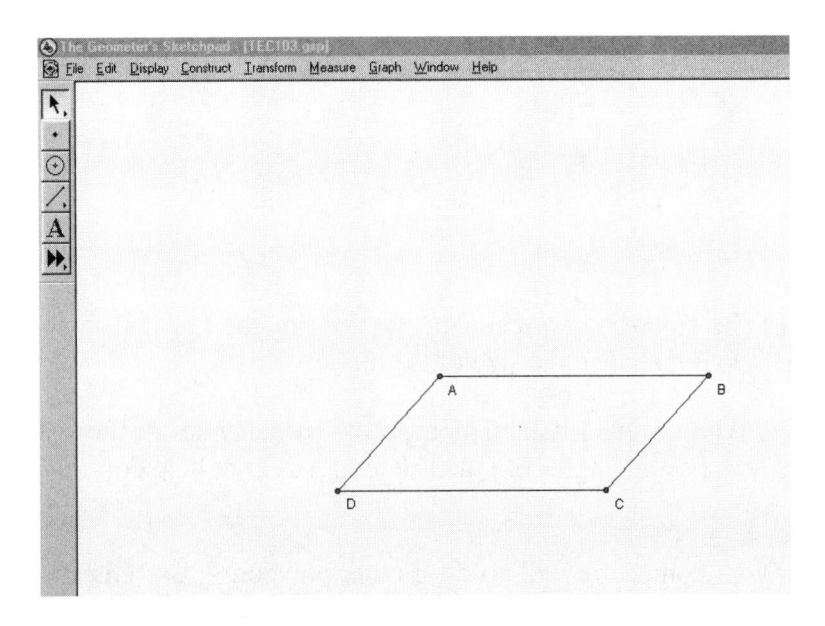

○ Create a square extending out from each side of the parallelogram. Be sure that the squares are maintained even when the parallelogram is distorted. You may measure lengths and angles to ensure that you have constructed squares.

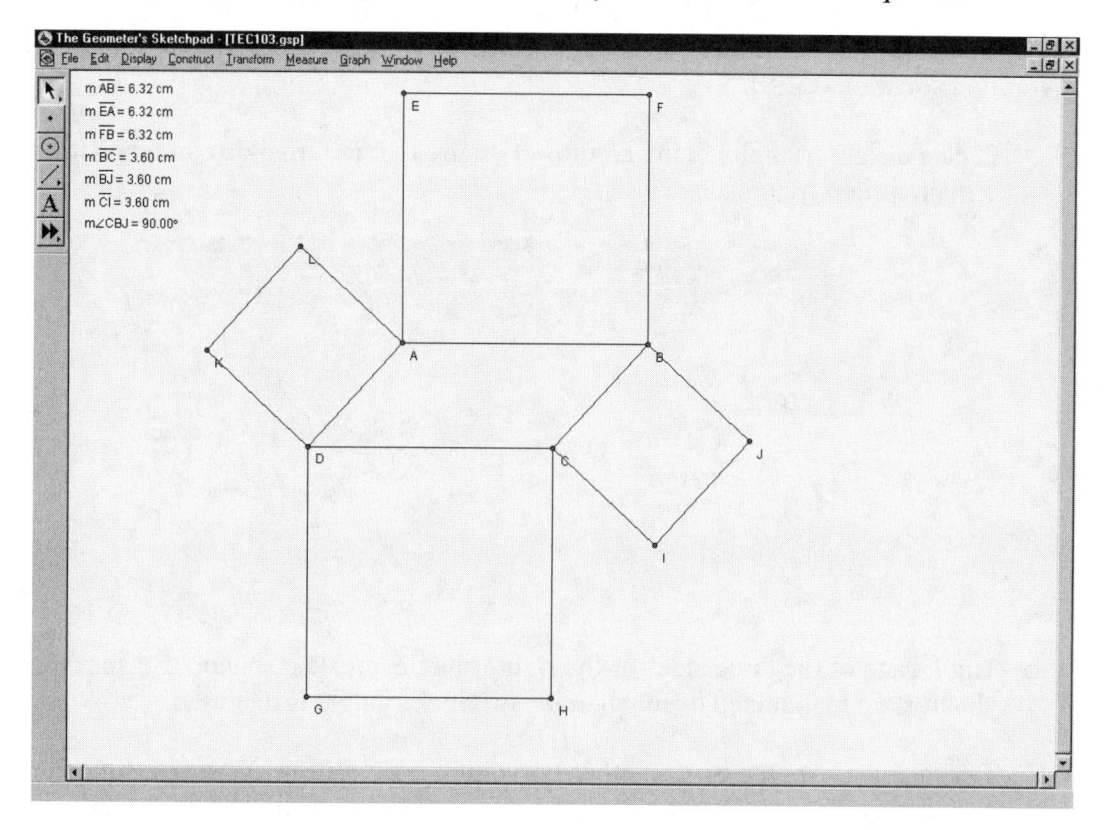

```
The Geometer's Sketchpad - [TEC103.gsp]
File Edit Display Construct Transform Measure Graph Window Help

m AB = 6.32 cm
m EA = 6.32 cm
m FB = 6.32 cm
m BC = 3.60 cm
m BJ = 3.60 cm
m CI = 3.60 cm
m∠CBJ = 90.00°
```

○ Locate the center of each square as the intersection point of the two diagonals of each square.

○ Connect these four center points in consecutive order. Identify the figure you have created.

Distort the original parallelogram and observe the new figure as it changes.

Summary Questions:
1. What results did you observe? Refer to geometric properties to explain what you observed.

2. If the original figure had been some other type of quadrilateral, would your results have been the same? Explore the problem and explain your prediction.

232   Chapter 10: Introducing Geometry

TECHNOLOGY ACTIVITY 10.3

Right Triangle Relationships

For this activity you will need to use The Geometer's Sketchpad® or a similar geometry exploration software (GES).

- Create a right triangle, being careful to assure that the triangle can be distorted yet remain a right triangle.

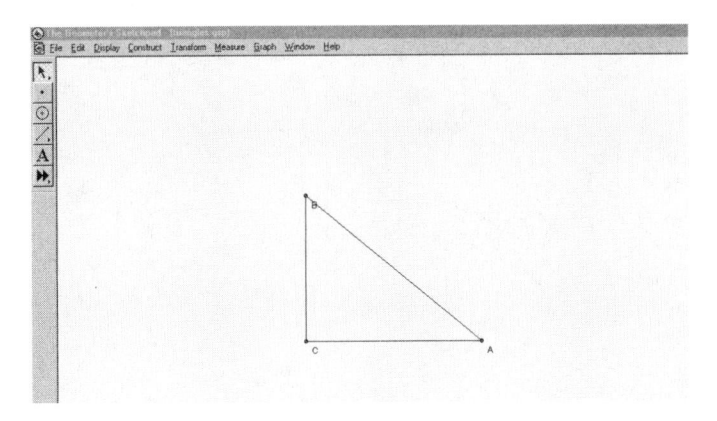

- Upon each of the three sides of the right triangle, create a square. Be sure that the squares are maintained even when the original triangle is distorted.

Because the hypotenuse is neither horizontal nor vertical, creating a square on the hypotenuse is slightly more difficult then on either of the two legs. One way to create a square is to make use of the rotate feature of the GES. To do this, double click on an endpoint of the line segment you want rotated and then click on the line segment. In the diagram above you would double click on Point *A* and click on Line Segment *AB*. Under the **Transform** menu choose **Rotate**. For this example you would want the angle of rotation to be -90^0.

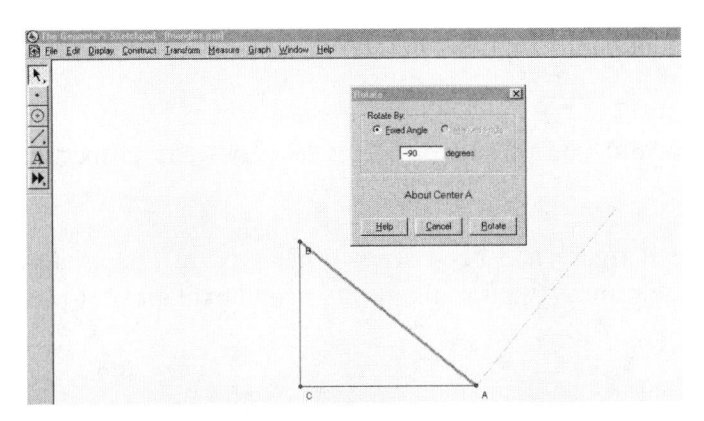

Click on the Rotate button or press enter.

Repeat the process to construct a third side of the square, rotated about Point B. Then using the **Line Tool**, connect the ends of the rotated line segments to enclose the square. Create the other two squares on the legs of the right triangle. Since the sides should be horizontal or vertical lines, you can create line segments and measure their lengths instead of using the rotate feature.

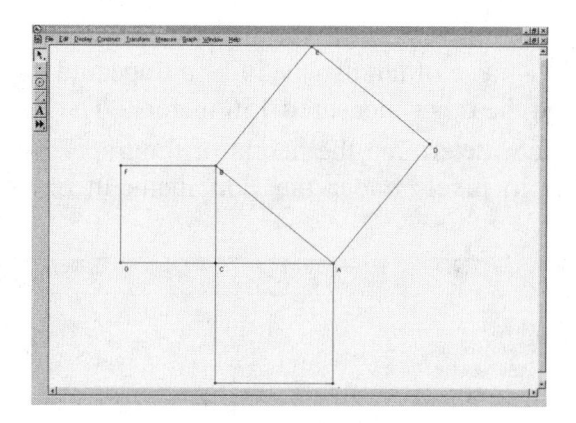

o Calculate the areas of the three squares you created.

Summary Questions:
1. What familiar geometric relationship is revealed in your area calculations?

2. Repeat the steps above with a new right triangle, but this time create an equilateral triangle on each of the three sides of the triangle.

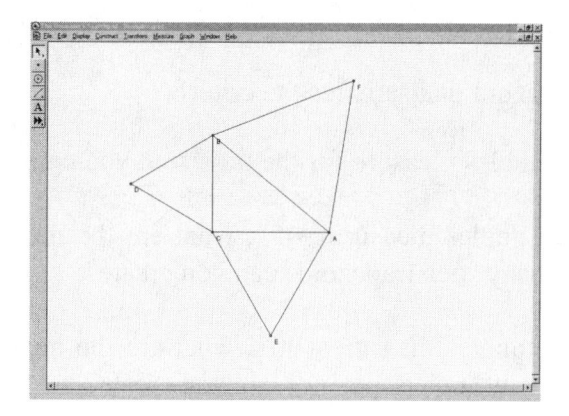

Does the relationship in Question 1 still hold? After exploring this relation in the GES, justify your assertion utilizing the Pythagorean theorem, Triangle Relationships (See page 562 of your text.), and the fact that the area of a triangle is $A = \frac{1}{2}bh$ where b is the base and h is the height. This formula is mentioned on page 529 and will be justified in Section 12.2 of your text.

3. What other shapes can be constructed on the sides of a right triangle and maintain the relationship in Question 1? Use the GES to explore this idea.

TECHNOLOGY ACTIVITY 10.4

Property Lines

For this activity you will need to use The Geometer's Sketchpad® or a similar geometry exploration software (GES).

Nadia and Adam bought a piece of land shaped like a trapezoid. One of the parallel sides measured 388 meters and the other measured 156 meters. The land encompassed 49,232 meters^2. Using your GES, determine the height of the trapezoid formed. Change your distance unit preference to pixels under the Edit menu in order to allow for ease of measurements.

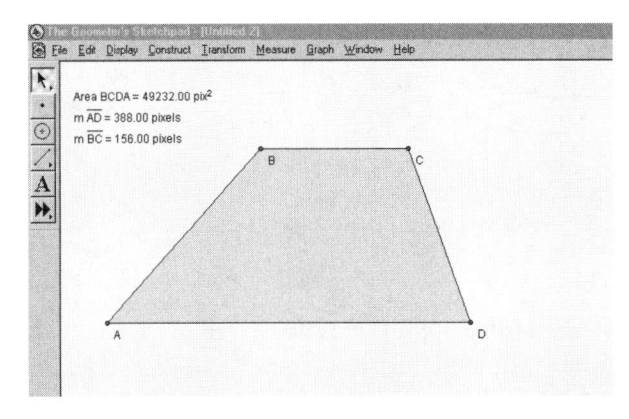

Part A Summary Questions:
1. What strategy did you use to find the height of the trapezoid?

2. Is there only one trapezoid that satisfies the criteria?

3. What do the interior angles measure for the trapezoid you constructed?

4. If one of the interior angles measures $45°$, what are the measurements of the other three angles? How many such trapezoids can you create?

5. If one of the interior angles measures $90°$, what are the measurements of the other three angles? How many such trapezoids can you create?

Suppose Nadia and Adam wish to divide the land into two trapezoidal pieces with the same area, how much fencing would they need to create boundaries?

Part B Summary Questions:
1. What strategy did you use to find the amount of fencing?

2. Is your answer unique? Justify using the GES.

3. Is it possible to divide the land into two triangular pieces with the same area? Justify using the GES.

TECHNOLOGY ACTIVITY 10.5

Triangle Explorer

Go to the Triangle Explorer feature on the Interactiviate disk.

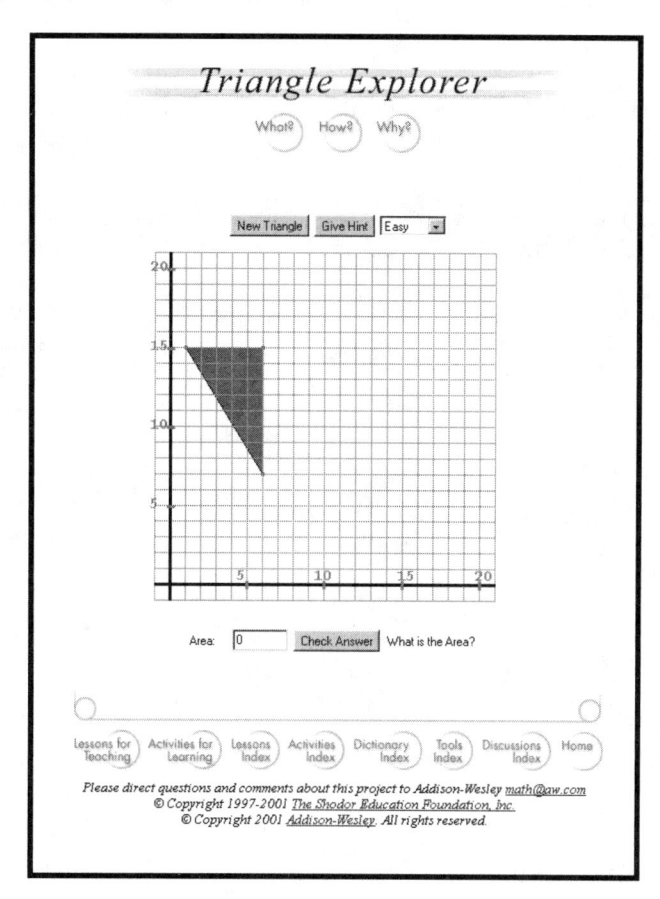

- Perform the activity five times under the Easy level of difficulty.

- Perform the activity five times under the Medium level of difficulty.

- Perform the activity five times under the Hard level of difficulty.

Summary Questions:
1. What are the differences in the triangles in terms of type and orientation on the grid for the three levels of difficulty?

2. In each of the three levels, what does the Hint button reveal? What are the differences among the three levels of difficulty?

3. In the three levels of difficulty, how is the Hint supposed to assist you in obtaining the area of the triangle shown?

TECHNOLOGY ACTIVITY 10.6

Triangles in Triangles

For this activity you will need to use The Geometer's Sketchpad® or a similar geometry exploration software (GES).

Construct a triangle and a line segment parallel to one of the sides and endpoints on the other two sides.

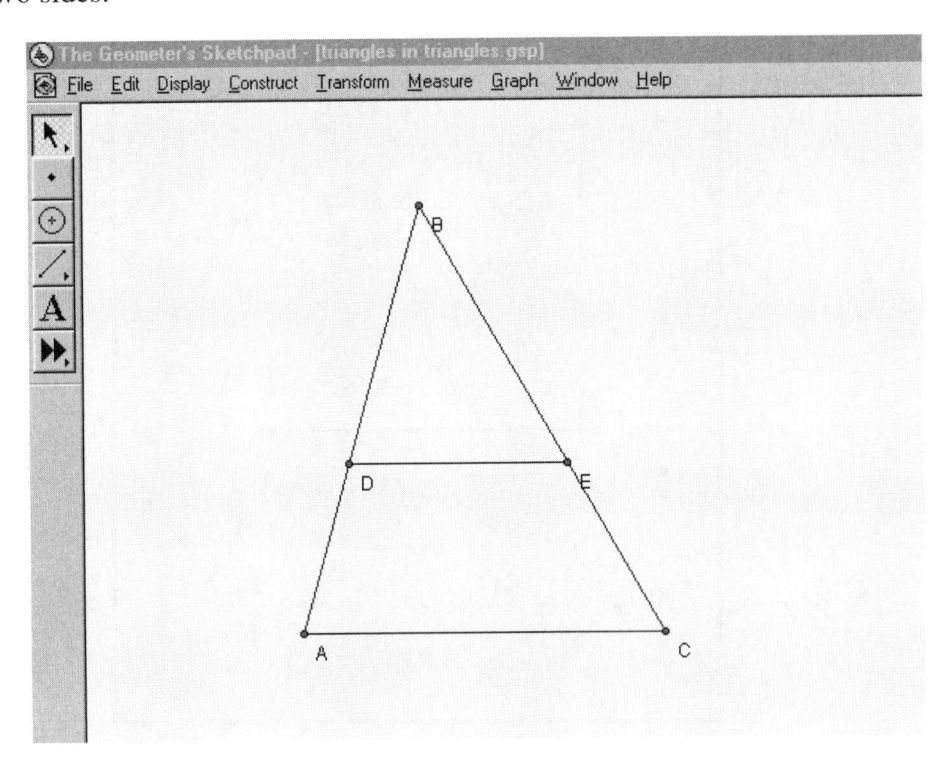

According to the labeling of the above, measure the length of $\overline{AC}$, $\overline{DE}$, $\overline{BD}$, and $\overline{AB}$. Calculate the ratio of $\overline{DE}$ to $\overline{AC}$ and $\overline{BD}$ to $\overline{AB}$.

Summary Questions:
1. What do you notice?

2. Refer to page 355 of your textbook. Would it be correct to state that $\triangle CAB$ is similar to $\triangle BDE$? Explain.

3. Measure the length of $\overline{BC}$. What would you predict the measurement of $\overline{BE}$ to be based upon your observations? Verify your prediction by using the GES to measure the length.

4. If you consider the statement made on page 556 of your textbook regarding congruent triangles, what statement(s) can you make about similar triangles?

5. If you construct a right triangle with an altitude as shown below, what would you predict would be the relationship between altitude $\overline{CD}$, $\overline{AD}$, and $\overline{DB}$? Hint: First state what triangles are similar. Verify your prediction by performing the construction with the GES and measuring the appropriate lengths.

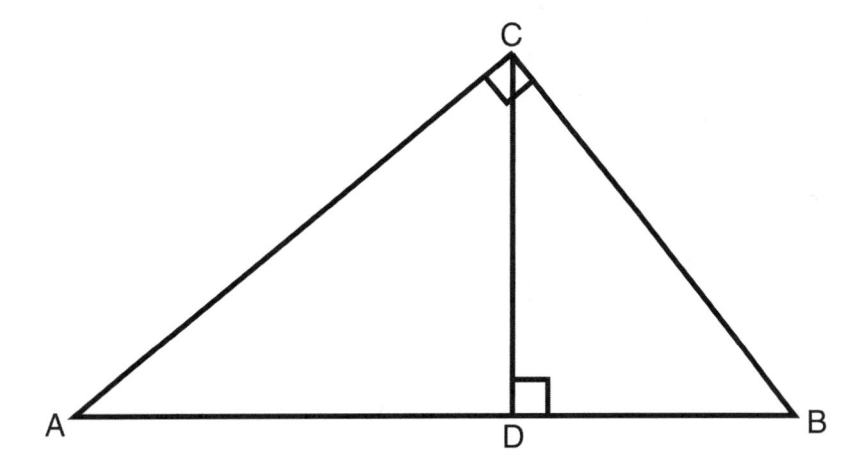

CHAPTER 11: EXTENDING GEOMETRY

INVESTIGATION 11.1

Magnification

Discuss in a small group what methods you would use to easily make a fairly accurate, larger copy of this little cat.

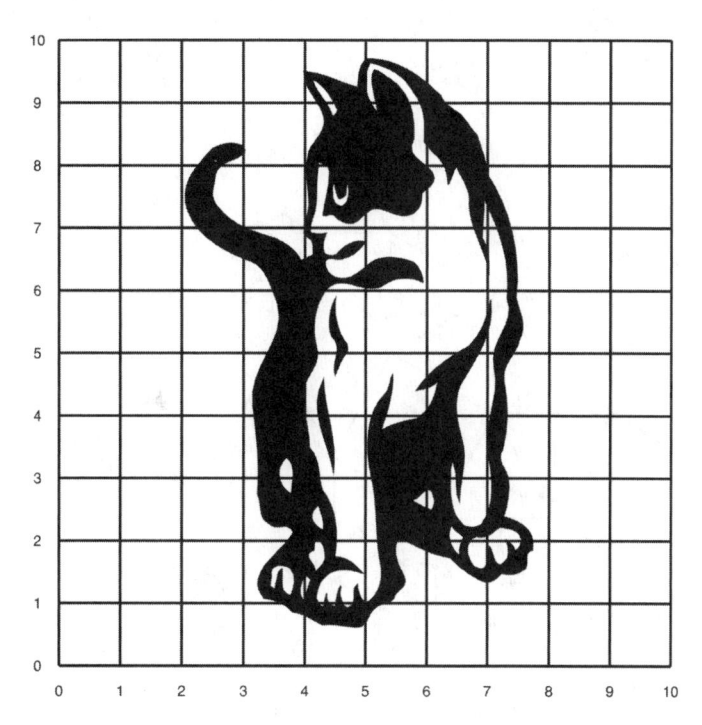

Summary Questions:
1. How could you use a larger grid-size piece of graph paper to make a larger copy? Describe the procedure you could use, and make the copy.

2. How could you use a size transformation to make a larger copy? Describe the procedure you could use, and make the larger copy.

3. Can your group think of any other methods to make a larger copy? If so describe them.

4. How does the procedure that involves using larger grid-size graph paper in Question 1 relate to the idea of size transformation? (Hint: Think about a three-dimensional situation, with the two different grid-size graph paper sheets in different parallel plane.)

5. Which method (the one in Question 1, or 2, or another) do you think is easiest? Which do you think is most accurate?

239

240 Chapter 11: Extending Geometry

INVESTIGATION 11.2

Tessellations from Tessellations

An interior designer didn't like the wallpaper pattern shown below made up of squares and equilateral triangles. Her assistant said, "No problem, we can make it into a tessellation of regular pentagons by drawing lines between the centers of all of the figures in this tessellation, and then repainting." Do you agree that the assistant is correct? Explain.

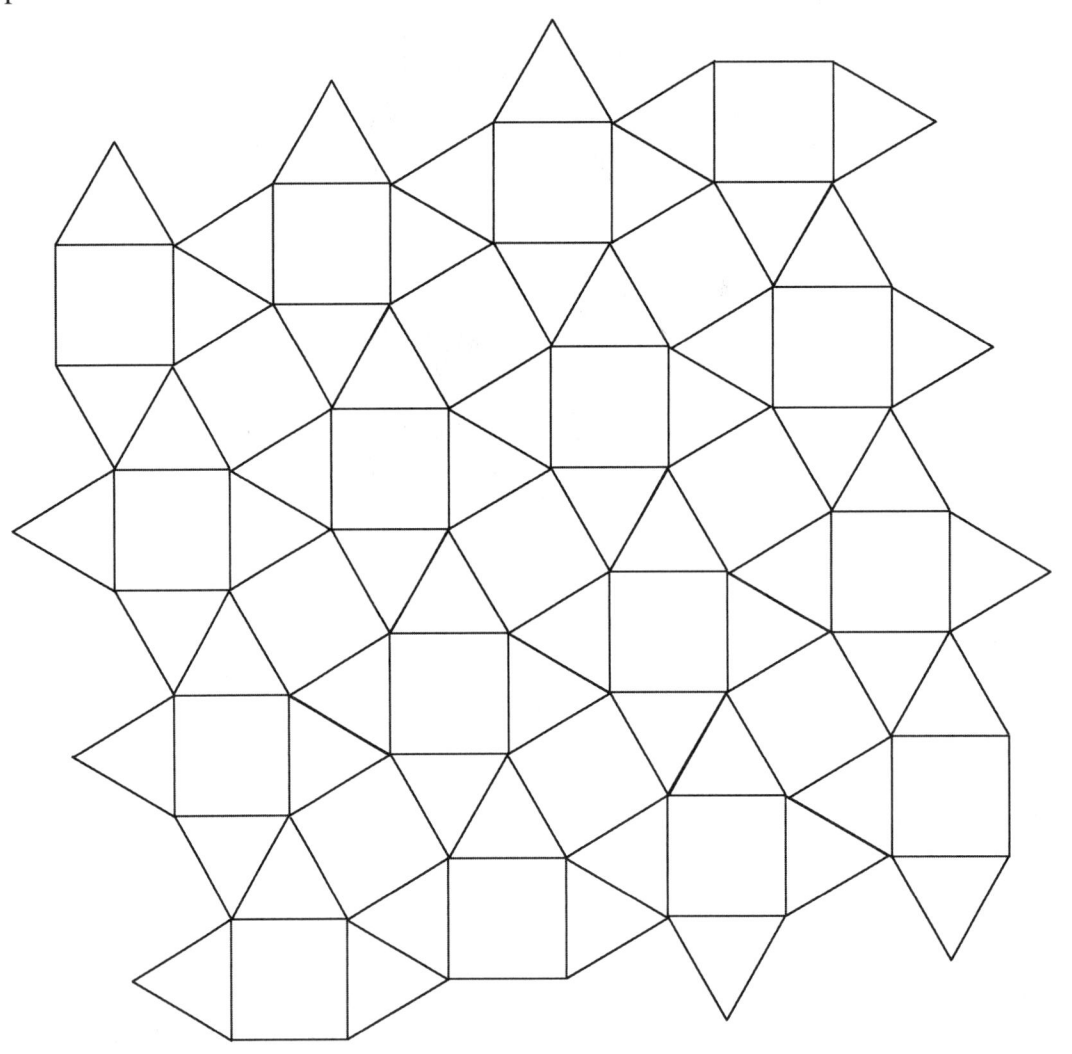

Summary Questions:
1. How would you describe the tessellation formed by joining the centers of all the figures in the above tessellation?

2. Suppose the assistant had suggested that the midpoints of the edges that come together at each vertex be joined to form a new tessellation. How would you describe this tessellation, and how is it like or different from the tessellation you described in Question 1?

INVESTIGATION 11.3

Euler's Formula

One corner of a cube, octahedron, and tetrahedron is shown to be cut off in the figures below. Consider if each corner of a cube, octahedron, and tetrahedron was cut off. Would Euler's formula hold true for the resulting figures?

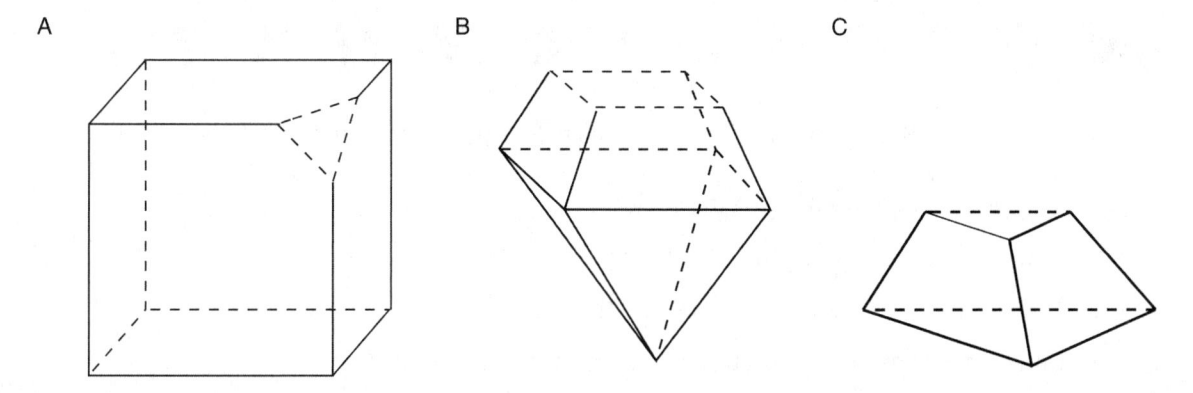

A   B   C

Summary Questions:

1. How many faces, edges, and vertices does a cube have? How would you find, without counting all of them, the number of faces, edges, and vertices of Figure A with all corners cut off?

2. How many faces, edges, and vertices does an octahedron have? How would you find, without counting all of them, the number of faces, edges, and vertices of Figure B with all corners cut off?

3. How many faces, edges, and vertices does a tetrahedron have? How would you find, without counting all of them, the number of faces, edges, and vertices of Figure C with all corners cut off?

4. Does Euler's formula hold true for Figures A, B, and C, when all the corners are cut off? Justify your conclusion.

INVESTIGATION 11.4

Symmetries in the Alphabet

Consider the 26 letters of the English alphabet.

**A B C D E F G H I J K L M
N O P Q R S T U V W X Y Z**

Many of these letters display rotational and/or reflectional symmetries.

Categorize the letters according to the following.

- Letters that have rotational symmetry
- Letters that have reflectional symmetry
- Letters that have both rotational and reflectional symmetry
- Letters that have neither rotational nor reflectional symmetry

Summarize your findings in a Venn diagram like the one below.

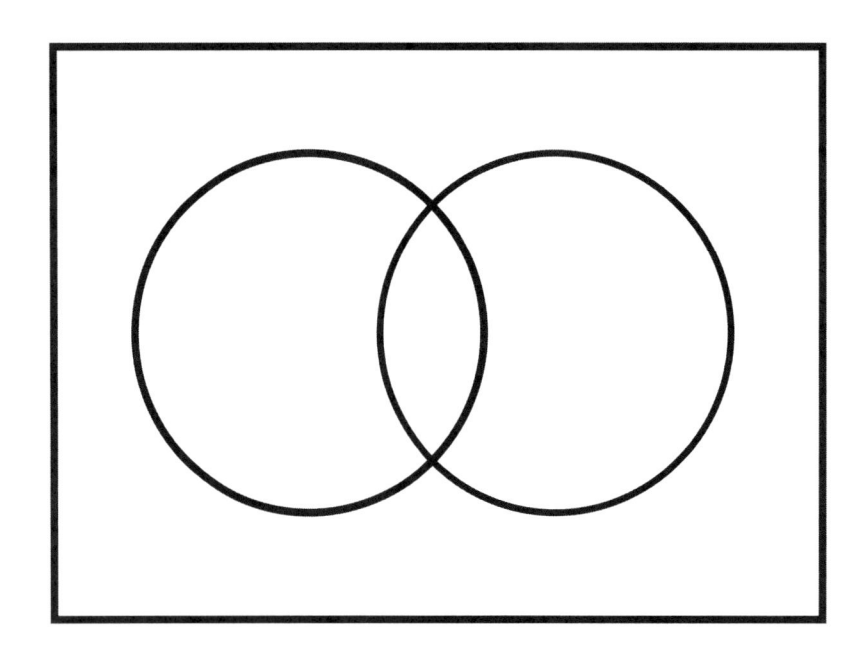

Summary Question:
Of the letters that have reflectional symmetry, how can you further classify them? If you were to place them in a Venn diagram, how many circles would you need?

INVESTIGATION 11.5

Three Short Problems VI

Consider a regular hexagon. Calculate the measure of an interior angle.

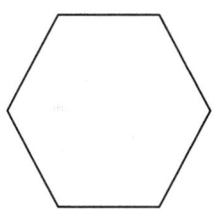

Part A Summary Question:
How could you convince someone that no regular polygon with more than six sides will tessellate the plane?

Consider prisms and pyramids like the ones shown below.

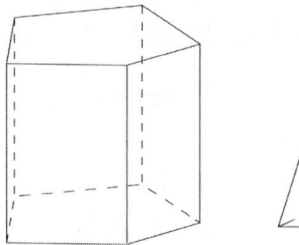

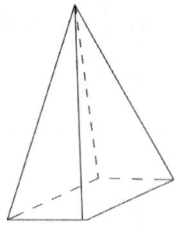

Part B Summary Question:
1. Does Euler's formula hold for these figures? Explain.

2. Do you believe Euler's formula will hold for prisms and pyramids in general? Explain.

Consider the Figure 11.25 on page 617 of your textbook.

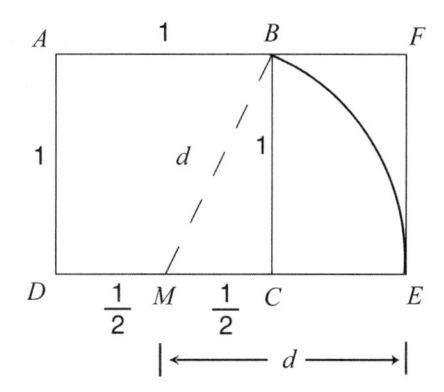

Part C Summary Question:
How would you convince someone that Rectangle *BFEC* is a golden rectangle?

MANIPULATIVE ACTIVITY 11.1

The Box Pattern Report

For this activity you will need several 2-inch by 2-inch squares, tape, and 1-inch graph paper. You can visit http://wps.aw.com/aw_odaffer_mathematic_2 to download graph paper if you choose.

Work in a small group to solve the following problem. Use graph paper to draw the patterns if helpful.

> A box factory manager wanted to use a pattern consisting of six squares, connected only by common sides that could be folded to make a box with a top. The machines could use the pattern more effectively of it had four squares in a line. The manager asked the engineer to find all possible such patterns so he could compare them. His engineer claimed to his assistant that there were only six possible such box patterns. If turned or flipped patterns counted the same as the pattern that was turned or flipped.

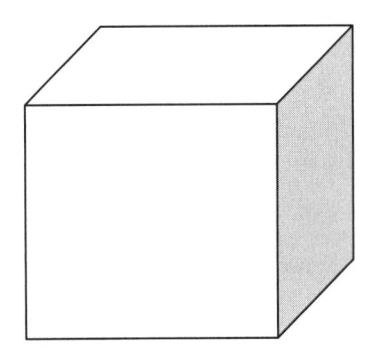

Prepare the engineer's report, including a convincing argument that you have found all possible patterns.

Verify your solution by using taped 2-inch by 2-inch squares or graph paper cut-outs to make models of the patterns you found. Show how the patterns can be folded to make closed top boxes, or cubes.

Summary Questions:
1. What is an example of a six-square pattern with four squares in a row that cannot be folded to form a cube?

2. What is an example of a six-square pattern without four squares in a row that can be folded to form a cube?

MANIPULATIVE ACTIVITY 11.2

Showing Pattern and Cube Symmetry

For this activity you will need several 2-inch by 2-inch squares, tape, scissors, 1-inch graph paper, and some drinking straws. If you wish, you can visit http://wps.aw.com/aw_odaffer_mathematic_2 to download graph paper.

A. Use the results from Manipulative Activity 11.1 to help you find those of the 11 possible different patterns consisting of six squares, connected only by common sides, that can be folded to make a cube and show them on graph paper. Note that turned or flipped patterns are counted the same as the pattern that was turned or flipped.

B. Describe a way of classifying the patterns you found in Part A in terms of their rotational and reflectional properties.

C. From the 11 patterns you found in Part A, select the one that has a line of reflectional symmetry and forms a capital letter of the alphabet. Fold this pattern to make a cube.

D. Cut holes in the cube as needed to put straws through the cube to show three different types of axes of rotational symmetry. Write a description of these different types of axes of rotational symmetry, and identify the degrees of rotational symmetry involved.

Summary Question:
How could you make a model showing the different planes of reflectional symmetry for a cube?

246 Chapter 11: Extending Geometry

MANIPULATIVE ACTIVITY 11.3

Try Some Tiling!

For this activity you need to cut out several copies of an equilateral triangle, a square, a regular hexagon, a regular octagon, and a regular dodecagon. The sides of all of these polygons should be the same length. If you wish, you can visit http://wps.aw.com/aw_odaffer_mathematic_2 to download these figures to be cut out. You will need to print multiple copies.

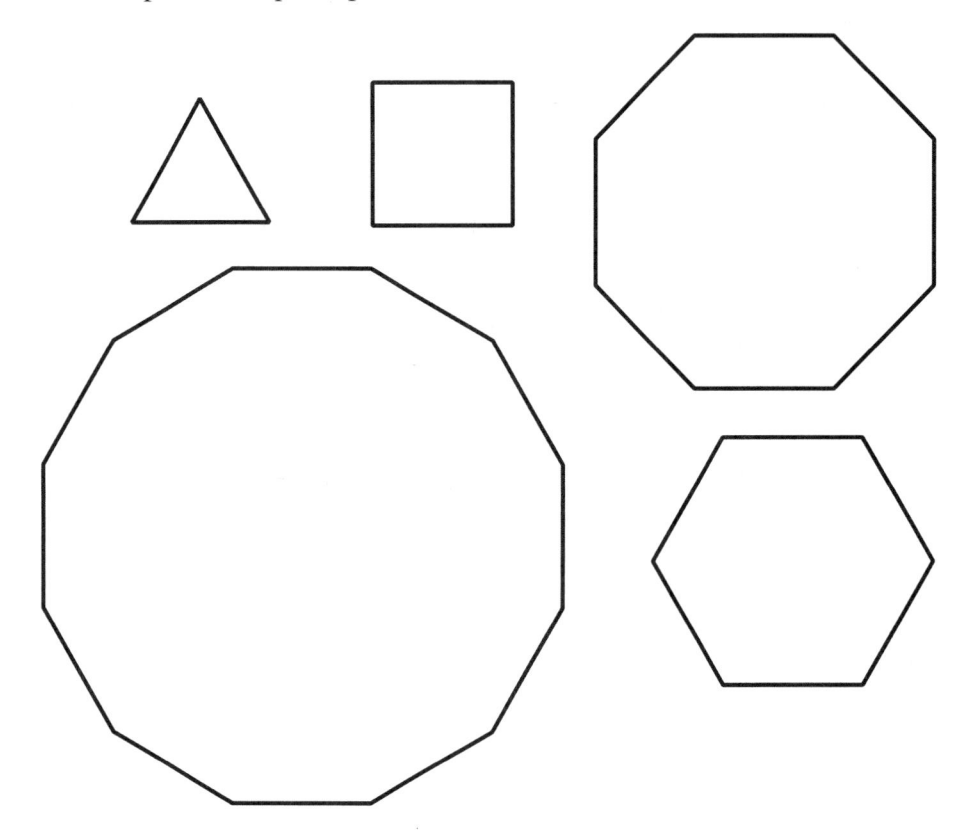

- Find how many ways you can fit three of these polygons around a point. A particular polygon may be repeated in the arrangement. Record each of the arrangements you found.

- Find how many ways you can fit four, five, six, or more of these polygons around a point. Record each of the arrangements you found.

- Devise a notation to describe each arrangement you found.

Summary Question:
Only eight of the arrangements that could be found above can continue to tessellate the plane. How would you go about identifying with eight these are?

MANIPULATIVE ACTIVITY 11.4

Flipping Out!

For this activity you will need a ruler to draw straight lines and measure lengths.

Step A: On a piece of paper draw two parallel lines, r and s, 5 inches apart. Cut out a scalene triangle as shown below. Draw around the triangle to show the original Triangle A.

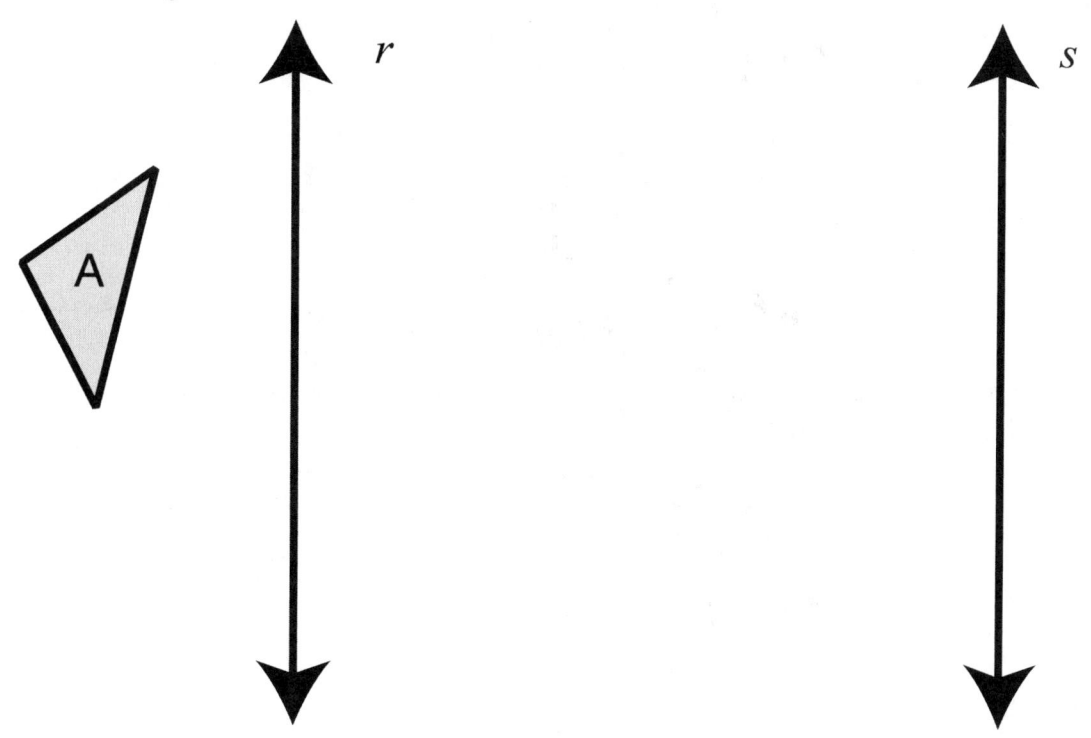

Step B: Construct lines from two vertices of Triangle A, perpendicular to Line r, and reflect Triangle A over Line r. Draw around Triangle A to show the reflection image, Triangle A'.

Step C: Extend the lines in Step B and reflect the triangle over Line s. Draw around the triangle to show the reflection image, Triangle A".

Summary Questions:
1. What transformations would have the same effect as M_r followed by M_s? How does the distance the original triangle was moved compare with the distance between lines r and s? State a possible generalization about this situation.

2. How would you set up a similar situation involving two intersecting lines, r and s, instead of two parallel lines? What generalizations might be true about M_r followed by M_s in this case?

248 Chapter 11: Extending Geometry

MANIPULATIVE ACTIVITY 11.5

Footprints in the Sand

For this activity you will need to copy a 1-inch by 2-inch footprint. You will also need $\frac{1}{2}$ inch by $\frac{1}{2}$ inch square grid paper. Appropriately sized footprints and grid paper are available for download at http://wps.aw.com/aw_odaffer_mathematic_2.

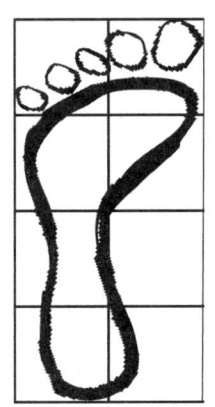

With your grid paper and footprints recreate the following walking path. The drawing below has been scaled to fit on the page.

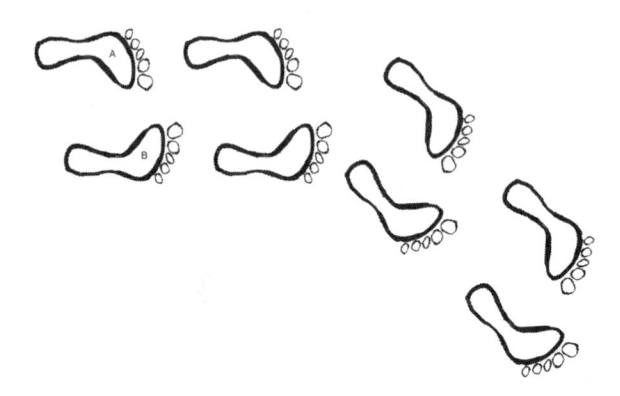

- Starting with Foot A, describe the footprints created as translations, rotations, and/or reflections.

- Starting with Foot B, describe the footprints created as translations, rotations, and/or reflections.

Summary Questions:
1. Did you have to make any assumptions about the path of the footprints? If so, what assumptions did you make?

2. How would you describe the starting position for Foot A? Foot B?

3. What are the differences in the transformations you made between starting Foot A and starting Foot B?

TECHNOLOGY ACTIVITY 11.1

Transformations

For this activity you will need to use The Geometer's Sketchpad® or a similar geometry exploration software (GES). Your software should allow you to plot points and carry out various transformations of geometric shapes on a rectangular grid.

With a coordinate grid visible on your GES, create a Quadrilateral *PINE* with vertices at $P = (2, 2)$, $I = (2, -2)$, $N = (-2, -2)$, and $E = (-2, 2)$. Now plot Point X at $(4, 0)$ and Point Y at $(8, 4)$. To do this, under the **Graph** menu choose **Define Coordinate System**. Under the **Graph** menu you will find **Plot Points**. Separately enter the coordinates for the six points to be plotted. If you right click on any of the points and choose **Properties**, you can label the six points as shown below.

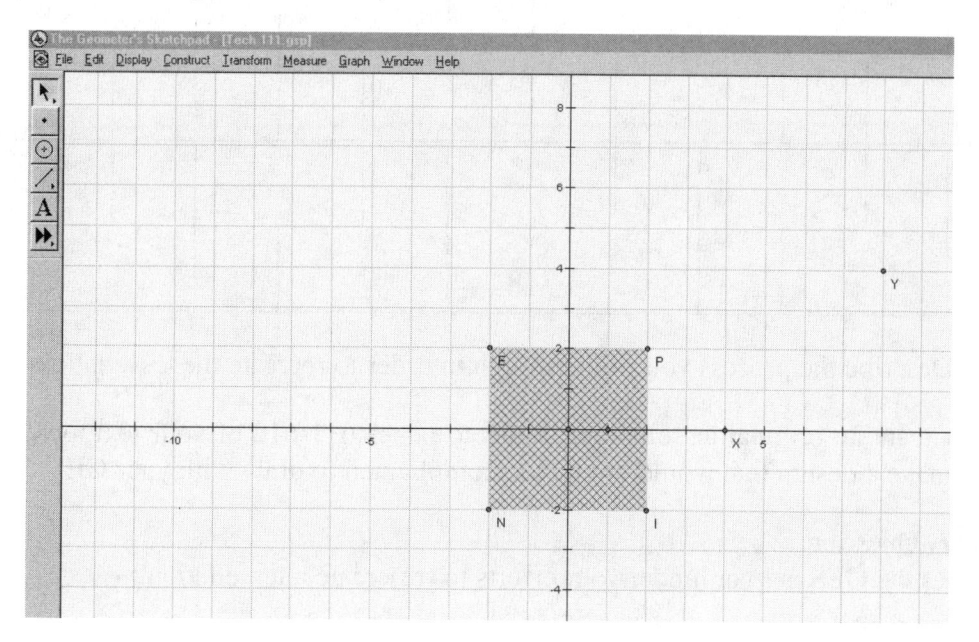

Use the GES to carry out the following transformations of Quadrilateral *PINE*. Sketch or print out the image of each transformation. These transformations are described in Section 11.1 of your textbook. All of the transformations will require features found under the **Transform** menu. You will need to choose points that the quadrilateral will be transformed about. Also, in Part D you will need to utilize the **Mark Mirror** feature under the **Transform** menu.

A. T_{XY}

B. $R_{X, 45°}$

C. M_l, where l contains points X and Y

D. $S_{Y, 0.5}$

Summary Question:
What set of ordered pairs correspond to images of P, I, N, and E under each of the transformations? Refer to geometric properties to explain your results.

TECHNOLOGY ACTIVITY 11.2

Create Your Own Tessellations

For this activity you will need to use The Geometer's Sketchpad® or a similar geometry exploration software (GES).

- Using your GES, recreate the following tessellation.

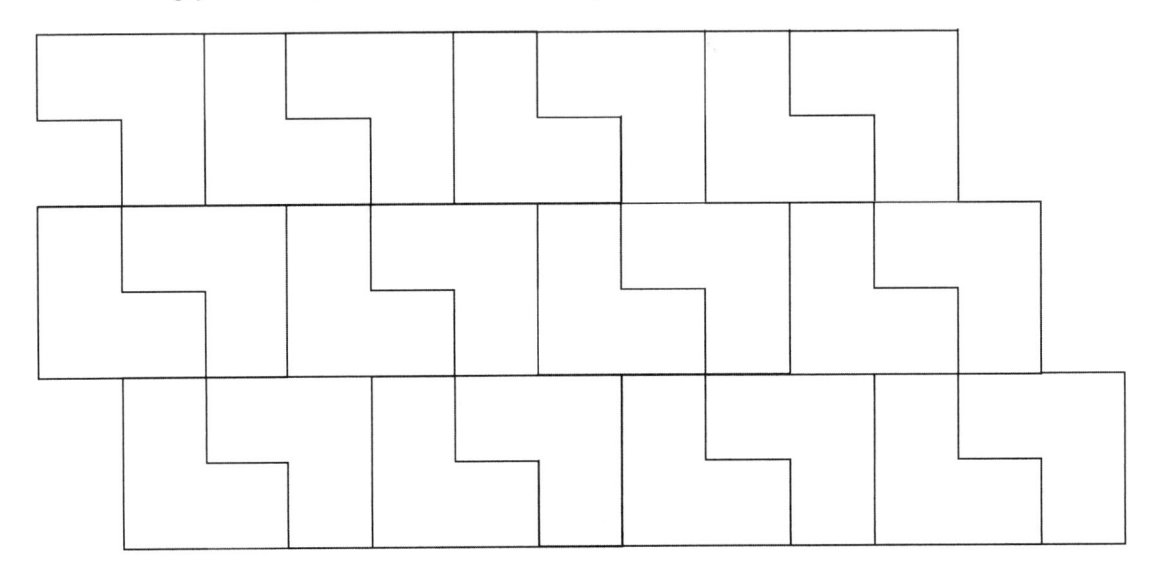

  Describe the process you went through in order to recreate the tessellation.

- Create an original tessellation. Refer to pages 611-612 of your textbook. Try to make a design that would not be too complicated to draw with your GES.

Summary Question:
How does the GES help or hinder your efforts to (re)create a tessellation?

TECHNOLOGY ACTIVITY 11.3

Regular Polygons

For this activity you will need to use The Geometer's Sketchpad® or a similar geometry exploration software (GES).

Refer to pages 617-619 of your textbook.

- With your GES begin with $\left\{\frac{5}{2}\right\}$ and create the first five star polygons of the form $\left\{\frac{n}{2}\right\}$.

- With your GES create the two regular n-gons that exist within each star polygon. The larger of these is the $\left\{\frac{n}{1}\right\}$ polygon within each image and the smaller is the regular polygon formed at the center of the star polygon. The two regular pentagons are shaded in the $\left\{\frac{5}{2}\right\}$ star polygon illustrated below.

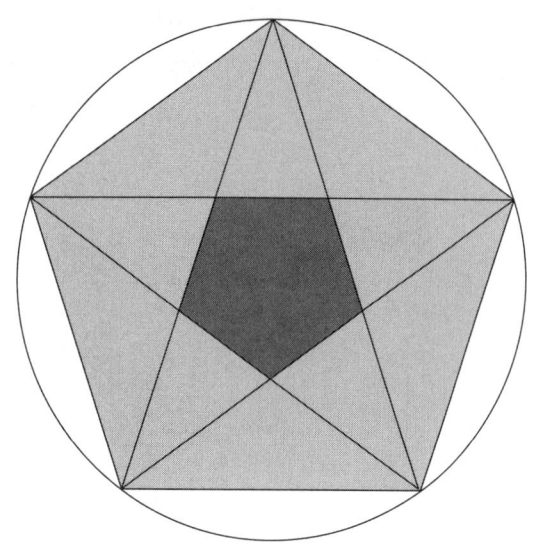

For each star polygon, calculate the ratio of the area of the larger regular polygon to the area of the smaller regular polygon. Use GES to expand and contract the circle for each star polygon and observe how each areas ratio changes. Write a conjecture to described your observations.

Summary Question:
Based on the five cases you have explored, what can you predict about the area ratios for $\left\{\frac{n}{2}\right\}$ star polygons as n grows larger and larger? Explain.

252 Chapter 11: Extending Geometry

TECHNOLOGY ACTIVITY 11.4

Perspective Drawings

For this activity you will need to use The Geometer's Sketchpad® or a similar geometry exploration software (GES).

Using your GES create a perspective drawing of a rectangular solids, similar to the one shown here and on pages 637-638. Here are some suggestions to help you create the drawing.

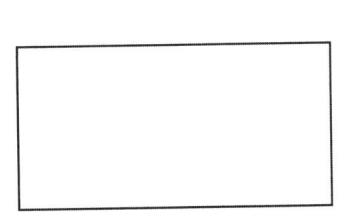

Draw a rectangle for the front of the box.

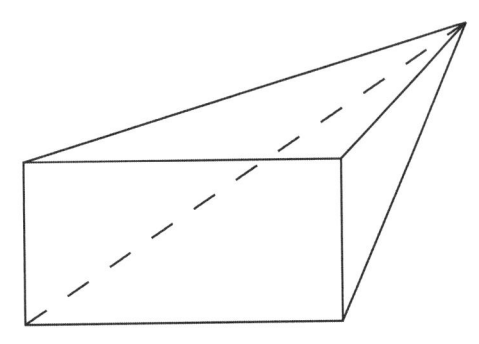

Choose a vanishing point and create segments from each vertex of the rectangle to that point.

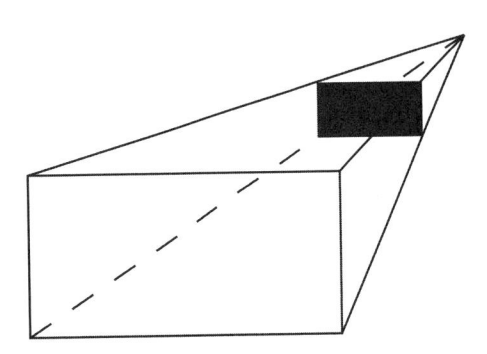

Draw the back of the box by creating segments parallel to corresponding sides of the front of the box.

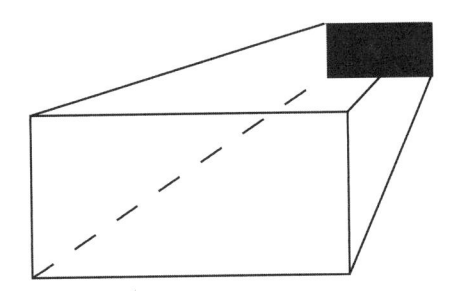

Hide all unnecessary lines.

When you have completed the drawing, use the GES to distort the image. Move the box, elements of the box, or the vanishing point itself.

Summary Question:
How does the drawing change as you distort the elements of the figure? Refer to geometric properties in your explanation.

TECHNOLOGY ACTIVITY 11.5

Tessellate!

Go to the Tessellate! feature on the Interactiviate disk. This program will allow you to create tessellations with a triangle, quadrilateral, and a hexagon.

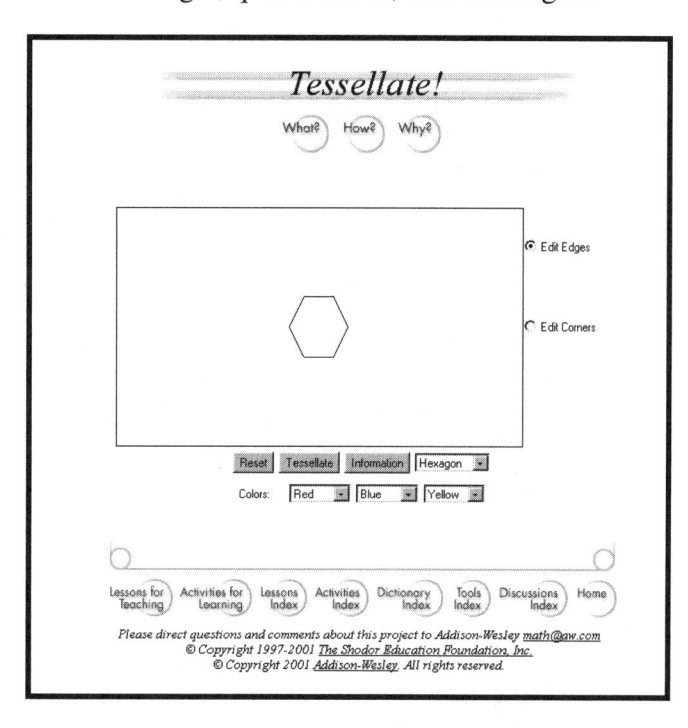

o For the triangle, rectangle, and hexagon options, perform the tessellation activity without altering any of the settings.

Part A Summary Questions:

1. How are the three types of tessellations created? Describe the process of each.

2. The triangle and rectangle mode each are displayed in two colors. Why does the hexagon mode display three colors?

In each of the modes (triangle, rectangle, and hexagon), it is possible to alter the figures to be tessellated. Alter the figures in each of the modes and predict what the tessellation will look like.

Part B Summary Questions:

1. Were you predictions correct? Explain.

2. What is the difference between editing the edges and editing the corners of the figures?

3. Is it possible to create a figure to be tessellated that has more than six sides? If so, how and does it require more colors?

CHAPTER 12: MEASUREMENT

INVESTIGATION 12.1

Analyzing The Concept of Measure

Consider the following statements. Decide which statements are reasonable and which ones are flawed.

A. John Nolan must have a larger floor than mine because the contractor said it would take only 200 tiles to cover my floor and John's contractor said it would take 300 tiles to cover his.

B. It took me five glasses of water to fill my container and seven of the same glasses to fill your container. Your container must be larger than mine.

C. There is a lot more water in Jenin's pond than Beth's pond because Jenin's pond is a much deeper pond.

D. I used the width of my hand to measure the length of both tables. The first table is much longer than the second table.

E. Yesterday it took me two hours to drive from Jacksonville to Savannah and today it took me three hours to drive from Jacksonville to Orlando. Orlando must be 50% further from Jacksonville than Savannah.

F. My dog is about one-half her adult size. My dog is currently 18 inches tall and therefore will be 36 inches tall when she reaches her full-grown size.

Summary Questions:
1. What is wrong with the statements that you identified as being flawed?

2. In order to compare two measurements, what conditions must hold true?

3. Compare your results with a classmate. Did your responses to Questions 1 and 2 agree?

256 Chapter 12: Measurement

INVESTIGATION 12.2

Analyzing the Concept of Area

Find a map of the continental United States. Assume the state of Vermont represents one square unit. Estimate the number of units of area in the following states.

A. Maine

B. Connecticut

C. Florida

D. Texas

E. California

A larger printable version of the following map is available if you visit http://wps.aw.com/aw_odaffer_mathematic_2 .

Describe the procedure you implemented in order to determine the approximate areas of the five states.

Summary Questions:
1. What kinds of questions can the above comparisons answer? Explain your reasoning.

2. What kinds of questions can the above comparisons not answer? Explain your reasoning.

3. How could you determine if your estimations were accurate or not?

INVESTIGATION 12.3

Analyzing Measure of Surface Area and Volume

Consider a ball packed in the following containers. The ball should fit snugly into each of the containers so that it touches all surfaces. Determine the amount of material required to make each container as well as the volume of each.

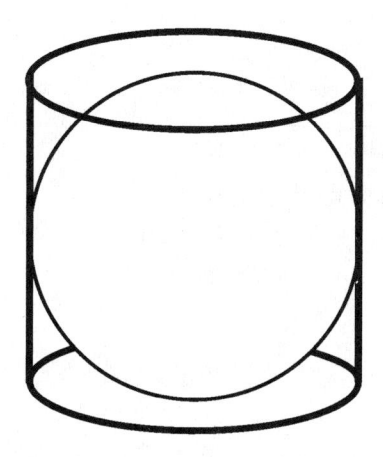

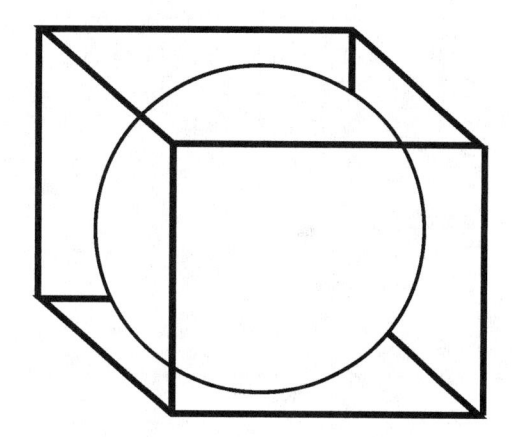

Summary Questions:
1. What assumptions did you need to make in order to make your calculations?

2. Compare the amount of material needed to make each container. Which one took more? Explain.

3. If the two containers were to hold water, which would hold more? Do you need to consider whether the ball is in or out of the container in order to answer this question? Explain.

4. If you had to choose between the two types of containers for packing a ball, which container would you use? Explain your reasoning.

5. The size of the ball was not given. Why is it not necessary to know in order to make comparisons?

258 Chapter 12: Measurement

INVESTIGATION 12.4

Sewing a Flag

In order to make a U.S. flag in correct proportions, the ratio of the width of a flag to its length should be 10 to 19. The following yields this specification along with others pertaining to the stars and stripes.

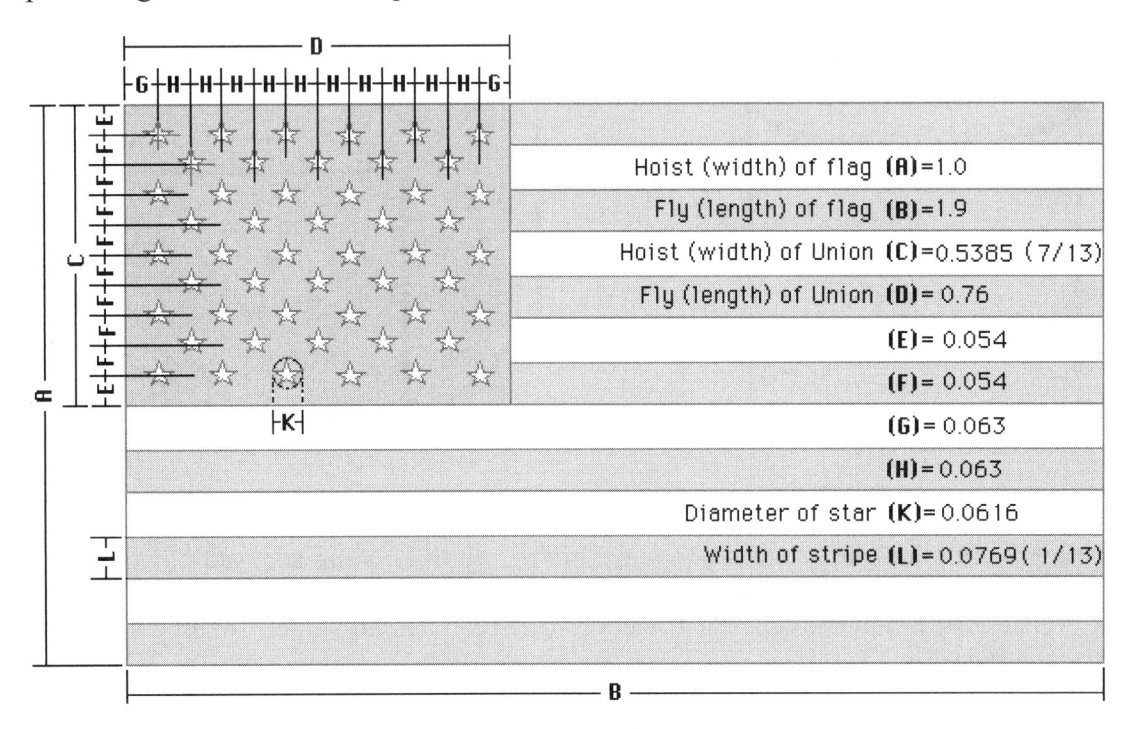

Hoist (width) of flag (A)	=1.0
Fly (length) of flag (B)	=1.9
Hoist (width) of Union (C)	=0.5385 (7/13)
Fly (length) of Union (D)	=0.76
(E)	=0.054
(F)	=0.054
(G)	=0.063
(H)	=0.063
Diameter of star (K)	=0.0616
Width of stripe (L)	=0.0769 (1/13)

Suppose you wanted to make a U.S. flag in the correct proportions and it needed to be 26 feet in width. You want to determine how many square yards will be needed for the red, white, and blue material. For each of the three colors, round your answer up to the next square yard. Assume each star will be cut from a circle that circumscribes it. Also assume the stars are to be sewed upon the blue (Union).

Summary Questions:
1. How many square yards of red material would you need?

2. How many square yards of blue material would you need?

3. How many square yards of white material would you need?

4. Which amount of material, the red, white, or blue was the hardest to determine and why?

INVESTIGATION 12.5

Area and Perimeter Connections

Consider a rectangle that has length and width measurements that are natural numbers. Given the condition, if it is possible to create such a rectangle, then determine length and width measurements for two examples. If it is not possible to create such a rectangle, explain why.

A. The area is 24 square units.

B. The perimeter is 24 units.

C. The area is 15 square units.

D. The perimeter is 15 units.

E. The area is represented by an even natural number.

F. The perimeter is represented by an even natural number.

G. The area is represented by an odd natural number.

H. The perimeter is represented by an odd natural number.

I. The area is represented by a prime number.

J. The perimeter is represented by a prime number.

Summary Question:
Are there any generalizations you can make regarding area, perimeter, and relationships between area and perimeter of a rectangle? If so, what are they? Consider only natural numbers in your generalizations.

260 Chapter 12: Measurement

MANIPULATIVE ACTIVITY 12.1

Determining Volume

For this activity you will need PopCubes®.

Working with a partner, estimate the volume of each figure. Build each figure with your PopCubes® and count the number of cubes. Compare your estimate for each figure to the actual number of blocks to determine the accuracy of your estimate of each volume.

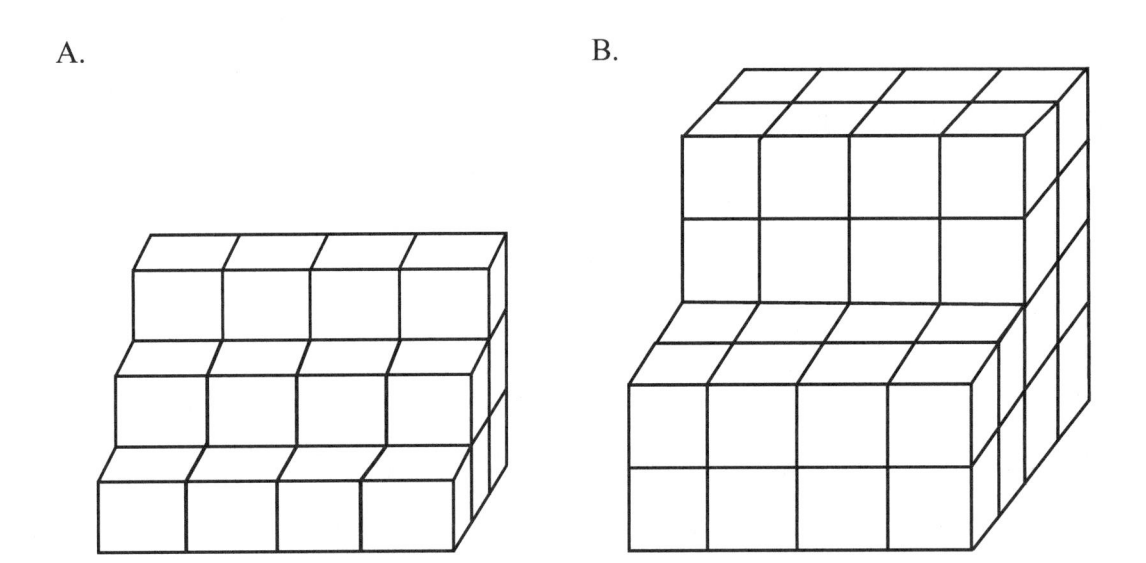

A.

B.

Summary Questions:
1. How did you determine the estimated volumes? Describe the process.

2. What are two different ways that the volumes of the figures can be determined before they are actually constructed?

3. In each of the two examples above, how many of the blocks are not visible in the drawings? Should the sum of the number of visible blocks plus the number of blocks not visible equal the volume of the figure? Explain your reasoning.

MANIPULATIVE ACTIVITY 12.2

Surface Area of Similar Solids

For this activity you will need paper, ruler, and scissors. If you wish you may visit http://wps.aw.com/aw_odaffer_mathematic_2 for pre-measured figures to be cut out for this activity.

A. Cut out a pattern like the one shown below for a square pyramid with a base of 1 inch by 1 inch and lateral faces that are equilateral triangles. Determine the surface area.

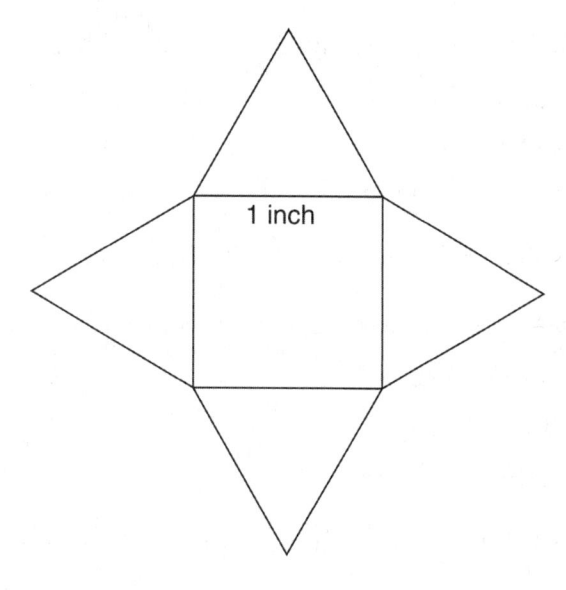

B. Cut out a pattern like the one shown above for a square pyramid with a base of 2 inches by 2 inches and lateral faces that are equilateral triangles. Determine the surface area.

C. Cut out a pattern like the one shown above for a square pyramid with a base of 1.5 inches by 1.5 inches and lateral faces that are equilateral triangles. Determine the surface area.

Summary Questions:
1. When each edge of the square pyramid is doubled, how does the surface area of the pyramid change?

2. When each edge of the square pyramid is 1.5 times its original size how does the surface area of the pyramid change?

3. If a pyramid was made with an equilateral triangle for a base and equilateral triangles for faces 1 inch on a side, and another was made with an equilateral base and faces of 2 inches on a side, would the relationship you discovered in Question 1 still hold true? Explain your reasoning.

MANIPULATIVE ACTIVITY 12.3

Volumes of Solids

For this activity you will need PopCubes®.

Working with at least three partners (You will need four sets of PopCubes®.) you will make rectangular prisms in which one or more dimensions are doubled or tripled. For each of the following parts, compare the affect on the volume of the first solid when the dimensions are altered.

A. Use your PopCubes® to construct rectangular prisms with the following dimensions.
   a. 1 cube × by 2 cubes × 3 cubes
   b. 2 cubes × by 2 cubes × 3 cubes
   c. 3 cubes × by 2 cubes × 3 cubes

   Record the number of cubes in each solid to determine the volume.

B. Use your PopCubes® to construct rectangular prisms with the following dimensions.
   a. 1 cube × by 2 cubes × 3 cubes
   b. 2 cubes × by 4 cubes × 3 cubes
   c. 3 cubes × by 6 cubes × 3 cubes

   Record the number of cubes in each solid to determine the volume.

C. Use your PopCubes® to construct rectangular prisms with the following dimensions.
   a. 1 cube × by 2 cubes × 3 cubes
   b. 2 cubes × by 4 cubes × 6 cubes
   c. 3 cubes × by 6 cubes × 9 cubes

   Record the number of cubes in each solid to determine the volume.

Summary Questions:
1. How does doubling one dimension of a rectangular prism change the volume? Tripling?

2. How does doubling two dimensions of a rectangular prism change the volume? Tripling?

3. How does doubling three dimensions of a rectangular prism change the volume? Tripling?

4. What general statement can you make about your observations in Questions 1 - 3?

MANIPULATIVE ACTIVITY 12.4

Tangram

For this activity you will need to visit http://wps.aw.com/aw_odaffer_mathematic_2 to download a tangram puzzle in an 8-inch by 8-inch square and a tangram puzzle in a 2-inch by 2-inch square.

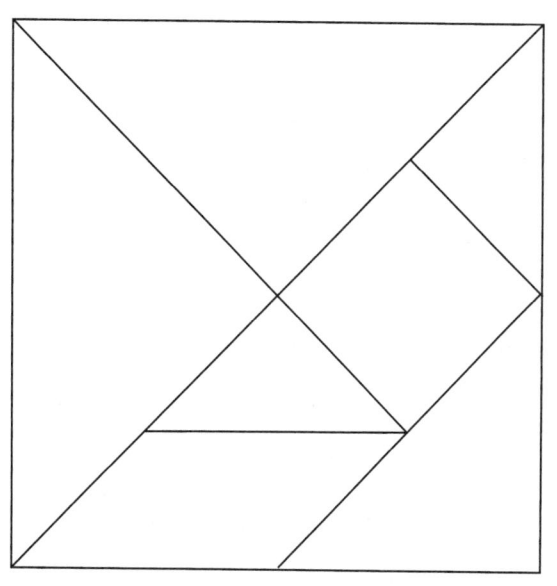

Determine the following for the tangram puzzle in an 8-inch by 8-inch square.

A. The actual areas of each of the figures in the tangram

B. The actual perimeters of each of the figures

Summary Questions:

1. Which two pieces have the same area and the same perimeter? How could you verify this without doing any measurements?

2. Suppose the 8-inch by 8-inch square represented one square unit. What would the areas of the other figures be?

3. Suppose the square in the tangram represented one square unit. What would the areas of the other figures be?

4. Suppose a small triangle in the tangram represented one square unit. What would the areas of the other figures be?

5. Did you use a ruler for either Parts A or B? If so, when and did you really need to?

6. Perform Parts A and B for the tangram puzzle in a 2-inch by 2-inch square and answer Questions 1 - 3. Which responses yield different values? How do they differ? Of those responses that were the same as before, why were they the same?

264 Chapter 12: Measurement

MANIPULATIVE ACTIVITY 12.5

Looking at a Cone from a Different Angle

In Exercises 35 and 36 on page 675 of your textbook, arc lengths and areas of sectors (pie-shaped figures) are explored. Consider the following sector in Figure A.

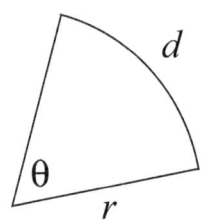

Figure A

To solve for the arc length, we set up a proportion to solve for d.

$$\frac{\theta}{360^0} = \frac{d}{2\pi r}$$

$$d = \frac{\theta r \pi}{180^0}, \text{ where } \theta \text{ is in degrees}$$

Part A Summary Question:
What is a similar proportion that can be set up to determine the area of the sector? What is the formula for the area of a sector?

The formula for the surface area of a cone is justified on page 662 of your textbook by looking at the limiting value of the surface area of an inscribed right pyramid. The formula is $SA = \pi r^2 + \pi r l$, where r is the radius of the circular base and l is the slant height of the cone. In the formula, πr^2 naturally represents the area of the circular base. An alternate approach to justifying the remaining term is to investigate a figure such as the one below in Figure B. On a piece of paper cut out a circle and then cut out a sector. You should be able to now create a cone without a bottom.

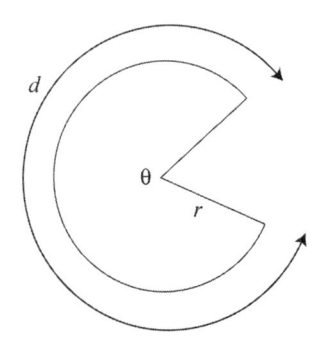

Figure B

Compare Figure B with Figure 12.22 on page 682 of your textbook, using the cone you made as a guide.

Part B Summary Questions:
1. What does the r in Figure B correspond to in Figure 12.22?

2. What does the d in Figure B correspond to in Figure 12.22?

To determine the remaining term in the surface area of a cone formula do the following.

- Set up a proportion to find the area of Figure B. Solve the formula for the area.

- Substitute what the r in Figure B corresponds to in Figure 12.22.

- Set up a proportion to solve for d in Figure B. Substitute what the r in Figure B corresponds to in Figure 12.22.

- Solve the formula for d and set it equal to what the d in Figure B corresponds to in Figure 12.22.

Part C Summary Question:
How can you use what you have found to justify that the remaining term in the surface area of a cone formula is indeed $\pi r l$?

TECHNOLOGY ACTIVITY 12.1

Watering a Garden

For this activity you will need to use The Geometer's Sketchpad® or a similar geometry exploration software (GES).

A triangular garden plot has a sprinkler at each vertex. The sprinklers located at S_1, S_2, and S_3 can be adjusted to vary both the sector of the circle it waters and the radius of that circle. A sample region is shown for the sprinkler at S_2.

Using your GES create a dynamic demonstration of the changes in sprinkler radii. Include triangle and sector measurements in your sketch.

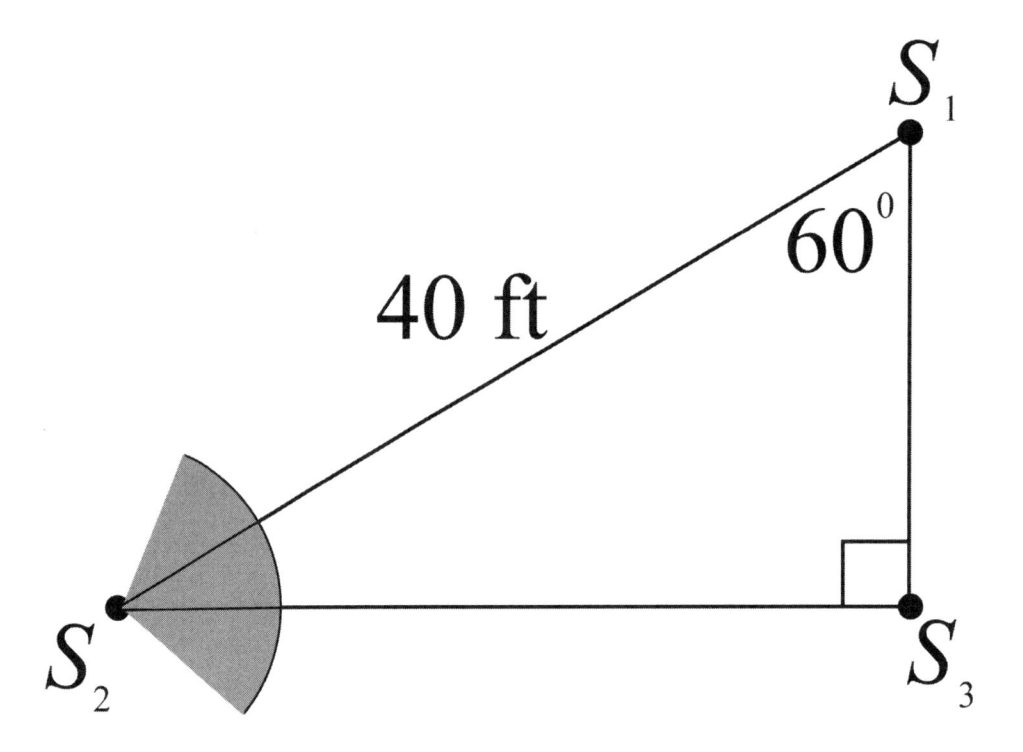

Summary Questions:
1. How should the sprinklers be adjusted so that the entire triangular plot is watered with the least amount of overlap? State the appropriate angle and sprinkling radius for each sprinkler.

2. Would it be more effective to use just one sprinkler, appropriately placed, to water the entire plot? Explain.

TECHNOLOGY ACTIVITY 12.2

Pick a Box

For this activity you will need to use a spreadsheet program such as Excel®. If such a program is not available, a calculator can be used.

An Internet packing supply company offers shipping boxes in various sizes. The following is a price list for their in-stock boxes. All boxes come in bundles of 25.

Size	Price per bundle	Size	Price per bundle
$4'' \times 4'' \times 4''$	$12.18	$6\frac{11}{16}'' \times 4\frac{1}{4}'' \times 10\frac{3}{8}''$	$18.30
$7'' \times 7'' \times 12\frac{3}{8}''$	$14.00	$6'' \times 6'' \times 6''$	$13.27
$9\frac{3}{4}'' \times 9\frac{3}{4}'' \times 14$	$30.25	$8'' \times 8'' \times 7''$	$14.99
$12'' \times 12'' \times 9''$	$23.53	$10'' \times 6'' \times 4''$	$24.61
$12'' \times 12'' \times 12''$	$20.75	$10'' \times 10'' \times 8''$	$18.59
$12'' \times 10'' \times 8''$	$21.30	$10'' \times 8'' \times 6''$	$15.97
$14'' \times 14'' \times 9''$	$39.98	$13\frac{1}{2}'' \times 12\frac{3}{4}'' \times 10\frac{1}{2}''$	$37.98
$16'' \times 15'' \times 10\frac{5}{8}''$	$37.00	$15'' \times 12'' \times 10''$	$36.98
$16'' \times 16'' \times 8''$	$49.00	$15'' \times 15'' \times 15''$	$48.49
$6\frac{1}{2}'' \times 4'' \times 3\frac{3}{4}''$	$13.39	$17\frac{1}{4}'' \times 11\frac{1}{4}'' \times 12\frac{1}{2}''$	$45.00

Place the dimensions of the above twenty boxes into a spreadsheet. For each box, calculate the surface area and volume when closed. Don't figure in any overlap in the top flaps when folded. Also determine the cost per square inch and cubic inch for each box. The cost given in the table is for a bundle, not each box.

Summary Questions:
1. Which box is the best value in terms of surface area?

2. Which box is the best value in terms of volume?

3. Which do you think is more important in determining the value of a box, its surface area or its volume? Explain.

TECHNOLOGY ACTIVITY 12.3

Heron's Formula

For this activity you will need to use The Geometer's Sketchpad® or a similar geometry exploration software (GES).

A formula to determine the area of a triangle give the lengths of the three sides is named after the Greek mathematician Heron. The formula states that given a triangle with sides a, b, and c, the area is given by

$$A = \sqrt{s(s-a)(s-b)(s-c)}, \text{ where } s = \frac{a+b+c}{2}.$$

Using your GES construct an acute, right, and obtuse triangle. For each of the triangles, use Heron's formula to determine the area.

Part A Summary Questions:
1. How could you use Heron's formula to determine the three altitudes of a triangle if you are only given the measures of the three sides?

2. In the formula, what does $s = \frac{a+b+c}{2}$ represent?

3. How could you justify that no factor under the radical in Heron's formula will result in a negative value?

In Section 12.2 of your textbook, the area of an equilateral triangle is derived to be $A = \frac{\sqrt{3}\,s^2}{4}$, where s is the length of each side. Use Heron's formula to verify this formula.

Part B Summary Question:
What assumption(s), if any, are made in the proof given for the formula of the area of an equilateral triangle?

TECHNOLOGY ACTIVITY 12.4

Shape Explorer

Go to the Shape Explorer feature on the Interactiviate disk. This program will draw different shapes that are made up of squares. There are fourteen levels and each level (except the first) offers a variety of shapes.

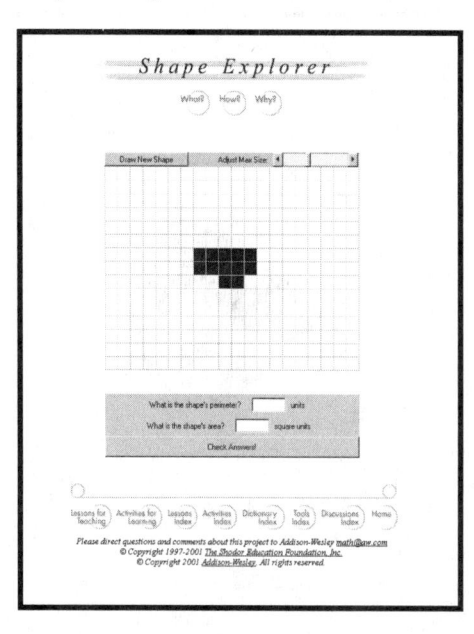

For each of the fourteen levels do the following.

- Draw at least one of the figures that is generated. It may be helpful to draw these figures on grid paper.
- Determine the perimeter and area of each and check your answers with the software.
- Determine how many grid lines intersect on the boundary of the figure and how many are in the interior.
- Draw a rectangle around each of your figures so that no part is outside your rectangle. Make as small as rectangle as possible.

Summary Questions:

1. Is there a relationship between the perimeter of your figure and the number of grid-line intersections on the boundary and interior? If so, what is it?

2. Is there a relationship between the area of your figure and the number of grid-line intersections on the boundary and interior? If so, what is it?

3. How could you use the rectangle you created around each of the figures to determine the area/perimeter of the figure? In which figures would it be helpful to create such a rectangle?

TECHNOLOGY ACTIVITY 12.5

Surface Area and Volume

Go to the Surface Area and Volume feature on the Interactiviate disk. This program will create and manipulate rectangular are triangular right prisms.

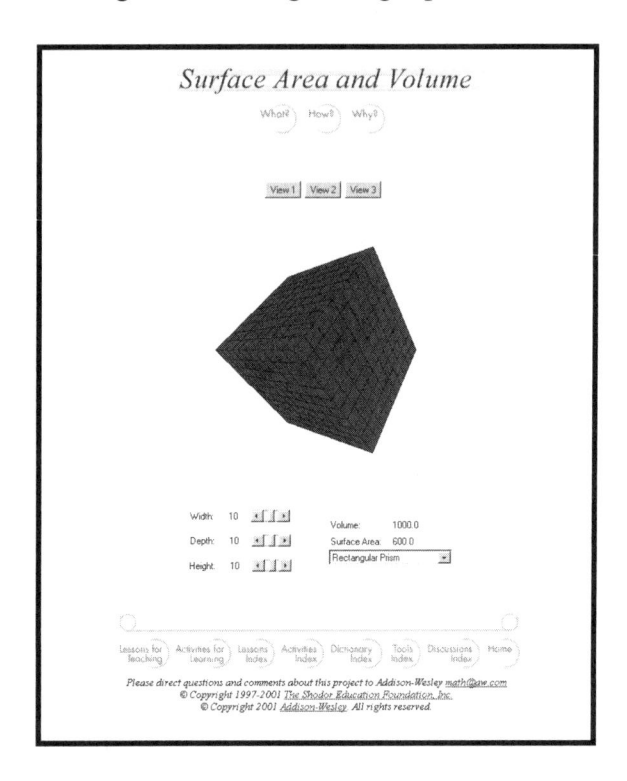

Create four sets of rectangular and triangular prisms. Each of the prisms within a set should have the same width, depth, and height measurements. Draw these prisms on paper and record the measurements, volume and surface area.

Summary Questions:
1. How are the width, depth, and height measurements indicated on the figure for the rectangular and triangular prisms? You may choose to draw a diagram.

2. Within a set is there a relationship between the volume of the rectangular prism and the triangular prism? If so, what is it?

3. Within a set is there a relationship between the surface area of the rectangular prism and the triangular prism? If so, what is it?

4. The triangular bases of the triangular right prisms are all isosceles triangles. Would the relations you found in the responses to Questions 2 and 3 still hold true if the triangular bases were not isosceles?

CHAPTER 13: EXPLORING IDEAS OF ALGEBRA AND COORDINATE GEOMETRY

INVESTIGATION 13.1

Garden Expressions

One-foot square tiles are to be placed around the edges of a square garden. Let s be the length of each side of the garden in feet and n be the number tiles needed all together.

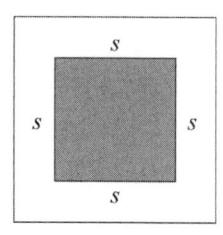

A. Write an equation that shows how the number of tiles, n, is related to the side length of the garden s.

B. Find a different, but equivalent, way to express this relationship. Show why the two equations are equivalent.

Below is another drawing of the garden shown above with the 1-foot tiles in each corner shown.

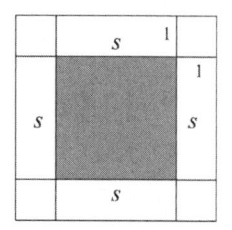

Each equation below is a correct representation for the relationship between the length of each side of the garden and the number of tiles needed to surround the garden. Draw a picture and explain why *each* equation makes sense.

C. $s + s + s + s + 4 = n$

D. $4(s + 1) = n$

E. $4(s + 2) - 4 = n$

F. $2s + 2(s + 2) = n$

Summary Question:
What does it mean for two expressions to be equivalent?

272 Chapter 13: Exploring Ideas of Algebra and Coordinate Geometry

INVESTIGATION 13.2

The Ups and Downs of Life

These graphs show how the amount of punch in a bowl at a party changes over the course of the evening. Write an explanation of what might have occurred to produce the relationship shown.

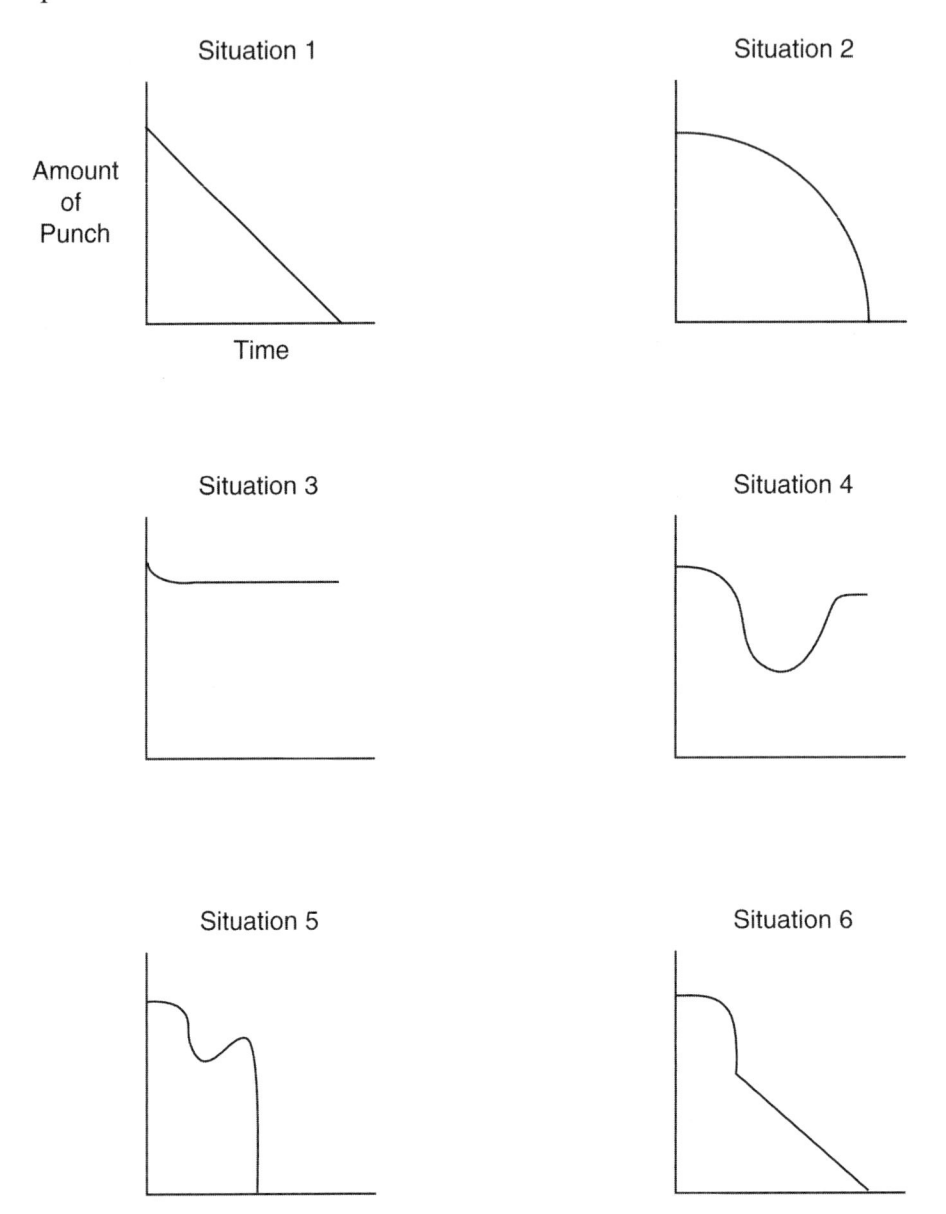

Situation 1

Amount of Punch

Time

Situation 2

Situation 3

Situation 4

Situation 5

Situation 6

Summary Questions:
1. What does the horizontal line mean on the graphs above?

2. What does a nearly vertical line mean on the graphs above?

3. What does a steep line mean on these graphs?

INVESTIGATION 13.3

Seeing Double

For this activity you will need grid paper. If grid paper is not available, you can visit http://wps.aw.com/aw_odaffer_mathematic_2 for a download.

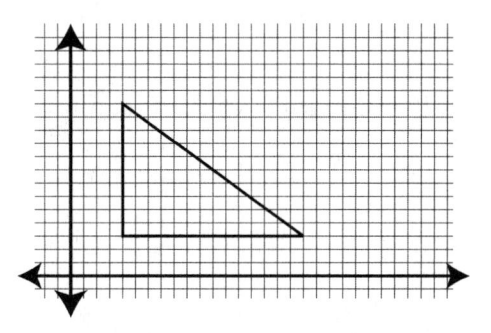

Draw a right triangle on a coordinate grid. Write the coordinates of each vertex on the grid. Double each coordinate. For example, coordinate (a, b) becomes $(2a, 2b)$. Draw the enlarged triangle represented by the new coordinates.

  A. How do the angles in the original triangle compare to the angles in the enlarged triangle?
  B. What is the length of each side of the original triangle? The enlarged triangle?
  C. What is the area of the original triangle? The enlarged triangle?

Draw a rectangle on a coordinate grid. Write the coordinates of each vertex on the grid. Double each coordinate. Draw the enlarged rectangle represented by the new coordinates.

  D. How do the angles in the original rectangle compare to the angles in the enlarged rectangle?
  E. What is the length of each side of the original rectangle? The enlarged rectangle?
  F. What is the area of the original rectangle? The enlarged rectangle?

Summary Questions:
1. What patterns do you see when comparing the angles in the original figure to the angles in the enlarged figure?

2. What patterns do you see when comparing the side lengths of the original figure to the side lengths of the enlarged figure?

3. What patterns do you see when comparing the area of the original figure to the area of the enlarged figure?

4. If you wanted to justify that the patterns you found for Questions 2 and 3 were valid for *any* triangle/rectangle, how would you do it?

INVESTIGATION 13.4

The Cat's-Eyes Have It

There are two piles of cat-eye marbles. The task is to find the number in each pile for the given situation.

For each situation,

- let *n* represent the number of marbles in the first pile.
- write an expression in terms of *n* for the number of marbles in the second pile.
- write an equation showing equivalent expressions for the total number in the two piles.
- solve the equation and check.

A. There are 85 marbles in the two piles. The second pile has 17 more marbles than the first.

B. There are 100 marbles in the two piles. The second pile has 28 fewer marbles than the first.

C. There are 66 marbles in the two piles. The second pile has twice as many as the first.

D. There are 90 marbles in the two piles. The second pile has half as many as the first.

E. There are 37 marbles in the two piles. The second pile has 5 less than twice the number in the first pile.

Summary Questions:

1. In which situation(s) was the number in the second pile given as an addition expression?

2. In which situation(s) was the number in the second pile given as a subtraction expression?

3. In which situation(s) was the number in the second pile given as a multiplication expression?

4. In which situation(s) was the number in the second pile given as an expression involving more than one operation?

Make up two statements like those above. Exchange them with a classmate to write and solve the equations.

INVESTIGATION 13.5

Changing Population Densities

Use any type of calculator for this activity.

Here is some information about ten states with the highest population according to the 2000 Census.

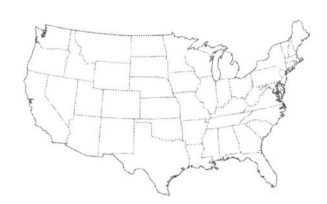

State	Population Estimate	Land Area	Population Density
California	33,871,648	163,696 sq. mi.	
Texas	20,851,820	268,581 sq. mi.	
New York	18,976,457	54,556 sq. mi.	
Florida	15,982,378	65,755 sq. mi.	
Illinois	12,419,293	57,914 sq. mi.	
Pennsylvania	12,281,054	46,055 sq. mi.	
Ohio	11,353,140	44,825 sq. mi.	
Michigan	9,938,444	96,716 sq. mi.	
New Jersey	8,414,350	8,721 sq. mi.	
Georgia	8,186,453	59,425 sq. mi.	

A. Determine the population density for each state.

B. Determine the number of people that would have to move from one state to another in order for Pennsylvania and Ohio to have the same population density.

C. Determine the percentage of people that would have to move from one state to another in order for Texas and New Jersey to have the same population density.

Summary Questions:
1. How did you determine the number of people in Parts B and C?

2. How did you determine which state the people were moving from?

3. How could you generalize your procedure Parts B and C for any two states? For the 10 given states?

MANIPULATIVE ACTIVITY 13.1

Expression Strips

For this activity you will need 5 *x*-strips and 20 unit squares. A download is available at http://wps.aw.com/aw_odaffer_mathematic_2.

The strip below represents an unknown quantity, *x*. It is called an *x*-strip. The small square represents 1 unit.

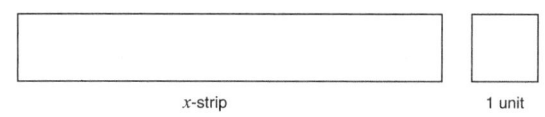

x-strip   1 unit

This arrangement of strips and squares shows $(3 \cdot x) + (3 \cdot 1)$.

This arrangement of strips and squares shows $3 \cdot (x + 1)$.

Use the *x*-strips and unit squares to show each expression. Draw a picture of what you are showing.

         A. $(2 \cdot x) + (2 \cdot 3)$ B. $2 \cdot (x + 3)$
         C. $(4 \cdot x) + (4 \cdot 1)$ D. $3 \cdot (x + 4)$
         E. $(2 \cdot x) + (4 \cdot x)$ F. $x \cdot (3 \cdot x)$
         G. $(3 \cdot x) + (2 \cdot x)$ H. $2 \cdot (x + 3) + 4$

Summary Questions:
1. What property is illustrated with the two arrangements at the top of the page?

2. How can you use the strips and units to show that $3x + 2 = 2 + 3x$?

3. Make up a strip and unit arrangement and, on separate paper, record the algebraic expression it represents. Exchange the strip arrangement with a classmate. Write the algebraic expression represented by your classmate's strip arrangement. Does it match the algebraic expression he or she wrote? If not, why not?

MANIPULATIVE ACTIVITY 13.2

Solving Equations with Cubes

For this activity you will need PopCubes®.

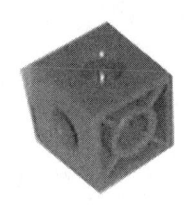

Working with at least three partners (You will need four sets of PopCubes®.) choose three different colors, 20 of each color. Use the PopCubes® to solve each of the following problems. If needed, you may substitute for the suggested colors.

A. There are 14 cubes in all. There are 2 more blue cubes than green cubes. There are 3 more green cubes than red cubes. How many cubes of each color are there?

B. There are 8 cubes in all. There is 1 fewer blue cube than red cubes. There are 2 fewer green cubes than blue cubes. How many cubes of each color are there?

C. There are 20 cubes in all. There are the same number of blue cubes and green cubes. There are 2 fewer blue cubes than red cubes. How many cubes of each color are there?

D. There are 4 times as many red cubes as green cubes. There is 1 fewer blue cube than red cubes. There are 17 cubes in all. How many cubes of each color are there?

E. There are half as many blue cubes as green cubes. There are 16 cubes in all. There is 1 more red cube than green cubes. How many cubes of each color are there?

F. There are one-fourth as many red cubes as blue cubes. There are 2 fewer green cubes than red cubes. There are 28 cubes in all. How many cubes of each color are there?

Summary Questions:
1. How did you solve each problem?

2. Did you use guess and check? Why or why not?

3. What reasoning did you use?

MANIPULATIVE ACTIVITY 13.3

Bouncing Ball Experiment

For this activity you will need a small ball to bounce, a meter stick or measuring tape, one sheet of graph paper, and a straight edge.

A. One person drops a ball from a certain height measured to the nearest centimeter. Another person uses the meter stick or measuring tape to estimate the height of the bounce to the nearest centimeter. Drop the ball from the same height four times and use the average of the four bounces as the true bounce height.

B. Make a table to record drop height and (average) bounce height. Record the data from Step A in the table.

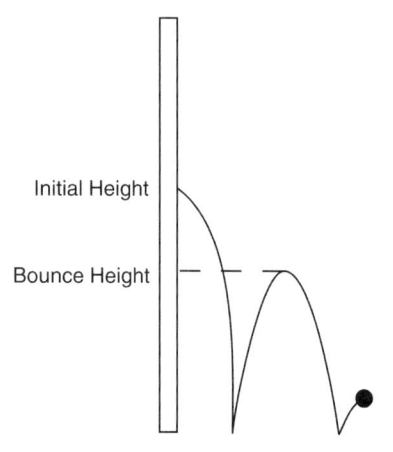

C. Repeat dropping the ball and measuring the bounce height using at least five different heights. Record the data for each drop height in your table.

D. Plot the data on a coordinate graph using the drop height on the horizontal axis and the bounce height on the vertical axis.

E. Use a straight edge and draw a line that passes as close to as many of the points as possible.

F. Find the equation of this line using any technique you choose.

G. Test your equation.
   o Choose a height from which to drop the ball.
   o Use the equation to predict the bounce height.
   o Drop the ball and measure the bounce height to test your prediction.

Summary Questions:
1. Do you think you can get your ball to bounce to any height? Explain.

2. Would the equation of the line be the same for all balls? Explain.

MANIPULATIVE ACTIVITY 13.4

Towers of Brahma

The Towers of Brahma (or the Towers of Hanoi or the Reve's puzzle) is an ancient puzzle from the Far East. In an ancient city, so the legend goes, monks in a temple had to move a pile of 64 sacred disks from one vertical diamond needle to another. There were basically only two rules

- The disks were fragile so only one could be carried at a time.
- A disk could not be placed on top of a smaller, less valuable disk.

In the temple there was only one other location besides the destination and starting place sacred enough for a pile of disks to be placed there. Using this intermediate location, the monks began to move disks around from the original pile to the pile at the new location, always keeping the largest on the bottom, smallest on the top. According to the legend, monks made one move each day and when they made the final move to complete the new pile in the new location, the temple would turn to dust and the world would end.

If you visit http://wps.aw.com/aw_odaffer_mathematic_2 you will find a download that contains nine sizes of "disks" and three "needles".

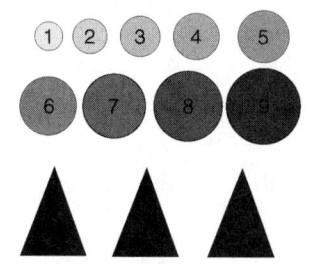

Using these disks, discover the formula for the minimum number of moves in terms of the number of disks. To do this, you will want to examine simpler problems.

- Working with a partner start with 1 disk, then 2 disks, then 3 disks and determine the minimum number of steps to complete the task.
- Keep track of these outcomes in a table. Hint: Each of these should be able to be performed in less than 8 moves.
- Based upon your observations, how many moves do you believe are required for 4 disks? Try performing the task with 4 disks to verify your results. Hint: It should be less than 16 moves.

Summary Questions:

1. What is the formula for the number of moves required in terms of the number of disks, n?

2. Three different types of functions are discussed in Section 13.1 of your textbook. What kind of function does this most resemble?

3. Suppose the Monks were allowed to move 10,000 disks per *second*. How long would it take the monks to finish their task?

MANIPULATIVE ACTIVITY 13.5

Flatten that Circle

For this activity you will need two pieces of string cut to about 11 centimeters each. We will want the actual length to be 10 cm when the string is tied. You will also need two pushpins, and two pieces of 1-centimeter grid paper. A download is available at http://wps.aw.com/aw_odaffer_mathematic_2 for the grid paper. You may also choose to obtain a piece of cardboard from a discarded box in order to have something for the pushpins to go into.

In Section 13.4 of your textbook a circle is defined to be the set of all points in a plane, (x, y), the same distance from a given point.

Tie the ends together on one of your pieces of string. Place a pushpin at origin of the grid paper and loop the string around the pushpin. With a pencil, stretch the string out. If properly made, the pencil should be able to cross the points $(0, 5)$, $(5, 0)$, $(0, -5)$, and $(-5, 0)$ when you trace a circle out. Find some points on the grid that the circle crossed through and verify that they satisfy the *Circle Equation Theorem-Center at the Origin* on page 762 of your textbook.

Part A Summary Questions:
1. Did the points you found on the circle satisfy the theorem? Why or why not?

2. What is the difference between the theorem on page 762 of your textbook and the one on page 763?

Now with the other string, tie each end to each of the two pushpins. The amount of string between the two pins should be 10 cm. Place one pin at $(-4, 0)$ and the other at $(4, 0)$ as shown below.

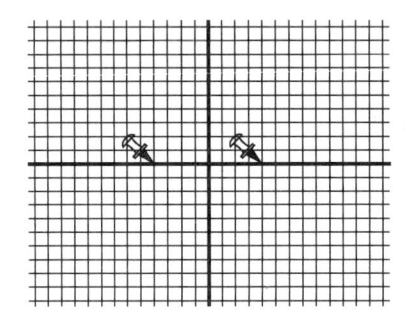

With a pencil, stretch the string out. If properly made, the pencil should be able to cross the points $(0, 3)$, $(5, 0)$, $(0, -3)$, and $(-5, 0)$ when you trace the figure out. You may have to move the string over the pushpins to get a complete loop.

What you have drawn is an ellipse. An ellipse is defined to be the set of all points in a plane, (x, y), in which the sum of the distances from two fixed points (called foci) is constant. For right now, we will consider the case where the ellipse is centered at the origin. Also, $d_1, d_2, a, b,$ and c represent distances. (x, y) is a point on the ellipse.

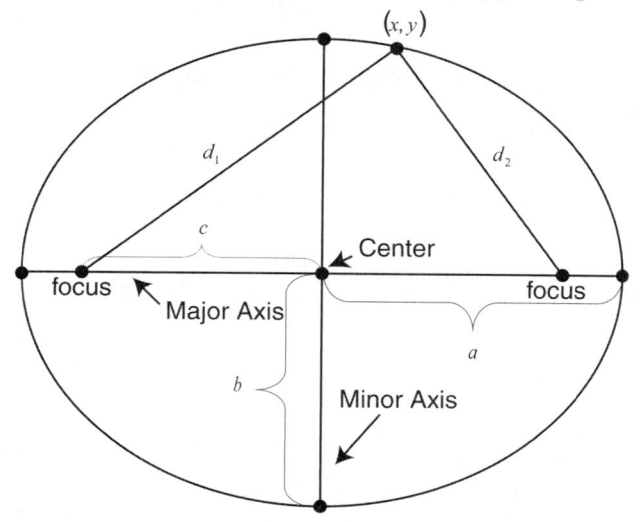

Part B Summary Questions:
1. If this ellipse is centered at the origin (like your drawing) what would the coordinates of the endpoints of the two axes be in terms of a and b?

2. What would the coordinates of the foci be?

3. If you move the point (x, y) to the top (or bottom) of the minor axis, then $d_1 = d_2$. What would the sum $d_1 + d_2$ be in terms of b and c? How can you justify that this sum is also equal to $2a$? How can you justify that this yields the relation $b^2 + c^2 = a^2$?

Now if you let (x, y) be any point on the ellipse then the sum, $d_1 + d_2$, must still be $2a$.

$$\sqrt{(x-(-c))^2 + y^2} + \sqrt{(x-c)^2 + y^2} = 2a$$

Using the relation $b^2 + c^2 = a^2$, it can be shown that this yields $\dfrac{x^2}{a^2} + \dfrac{y^2}{b^2} = 1$. Can you fill in the algebraic details?

Part C Summary Questions:
1. Refer to the ellipse you created on the grid paper. Find a point that is not on an axis and determine if it satisfies the equation $\dfrac{x^2}{a^2} + \dfrac{y^2}{b^2} = 1$. What are your values for a and b? Does your point satisfy the equation? Explain.

2. If the ellipse we've described was centered at the point (h, k), what would its equation be? Hint: Refer to your response to Question 2 in Part A.

282 Chapter 13: Exploring Ideas of Algebra and Coordinate Geometry

TECHNOLOGY ACTIVITY 13.1

What's One More Degree?

Linear (first degree) and quadratic (second degree) equations are examined in Section 13.2 of your textbook.

A linear equation of the form $ax + b = 0$, where $a \neq 0$, has a solution of $x = -\dfrac{b}{a}$.

A quadratic equation of the form $ax^2 + bx + c = 0$, where $a \neq 0$, has solutions $x = \dfrac{-b \pm \sqrt{b^2 - 4ac}}{2a}$.

A cubic equation of the form $ax^3 + bx^2 + cx + d = 0$, where $a \neq 0$, also has solutions and can be solved through formulas. Unfortunately these formulas are fairly complicated. If the graph of a cubic function crosses the x-axis in only one place then the following formula may be used to find that intercept or a solution to the equation $ax^3 + bx^2 + cx + d = 0$.

$$x = \sqrt[3]{\sqrt{\left(\dfrac{d}{2a} - \dfrac{bc}{6a^2} + \dfrac{b^3}{27a^3}\right)^2 + \left(\dfrac{c}{3a} - \dfrac{b^2}{9a^2}\right)^3} - \dfrac{d}{2a} + \dfrac{bc}{6a^2} - \dfrac{b^3}{27a^3}} - \sqrt[3]{\sqrt{\left(\dfrac{d}{2a} - \dfrac{bc}{6a^2} + \dfrac{b^3}{27a^3}\right)^2 + \left(\dfrac{c}{3a} - \dfrac{b^2}{9a^2}\right)^3} + \dfrac{d}{2a} - \dfrac{bc}{6a^2} + \dfrac{b^3}{27a^3}} - \dfrac{b}{3a}$$

Enlarged:

$$x = \sqrt[3]{\sqrt{\left(\dfrac{d}{2a} - \dfrac{bc}{6a^2} + \dfrac{b^3}{27a^3}\right)^2 + \left(\dfrac{c}{3a} - \dfrac{b^2}{9a^2}\right)^3} - \dfrac{d}{2a} + \dfrac{bc}{6a^2} - \dfrac{b^3}{27a^3}} -$$

$$\sqrt[3]{\sqrt{\left(\dfrac{d}{2a} - \dfrac{bc}{6a^2} + \dfrac{b^3}{27a^3}\right)^2 + \left(\dfrac{c}{3a} - \dfrac{b^2}{9a^2}\right)^3} + \dfrac{d}{2a} - \dfrac{bc}{6a^2} + \dfrac{b^3}{27a^3}} - \dfrac{b}{3a}$$

Consider the cubic function $f(x) = x^3 - 2x^2 + 3x - 6$. The graph looks like the following.

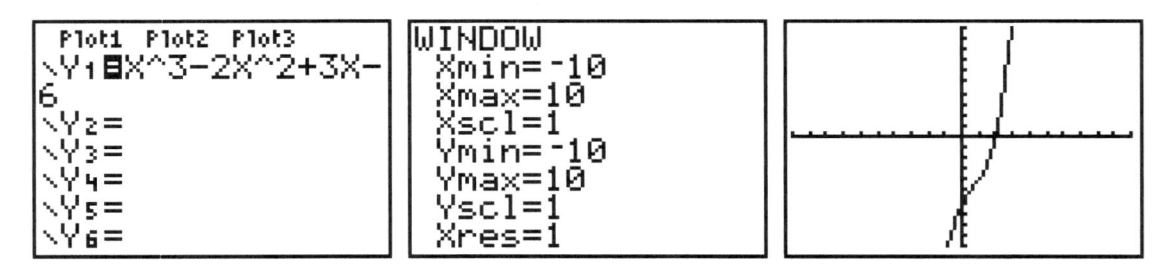

```
Plot1 Plot2 Plot3
\Y1■X^3-2X^2+3X-
6
\Y2=
\Y3=
\Y4=
\Y5=
\Y6=
```

```
WINDOW
Xmin=-10
Xmax=10
Xscl=1
Ymin=-10
Ymax=10
Yscl=1
Xres=1
```

Use the above formula to verify the location of the x-intercept of this function.

Part A Summary Question:
What solution does the formula yield for the equation $x^3 - 5x^2 + 3x - 15 = 0$? Provide graphical support.

For some cubic equations, you may simplify each of the three terms and end up with a solution that does not appear to be an integer value. For example if you consider the graph of the function $f(x) = x^3 - 3x^2 + 6x - 40$, you can see that it crosses the x-axis in only one place.

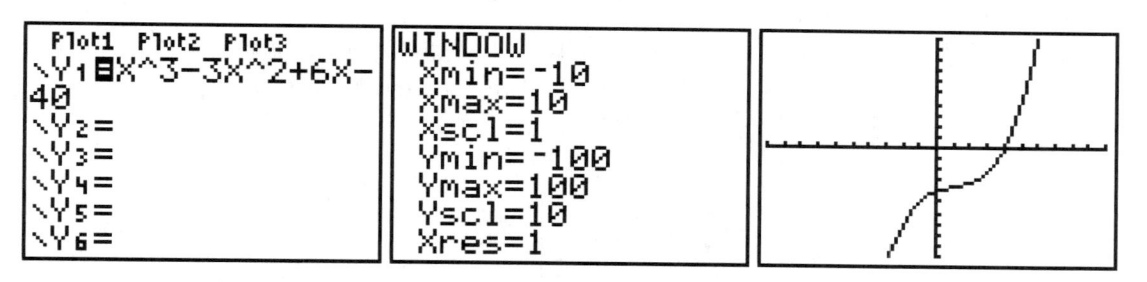

If you use the formula so solve the equation $x^3 - 3x^2 + 6x - 40 = 0$, you get $x = \sqrt[3]{5\sqrt{13} + 18} - \sqrt[3]{5\sqrt{13} - 18} + 1$. Using a calculator, verify that this yields *exactly* the x-intercept shown in the graph.

Part B Summary Question:
What solution does the formula yield for the equation $x^3 - 3x^2 + 4x - 12 = 0$? State the solution as three terms. Provide graphical support.

If your cubic equation crosses the x-axis in three places, the complete solution for the equation becomes quite cumbersome. Consider the cubic function

$$f(x) = (x-2)(x+3)(x+1) = x^3 + 2x^2 - 5x - 6.$$

You can see that the function crosses the x-axis in three places.

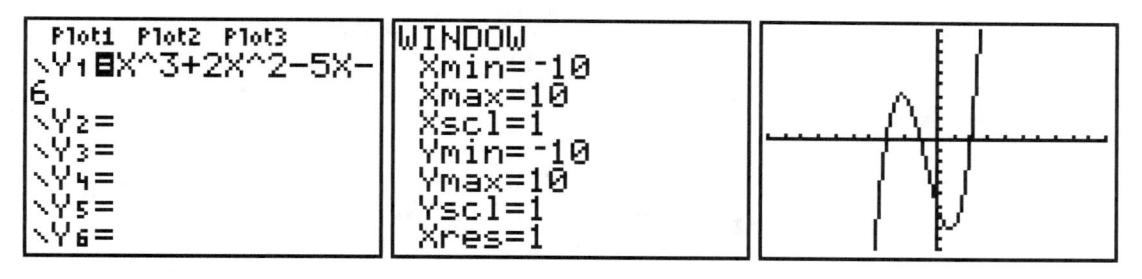

Part C Summary Questions:
1. What are the three x-intercepts? How can you tell from the function?

2. What kind of results do you get when you apply the formula?

TECHNOLOGY ACTIVITY 13.2

Another Fibonacci Sequence

For this activity you will need to use a spreadsheet program such as Excel®. If such a program is not available, a calculator can be used.

This activity requires the Fibonacci Sequence spreadsheet you may have created to solve Technology Activity 1.3.

Recall terms of the *Fibonacci Sequence* can be generated by adding two consecutive terms to get the next. When the first term is 1 and the second term is 1, the third term is $2 = 1 + 1$, the fourth term is $3 = 1 + 2$, and the fifth term is $5 = 2 + 3$. The next five terms are 8, 13, 21, 34, and 55.

	A	B
1	Term #	Fib. #
2	1	1
3	2	1
4	3	2
5	4	3
6	5	5
7	6	8
8	7	13
9	8	21
10	9	34
11	10	55

For this activity, we want to explore what happens when we change the first two terms to values different from 1.

A. Use a spreadsheet like the one you may have created to solve Technology Activity 1.3 and change the first two terms so that the third term of the sequence is 10.

B. Now change the first two terms so that the fifth term of the sequence is 50.

Summary Questions:
1. Is there more than one pair of value for the first two terms that satisfy Part A? Describe your strategies and results.

2. What strategies did you use to find the terms in Part B?

TECHNOLOGY ACTIVITY 13.3

Rectangles and Areas

For this activity you will need to use The Geometer's Sketchpad® or a similar geometry exploration software (GES).

- Create a square on a coordinate grid so that each of the four vertices are in different quadrants. Mark the coordinates of the vertices. For example, Square $ABCD$ has vertices $(-2, 1)$, $(1, 1)$, $(1, -2)$, and $(-2, -2)$.

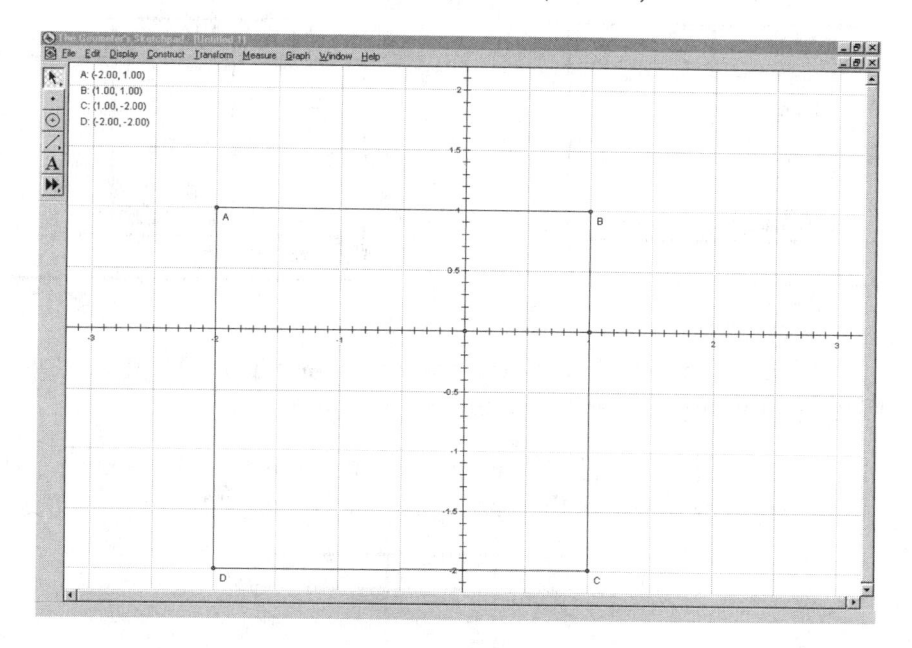

- Construct the diagonals of the square and their intersection point, the center of the square.

- Locate four points on the diagonals that represent the midpoint from the center to each of the vertices. Use these four new points to create a new square within the original square. Verify the location of these midpoints by using the *Theorem for Coordinates of the Midpoint* (page 747 of your textbook).

- Repeat the previous two steps with respect to the new square you just created. You should now have three squares nested within each other. Again, verify that the coordinates given by the GES are consistent with the Midpoint formula.

Summary Questions:
1. How does the area of the innermost square compare to the area of the original square?

2. Suppose we could repeat this process to construct infinitely many rectangles within an original rectangle. If the original rectangle measures 20 units by 16 units, what would the sum of the areas of all the rectangles be?

TECHNOLOGY ACTIVITY 13.4

Linear and Quadratic Graphs

For this activity you will need a graphing calculator to verify your results.

The table feature of a TI-83 calculator is displayed for two particular linear functions. Determine those functions by first finding the slope. Do this by looking at the Y column only. Determine the y-intercept by looking at a specific ordered pair.

A.

X	Y1
-3	-35
-2	-32
-1	-29
0	-26
1	-23
2	-20
3	

Y1 = -17

B.

X	Y1
-3	-5
-2	-5.25
-1	-5.5
0	-5.75
1	-6
2	-6.25
3	

Y1 = -6.5

Part A Summary Questions:
1. Which linear function has a positive slope and which has a negative slope? How can you tell by just looking at the values in the Y column?

2. If the following table was given, would you be able to determine the slope and y-intercept by using the same method as before? Explain.

X	Y1
-3	11
-1	7
1	3
3	-1
5	-5
7	-9
9	

Y1 = -13

The table feature of a TI-83 calculator is displayed for three particular quadratic functions. Determine those functions and use your graphing calculator to verify your results.

A.

X	Y1
-3	5
-2	0
-1	-3
0	-4
1	-3
2	0
3	

Y1 = 5

B.

X	Y1
-3	10
-2	4
-1	0
0	-2
1	-2
2	0
3	

Y1 = 4

C.

X	Y1
-3	5
-2	3
-1	3
0	5
1	9
2	15
3	

Y1 = 23

Part B Summary Question:
How did you determine the equation of each quadratic function?

TECHNOLOGY ACTIVITY 13.5

Possible or Not?

Go to the Possible or Not? feature on the Interactiviate disk. This program will draw ten different graphs of Distance or Profit verses Time.

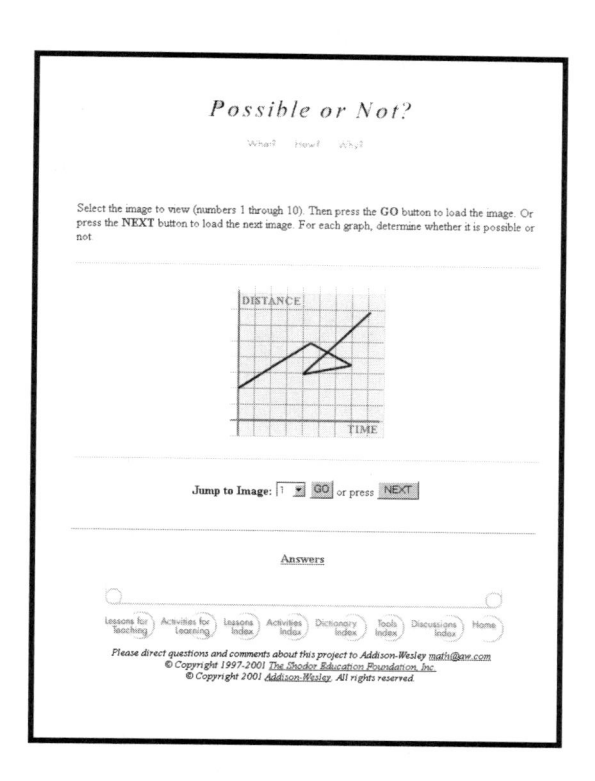

For each of the ten graphs do the following.

- Determine whether or not the graph is possible.
- For each graph that is possible, make up a story that could correlate to the graph.
- After you have examined all ten graphs, check your answers as to whether they are possible or not.

Summary Questions:

1. Which graphs are not possible?

2. What feature(s) does each impossible graph posses that makes it not possible?

3. Can any of the impossible graphs be altered so that they would become possible? If so, how?